BASIC AND CLINICAL SCIENCE COURSE

Glaucoma

Section 10

2012–2013

 AN
OF

The Basic and Clinical Science Course (BCSC) is one component of the Lifelong Education for the Ophthalmologist (LEO) framework, which assists members in planning their continuing medical education. LEO includes an array of clinical education products that members may select to form individualized, self-directed learning plans for updating their clinical knowledge. Active members or fellows who use LEO components may accumulate sufficient CME credits to earn the LEO Award. Contact the Academy's Clinical Education Division for further information on LEO.

The American Academy of Ophthalmology is accredited by the Accreditation Council for Continuing Medical Education to provide continuing medical education for physicians.

The American Academy of Ophthalmology designates this enduring material for a maximum of 10 *AMA PRA Category 1 Credits*™. Physicians should claim only the credit commensurate with the extent of their participation in the activity.

The BCSC is designed to increase the physician's ophthalmic knowledge through study and review. Users of this activity are encouraged to read the text and then answer the study questions provided at the back of the book.

To claim *AMA PRA Category 1 Credits*™ upon completion of this activity, learners must demonstrate appropriate knowledge and participation in the activity by taking the post-test for Section 10 and achieving a score of 80% or higher. For further details, please see the instructions for requesting CME credit at the back of the book.

The Academy provides this material for educational purposes only. It is not intended to represent the only or best method or procedure in every case, nor to replace a physician's own judgment or give specific advice for case management. Including all indications, contraindications, side effects, and alternative agents for each drug or treatment is beyond the scope of this material. All information and recommendations should be verified, prior to use, with current information included in the manufacturers' package inserts or other independent sources, and considered in light of the patient's condition and history. Reference to certain drugs, instruments, and other products in this course is made for illustrative purposes only and is not intended to constitute an endorsement of such. Some material may include information on applications that are not considered community standard, that reflect indications not included in approved FDA labeling, or that are approved for use only in restricted research settings. **The FDA has stated that it is the responsibility of the physician to determine the FDA status of each drug or device he or she wishes to use, and to use them with appropriate, informed patient consent in compliance with applicable law.** The Academy specifically disclaims any and all liability for injury or other damages of any kind, from negligence or otherwise, for any and all claims that may arise from the use of any recommendations or other information contained herein.

Cover image courtesy of M. Roy Wilson, MD.

Basic and Clinical Science Course

Gregory L. Skuta, MD, Oklahoma City, Oklahoma, *Senior Secretary for Clinical Education*

Louis B. Cantor, MD, Indianapolis, Indiana, *Secretary for Ophthalmic Knowledge*

Jayne S. Weiss, MD, New Orleans, Louisiana, *BCSC Course Chair*

Section 10

Faculty Responsible for This Edition

George A. Cioffi, MD, *Chair,* New York, New York

F. Jane Durcan, MD, Spokane, Washington

Christopher A. Girkin, MD, Birmingham, Alabama

Neeru Gupta, MD, PhD, Toronto, Ontario, Canada

Jody R. Piltz-Seymour, MD, Bristol, Pennsylvania

Thomas W. Samuelson, MD, Minneapolis, Minnesota

Angelo P. Tanna, MD, Chicago, Illinois

Keith Barton, MD, *Consultant,* London, United Kingdom

Sara S. O'Connell, MD, Overland Park, Kansas
Practicing Ophthalmologists Advisory Committee for Education

The Academy wishes to acknowledge Julie Falardeau, MD, *Committee on Aging,* and Mary Lou Jackson, MD, *Vision Rehabilitation Committee,* for their reviews of this edition.

The Academy also wishes to acknowledge the American Glaucoma Society for recommending faculty members to the BCSC Section 10 committee.

Financial Disclosures

Academy staff members who contributed to the development of this product state that they have no significant financial interest or other relationship with the manufacturer of any commercial product discussed in this course or with the manufacturer of any competing commercial product.

The authors state the following financial relationships:

Dr Barton: Alcon Laboratories, consultant; Allergan, consultant, lecturer; AqueSys, consultant, equity owner; Merck & Co, consultant, lecturer; New World Medical, grant support; Pfizer, consultant, grant recipient, lecturer

Dr Cioffi: Allergan, consultant

Dr Gupta: Johnson & Johnson, consultant

Dr Samuelson: Abbott Medical Optics, consultant; AcuMEMS, consultant/adviser; Alcon Laboratories, consultant, lecturer; Allergan, consultant; AqueSys, consultant; Endo Optiks, consultant; Glaukos Corporation, consultant, equity owner; Ivantis, consultant; Merck & Co, consultant; *Ocular Surgery News,* consultant; Pfizer Ophthalmics, consultant; QLT Phototherapeutics, consultant, equity owner; Santen, consultant; SLACK, consultant

Dr Tanna: Alcon Laboratories, consultant, grant recipient; Apotex, consultant; Merck & Co, consultant, lecturer; Sandoz, consultant; Watson Laboratories, consultant

The reviewers state the following financial relationships:

Dr Jackson: Opletec USA, grant recipient

The other authors and reviewers state that they have no significant financial interest or other relationship with the manufacturer of any commercial product discussed in the chapters that they contributed to this course or with the manufacturer of any competing commercial product.

Recent Past Faculty

Ronald L. Gross, MD
Peter A. Netland, MD
John R. Samples, MD

In addition, the Academy gratefully acknowledges the contributions of numerous past faculty and advisory committee members who have played an important role in the development of previous editions of the Basic and Clinical Science Course.

American Academy of Ophthalmology Staff

Richard A. Zorab, *Vice President, Ophthalmic Knowledge*
Hal Straus, *Director, Publications Department*
Christine Arturo, *Acquisitions Manager*
Stephanie Tanaka, *Publications Manager*
D. Jean Ray, *Production Manager*
Ann McGuire, *Medical Editor*
Steve Huebner, *Administrative Coordinator*

AMERICAN ACADEMY
OF OPHTHALMOLOGY
The Eye M.D. Association

655 Beach Street
Box 7424
San Francisco, CA 94120-7424

Contents

7   Medical Management of Glaucoma 159

8   Surgical Therapy for Glaucoma 179

General Introduction

The Basic and Clinical Science Course (BCSC) is designed to meet the needs of residents and practitioners for a comprehensive yet concise curriculum of the field of ophthalmology. The BCSC has developed from its original brief outline format, which relied heavily on outside readings, to a more convenient and educationally useful self-contained text. The Academy updates and revises the course annually, with the goals of integrating the basic science and clinical practice of ophthalmology and of keeping ophthalmologists current with new developments in the various subspecialties.

The BCSC incorporates the effort and expertise of more than 80 ophthalmologists, organized into 13 Section faculties, working with Academy editorial staff. In addition, the course continues to benefit from many lasting contributions made by the faculties of previous editions. Members of the Academy's Practicing Ophthalmologists Advisory Committee for Education serve on each faculty and, as a group, review every volume before and after major revisions.

Organization of the Course

The Basic and Clinical Science Course comprises 13 volumes, incorporating fundamental ophthalmic knowledge, subspecialty areas, and special topics:

1 Update on General Medicine
2 Fundamentals and Principles of Ophthalmology
3 Clinical Optics
4 Ophthalmic Pathology and Intraocular Tumors
5 Neuro-Ophthalmology
6 Pediatric Ophthalmology and Strabismus
7 Orbit, Eyelids, and Lacrimal System
8 External Disease and Cornea
9 Intraocular Inflammation and Uveitis
10 Glaucoma
11 Lens and Cataract
12 Retina and Vitreous
13 Refractive Surgery

In addition, a comprehensive Master Index allows the reader to easily locate subjects throughout the entire series.

References

Readers who wish to explore specific topics in greater detail may consult the references cited within each chapter and listed in the Basic Texts section at the back of the book. These references are intended to be selective rather than exhaustive, chosen by the BCSC faculty as being important, current, and readily available to residents and practitioners.

Related Academy educational materials are also listed in the appropriate sections. They include books, online and audiovisual materials, self-assessment programs, clinical modules, and interactive programs.

Study Questions and CME Credit

Each volume of the BCSC is designed as an independent study activity for ophthalmology residents and practitioners. The learning objectives for this volume are given on page 1. The text, illustrations, and references provide the information necessary to achieve the objectives; the study questions allow readers to test their understanding of the material and their mastery of the objectives. Physicians who wish to claim CME credit for this educational activity may do so by following the instructions given at the end of the book.

Conclusion

The Basic and Clinical Science Course has expanded greatly over the years, with the addition of much new text and numerous illustrations. Recent editions have sought to place a greater emphasis on clinical applicability while maintaining a solid foundation in basic science. As with any educational program, it reflects the experience of its authors. As its faculties change and as medicine progresses, new viewpoints are always emerging on controversial subjects and techniques. Not all alternate approaches can be included in this series; as with any educational endeavor, the learner should seek additional sources, including such carefully balanced opinions as the Academy's Preferred Practice Patterns.

The BCSC faculty and staff are continually striving to improve the educational usefulness of the course; you, the reader, can contribute to this ongoing process. If you have any suggestions or questions about the series, please do not hesitate to contact the faculty or the editors.

The authors, editors, and reviewers hope that your study of the BCSC will be of lasting value and that each Section will serve as a practical resource for quality patient care.

Objectives

Upon completion of BCSC Section 10, *Glaucoma,* the reader should be able to

- identify the epidemiologic features of glaucoma, including the social and economic impacts of the disease

- summarize recent advances in the understanding of hereditary and genetic factors in glaucoma

- describe the physiology of aqueous humor dynamics and the control of intraocular pressure (IOP)

- describe the clinical evaluation of the glaucoma patient, including history and general examination, gonioscopy, optic nerve examination, and visual field

- list the clinical features of the patient considered a "glaucoma suspect"

- describe the clinical features, evaluation, and treatment of primary open-angle glaucoma and normal-tension glaucoma

- list the various clinical features of and therapeutic approaches for the primary and secondary open-angle glaucomas

- explain the underlying causes of the increased IOP in various forms of secondary open-angle glaucoma and the impact these underlying causes have on management

- describe the mechanisms and pathophysiology of primary angle-closure glaucoma

- describe the pathophysiology of secondary angle-closure glaucoma, both with and without pupillary block

- outline the pathophysiology of and therapy for primary congenital and juvenile-onset glaucomas

- differentiate among the various classes of medical therapy for glaucoma, including efficacy, mechanism of action, and safety

- compare the indications for and techniques of various laser and incisional surgical procedures for glaucoma

- describe cyclodestructive therapy for refractory glaucoma

CHAPTER 1

Introduction to Glaucoma: Terminology, Epidemiology, and Heredity

Definitions

Glaucoma represents a group of diseases defined by a characteristic optic neuropathy that is consistent with excavation and undermining of the neural and connective tissue elements of the optic disc and by the eventual development of distinctive patterns of visual dysfunction. Although elevated *intraocular pressure (IOP)* is one of the primary risk factors, its presence or absence does not have a role in the definition of the disease. Normal aqueous humor flow in the eye is illustrated in Figure 1-1.

In most individuals with glaucoma, the optic nerve and visual field changes seen with this disease are determined by both the level of the IOP and the resistance of the optic nerve to damage. Although progressive changes in the visual field and optic nerve are

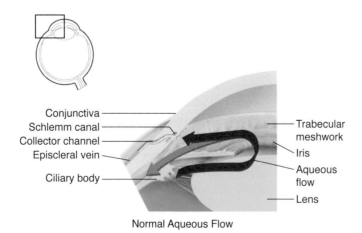

Conjunctiva
Schlemm canal
Collector channel
Episcleral vein
Ciliary body

Trabecular meshwork
Iris
Aqueous flow
Lens

Normal Aqueous Flow

Figure 1-1 Diagrammatic cross section of the anterior segment of the normal eye, showing the site of aqueous production (ciliary body), sites of conventional aqueous outflow (trabecular meshwork–Schlemm canal system and episcleral venous plexus), and the uveoscleral outflow pathway *(green arrow). Small white arrow* shows normal path of outflow and indicates that resistance in this illustration is relative, not total. *(Illustration by Cyndie C. H. Wooley.)*

often related to elevated IOP, in some glaucoma patients the IOP remains within statistically normal range (see Chapter 4). However, when considering whether glaucomatous damage is truly occurring in a patient with "normal" IOP, the ophthalmologist should take into account the measurement artifact that is caused by variation in central corneal thickness and that occurs with diurnal variation in IOP. In most cases of glaucoma, it is presumed that the IOP is too high for proper functioning of the optic nerve axons and that lowering the IOP will stabilize the damage. In cases involving other pathophysiologic mechanisms that may affect the optic nerve, however, the optic nerve may continue to be damaged despite lowering the IOP.

Preperimetric glaucoma is a term that is sometimes used to denote glaucomatous changes in the optic disc in patients with normal visual fields, as determined by white-on-white perimetry. Accurate diagnosis of this condition depends on the sensitivity of the visual function test that is used. Thus, the development of new, more sensitive tests may allow earlier confirmation of this form of glaucoma, while the patient is within this preperimetric phase.

Classification

Open-Angle, Angle-Closure, Primary, and Secondary Glaucomas

Traditionally, glaucoma has been classified as open angle or closed angle and as primary or secondary (Table 1-1). Differentiating open-angle glaucoma from closed-angle glaucoma is essential from a therapeutic standpoint (Figs 1-2, 1-3), and each type of glaucoma is discussed in detail in Chapters 4 and 5. The concept of primary and secondary glaucomas is also useful, but it reflects our lack of understanding of the pathophysiologic mechanisms underlying the glaucomatous process. There are separate anatomical, gonioscopic, biochemical, molecular, and genetic views of the classification of the glaucomas, among others, each with its own merit. Traditionally, open-angle glaucoma is classified as primary when there is no identifiable underlying anatomical cause of the events that led to obstruction of aqueous outflow and subsequent elevation of IOP (see Fig 1-2). The etiology of the outflow obstruction is generally thought to be an abnormality in the extracellular matrix of the trabecular meshwork and in trabecular cells in the juxtacanalicular region, although other views exist. Trabecular cells and their surrounding extracellular matrix are understood in fairly specific terms, and the basic scientific understanding of the outflow structures is constantly increasing. Glaucoma is traditionally classified as secondary when an abnormality is identified and a putative role in the pathogenesis can be ascribed to this abnormality. As knowledge of the mechanisms underlying the causes of glaucoma has grown, the primary/secondary classification has become increasingly artificial.

Other schemes for classifying glaucoma have been proposed. Classification of the glaucomas based on initial events and classification based on mechanisms of outflow obstruction are 2 schemes that have gained increasing popularity (Table 1-2).

Ritch R, Shields MB, Krupin T, eds. *The Glaucomas.* 2nd ed. St Louis: Mosby; 1996:722.

Table 1-1 Classification of the Glaucomas

Type	Characteristics
Open-angle glaucoma and related diagnoses (Fig 1-2)	
Primary open-angle glaucoma (POAG)	Not associated with known ocular or systemic disorders that cause increased resistance to aqueous outflow or damage to optic nerve; usually associated with elevated IOP
Normal-tension glaucoma (NTG)	Considered in continuum of POAG; terminology often used when IOP is not elevated
Juvenile open-angle glaucoma (JOAG)	Terminology often used when open-angle glaucoma diagnosed at young age (typically 4–35 years of age)
Ocular hypertension	Normal optic disc and visual field associated with elevated IOP
Glaucoma suspect	Suspicious optic disc or visual field regardless of IOP
Secondary open-angle glaucoma	Increased resistance to trabecular meshwork outflow associated with other conditions (eg, pigmentary glaucoma, phacolytic glaucoma, steroid-induced glaucoma, exfoliation syndrome, angle-recession glaucoma)
	Increased posttrabecular resistance to outflow secondary to elevated episcleral venous pressure (eg, carotid cavernous sinus fistula)
Angle-closure glaucoma (Fig 1-3)	
Primary angle-closure glaucoma (PACG) with pupillary block	Movement of aqueous humor from posterior chamber to anterior chamber restricted at the point of iridolenticular contact; resulting in anterior iris bowing and contact with trabecular meshwork
Acute angle-closure glaucoma	Occurs when IOP rises rapidly as a result of relatively sudden blockage of the trabecular meshwork
Subacute angle-closure (intermittent angle-closure) glaucoma	Repeated, brief episodes of angle closure with mild symptoms and elevated IOP, often a prelude to acute angle closure
Chronic angle-closure glaucoma	IOP elevation caused by variable portions of anterior chamber angle being permanently closed by peripheral anterior synechiae
Secondary angle-closure glaucoma with pupillary block	Pupillary block occurs as a result of a mechanism other than the anatomical configuration of the anterior segment (eg, an intumescent lens or a secluded pupil).
Secondary angle-closure glaucoma without pupillary block	Posterior pushing mechanism: lens–iris interface pushed forward (eg, posterior segment tumor, scleral buckling procedure, uveal effusion)
	Anterior pulling mechanism: anterior segment process pulling iris forward to form peripheral anterior synechiae (eg, iridocorneal endothelial syndrome, neovascular glaucoma, inflammation)
Plateau iris syndrome	An anatomical variation in the iris root in which narrowing of the angle occurs independent of pupillary block
Childhood glaucomas	
Primary congenital glaucoma (PCG)	Primary glaucoma presents at birth or within the first few years of life
Glaucoma associated with congenital anomalies	Associated with ocular disorders (eg, anterior segment dysgenesis, aniridia)
	Associated with systemic disorders (eg, Sturge-Weber syndrome, neurofibromatosis 1)
Secondary glaucoma in infants and children	Associated with acquired disorders (eg, inflammation, retinoblastoma, trauma)

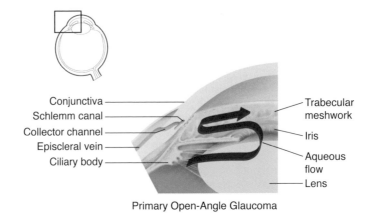

Primary Open-Angle Glaucoma

Figure 1-2 Schematic of open-angle glaucoma with resistance to aqueous outflow through the trabecular meshwork–Schlemm canal system in the absence of gross anatomical obstruction. *(Illustration by Cyndie C. H. Wooley.)*

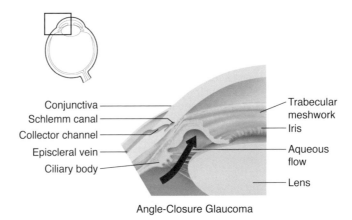

Angle-Closure Glaucoma

Figure 1-3 Schematic of angle-closure glaucoma with pupillary block leading to peripheral iris obstruction of the trabecular meshwork. *(Illustration by Cyndie C. H. Wooley.)*

Combined-Mechanism Glaucoma

Most commonly, combined-mechanism glaucoma occurs in a patient who has been successfully treated for a narrow angle but who continues to demonstrate reduced outflow facility and elevated IOP in the absence of peripheral anterior synechiae (PAS). However, combined-mechanism glaucoma can appear in a patient who has open-angle glaucoma but develops secondary angle closure from other causes. In this condition, IOP elevation can occur as a result of the following:

- the intrinsic resistance of the trabecular meshwork to aqueous outflow in open-angle glaucoma
- the direct anatomical obstruction of the filtering meshwork by synechiae in angle-closure glaucoma

Table 1-2 Classification of the Glaucomas Based on Mechanisms of Outflow Obstruction*

Pretrabecular (Membrane Overgrowth)	Open-Angle Glaucoma Mechanisms		Angle-Closure Glaucoma Mechanisms		Developmental Anomalies of Anterior Chamber Angle
	Trabecular	Posttrabecular	Anterior ("Pulling")	Posterior ("Pushing")	
Fibrovascular membrane (neovascular glaucoma) Endothelial layer, often with Descemet-like membrane Iridocorneal endothelial syndrome Posterior polymorphous dystrophy Penetrating and non-penetrating trauma Epithelial downgrowth Fibrous ingrowth Inflammatory membrane Fuchs heterochromic iridocyclitis Luetic interstitial keratitis	Idiopathic Chronic open-angle glaucoma Juvenile open-angle glaucoma "Clogging" of trabecular meshwork Red blood cells Hemorrhagic glaucoma Ghost cell glaucoma Sickled red blood cells Macrophages Hemolytic glaucoma Phacolytic glaucoma Melanomalytic glaucoma Neoplastic cells Primary ocular tumors Neoplastic tumors Juvenile xanthogranuloma Pigment particles Pigmentary glaucoma Exfoliation syndrome (glaucoma capsulare) Melanoma Protein Uveitis Lens-induced glaucoma Viscoelastic agents α-Chymotrypsin–induced glaucoma Alterations of the trabecular meshwork Steroid-induced glaucoma Edema Uveitis (trabeculitis) Scleritis and episcleritis Alkali burns Trauma (angle recession) Intraocular foreign bodies (hemosiderosis, chalcosis)	Obstruction of Schlemm canal, eg, collapse at canal Elevated episcleral venous pressure Carotid cavernous fistula Cavernous sinus thrombosis Retrobulbar tumors Thyroid eye disease Superior vena cava obstruction Mediastinal tumors Sturge-Weber syndrome Familial episcleral venous pressure elevation	Contracture of membranes Neovascular glaucoma Iridocorneal endothelial syndrome Posterior polymorphous dystrophy Penetrating and nonpenetrating trauma Consolidation of inflammatory products	With pupillary block Pupillary block glaucoma Lens-induced mechanisms Phacomorphic lens Ectopia lentis Posterior synechiae Iris-vitreous block Pseudophakia Uveitis Without pupillary block Ciliary block (malignant) glaucoma Lens-induced mechanisms Phacomorphic lens Ectopia lentis Following lens extraction (forward vitreous shift) Anterior rotation of ciliary body Following scleral buckling Following panretinal photocoagulation Central retinal vein occlusion Intraocular tumors Melanoma Retinoblastoma Cysts of the iris and ciliary body Retrolenticular tissue contracture Retinopathy of prematurity (retrolental fibroplasia) Persistent fetal vasculature (persistent hyperplastic primary vitreous)	Incomplete development of trabecular meshwork–Schlemm canal Congenital (infantile) glaucoma Axenfeld-Rieger syndrome Peters anomaly Glaucomas associated with other developmental anomalies Iridocorneal adhesions Broad strands (Axenfeld-Rieger syndrome) Fine strands that contract to close angle (aniridia)

Plateau Iris Syndrome

*Clinical examples cited in this table do not represent an inclusive list of the glaucomas.

Modified with permission from Ritch R, Shields MB, Krupin T, eds. The Glaucomas. 2nd ed. St Louis: Mosby; 1996:722.

Epidemiologic Aspects of Glaucoma

Primary Open-Angle Glaucoma

Magnitude of the problem

Primary open-angle glaucoma (POAG) poses a significant public health problem. The estimated prevalence of POAG in the United States in individuals older than 40 years is 1.86% (95% confidence interval, 1.75%–1.96%), based on a meta-analysis of population-based studies. Applied to data from the 2000 US census, this percentage translates to nearly 2.22 million Americans affected. Estimates based on the available data indicate that between 84,000 and 116,000 of them have become bilaterally blind (best-corrected visual acuity ≤20/200 or visual field <20°). With the rapidly aging US population, the number of POAG patients is estimated to increase by 50%, to 3.36 million in 2020.

The World Health Organization (WHO) undertook an analysis of the literature to estimate the prevalence, incidence, and severity of the different types of glaucoma on a worldwide basis. Using data collected predominantly in the late 1980s and early 1990s, the WHO estimated the global population of persons with high IOP (>21 mm Hg) to be 104.5 million. The incidence of POAG was estimated at 2.4 million persons per year. Blindness prevalence for all types of glaucoma was estimated at more than 8 million persons, with 4 million cases caused by POAG. Glaucoma was theoretically calculated to be responsible for 12.3% of blindness. This makes glaucoma the second leading cause of blindness worldwide, following cataract.

Prevalence

The estimated prevalence (the total number of individuals with a disease at a specific time) varies widely across population-based samples, with the Rotterdam Study (northern European population) showing a prevalence of 0.8% and the Barbados Eye Study (Caribbean population) showing a prevalence of 7% in individuals older than 40 years. But in both of these studies, there is a significant increase in the prevalence of glaucoma in older individuals, with estimates for persons in their 70s being generally 3 to 8 times higher than those for persons in their 40s. In addition, multiple population-based surveys have demonstrated a higher prevalence of glaucoma in specific ethnic groups. Among whites aged 40 years and older, a prevalence of between 1.1% and 2.1% has been reported based on population-based studies performed throughout the world. The prevalence among black persons and Latino persons is up to 4 times higher compared to the prevalence among whites. Black individuals are also at greater risk of blindness from POAG, and this risk increases with age: in persons aged 46–65 years, the likelihood of blindness from POAG is 15 times higher among blacks than that among whites.

Friedman DS, Wolfs RC, O'Colmain BJ, et al. Prevalence of open-angle glaucoma among adults in the United States. *Arch Ophthalmol.* 2004;122(4):532–538.

Javitt JC, McBean AM, Nicholson GA, Babish JD, Warren JL, Krakauer H. Undertreatment of glaucoma among black Americans. *N Engl J Med.* 1991;325:1418–1422.

Varma R, Ying Lai M, Francis BA, et al. Prevalence of open-angle glaucoma and ocular hypertension in Latinos: the Los Angeles Latino Eye Study. *Ophthalmology.* 2004; 111(8):1439–1448.

Incidence

The incidence (the number of new cases of a disease that develop during a specific period) of POAG, which has been examined less than the prevalence of POAG in population-based studies, varies widely. The Barbados Eye Study demonstrated, in a predominantly black population, an overall incidence of 2.2% in subjects older than 40 years. A much lower incidence was demonstrated in the Visual Impairment Project, based in Melbourne, Australia (1.1% for definite and probable POAG); and in the Rotterdam Study (5-year risk of 1.8% for definite and probable POAG).

Risk factors

Strictly defined, a factor can be considered a risk factor only if it predates disease occurrence. In prospective studies, a number of risk factors have been found to be associated with progression of glaucoma, including elevated IOP, reduced perfusion pressure, advanced age, thin central corneas, racial background, and a positive family history (Table 1-3). The role of gender and of various systemic factors, such as diabetes, systemic hypertension, and atherosclerotic and ischemic vascular diseases, in the development of glaucoma has been widely debated, and currently available data are inconclusive.

In terms of the assessment of risk factors, the importance of diurnal variation in IOP has been increasingly recognized. Current evidence, obtained under sleep laboratory conditions, suggests that in most subjects, the peak IOP occurs at night and is therefore not seen in the routine clinical setting.

Dueker DK, Singh K, Lin SC, et al. Corneal thickness measurement in the management of primary open-angle glaucoma: a report by the American Academy of Ophthalmology. *Ophthalmology.* 2007;114(9):1779–1787.

Hennis AJ, Wu SY, Nemesure B, et al. Nine-year incidence of visual impairment in the Barbados Eye Studies. *Ophthalmology.* 2009;116(8):1461–1468. Epub 2009 Jun 4.

Table 1-3 Risk Factors for Glaucomatous Progression

Risk Factor	Prospective Study
Increasing age	AGIS, CIGTS, EGPS, EMGT, OHTS
African ancestry	AGIS, CIGTS, CNTGS, OHTS (univariate)
Visual field severity	AGIS, EGPS, EMGT, OHTS
Diabetes mellitus	AGIS, OHTS (protective)
Disc hemorrhage	CNTGS, EMGT
Follow-up IOP	CNTGS, EMGT
Cup–disc ratio	EGPS, OHTS
Corneal thickness	EGPS, OHTS
Pseudoexfoliation	EMGT
Initial IOP	EMGT
Female sex	CNTGS
Male sex	AGIS
Central corneal thickness	OHTS
Perfusion pressure	BES, LALES

AGIS = Advanced Glaucoma Intervention Study; BES = Barbados Eye Study; CIGTS = Collaborative Initial Glaucoma Treatment Study; CNTGS = Collaborative Normal-Tension Glaucoma Study; EGPS = European Glaucoma Prevention Study; EMGT = Early Manifest Glaucoma Trial; LALES = Los Angeles Latino Eye Study; OHTS = Ocular Hypertension Treatment Study.

Leske MC, Heijl A, Hyman L, et al. Predictors of long-term progression in the Early Manifest Glaucoma Trial. *Ophthalmology.* 2007;114(11):1965–1972.

Primary Angle-Closure Glaucoma

Race

The prevalence of primary angle-closure glaucoma (PACG) varies among different racial and ethnic groups. Among white populations in the United States and Europe, it is estimated at 0.1%. Inuit populations from the Arctic regions have the highest-known prevalence of PACG—20 to 40 times higher than that for whites. Although estimates of the prevalence of PACG in Asian populations vary widely, available data suggest that for most Asian population groups, the prevalence of PACG is between that for whites and that for the Inuit. Some studies have suggested that the prevalence of PACG among blacks is similar to that among whites, with most cases among black persons being of the chronic variety.

Gender

Acute angle-closure glaucoma has been reported more often in women than in men, and several population-based surveys show that women are at increased risk of angle-closure glaucoma. Studies of normal eyes have shown that women have shallower anterior chambers than men.

Age

The depth and volume of the anterior chamber decrease with age. These changes predispose the eye to pupillary block; thus, the prevalence of angle-closure glaucoma with pupillary block increases with age. Acute angle-closure glaucoma is most common between the ages of 55 and 65 years, but it can occur in young adults and has been reported in children.

Refraction

Although PACG may occur in eyes with any type of refractive error, it is typically associated with hyperopia. The depth and volume of the anterior chamber are reduced in hyperopic eyes, predisposing them to PACG.

Inheritance

Some of the anatomical features of the eye that predispose to pupillary block, such as a more anterior lens position and greater-than-average lens thickness, are inherited. Although generalizable estimates are lacking, a population-based survey in China suggests that a family history of glaucoma increases the risk of PACG sixfold.

Epstein DL, Allingham RR, Schuman JS, eds. *Chandler and Grant's Glaucoma.* 4th ed. Baltimore: Williams & Wilkins; 1997:641–646.

Ritch RM, Shields MB, Krupin T, eds. *The Glaucomas.* 2nd ed. St Louis: Mosby; 1996: 753–765.

Genetics, Environmental Factors, and Glaucoma

The precise mechanism of inheritance of glaucoma is not clear. To date, many of the glaucomas appear to have an autosomal dominant inheritance pattern that may involve more than 1 gene (polygenic); have a late or variable age of onset; demonstrate incomplete penetrance (ie, the disease may not develop even when the causative gene has been inherited); and may be substantially influenced by environmental factors. See also BCSC Section 2, *Fundamentals and Principles of Ophthalmology*, Part III, Genetics. A positive family history is a risk factor for the development of POAG. The prevalence of glaucoma among siblings of glaucoma patients is approximately 10%.

The first gene described for POAG, *GLC1A* (also called the trabecular meshwork inducible glucocorticoid response/myocilin gene *[TIGR/MYOC]*), codes for the TIGR protein and is a trabecular meshwork glucocorticoid gene, located on chromosome 1. Mutations in *GLC1A* are present in 3% of the general open-angle glaucoma population. In the mid-1990s, the gene responsible for mutations in the TIGR protein was identified. Since then, several additional open-angle glaucoma genes have been mapped, and many more potential genes are being explored. The percentage of genes known to be associated with specific types of glaucoma is small, most likely because of the complex nature of the disease and because of the complicated interactions between multiple genetic loci and environmental factors (Table 1-4). Researchers are increasingly applying genome-wide scanning techniques to large cohorts of glaucoma subjects. These techniques may be useful for determining which regions of the genome are associated with glaucoma.

Kass MA, Becker B. Genetics of primary open-angle glaucoma. *Sight Sav Rev.* 1978;48:21–28.

Table 1-4 Currently Mapped Glaucoma Genes

Locus	Chromosome Location	Phenotype	Inheritance	Gene
GLC1A	1q23	JOAG and adult POAG	Dominant	*TIGR/MYOC*
GLC1B	2cen-q13	NTG, adult POAG	Dominant	—
GLC1C	3q21-24	Adult POAG	Dominant	—
GLC1D	8q23	Adult POAG	Dominant	—
GLC1E	10P15-14	NTG, adult POAG	Dominant	*OPTN*
GLC1F	7q35	Adult POAG	Dominant	—
GLC1G	5q22	Adult POAG	Dominant, complex	*WDR36*
GLC1I	15q11-q13	Adult POAG	Complex	—
GLC1J	9q22	Early POAG	Dominant	—
GLC1K	20p12	Early POAG	Dominant	—
GPDS1	7q35-q36	PDS	Dominant	—
GLC3A	2p21	Congenital	Recessive	*CYP1B1*
GLC3B	1p36	Congenital	Recessive	—
GLC3C	14q24.3	Congenital	Recessive	—
NNO1	11p	Nanophthalmos	Dominant	—
VMD2	11q12	Nanophthalmos	Dominant	—
MFRP	11q23	Nanophthalmos	Recessive	—
RIEG1	4q25	Rieger syndrome	Dominant	*PITX2*
RIEG2	13q14	Rieger syndrome	Dominant	—
IRID1	6p25	Iridogoniodysgenesis	Dominant	*FOXC1*
	7q35	PDS	Dominant	—
NPS	9q34	Nail-patella syndrome	Dominant	*LMX1B*
	15q24	PXE		*LOXL1*

JOAG = juvenile open-angle glaucoma; POAG = primary open-angle glaucoma; NTG = normal-tension glaucoma; PDS = pigment dispersion syndrome; PXE = pseudoexfoliation.

Adapted from Wiggs JL. Genetic etiologies of glaucoma. *Arch Ophthalmol.* 2007;125(1):30–37.

Polansky JR, Fauss DJ, Chen P, et al. Cellular pharmacology and molecular biology of the trabecular meshwork inducible glucocorticoid response gene product. *Ophthalmologica.* 1997;211(3):126–139.

Stone EM, Fingert JH, Alward WL, et al. Identification of a gene that causes primary open angle glaucoma. *Science.* 1997;275(5300):668–670.

Wolfs RC, Klaver CC, Ramrattan RS, van Duijn CM, Hofman A, de Jong PT. Genetic risk of primary open-angle glaucoma: population-based familial aggregation study. *Arch Ophthalmol.* 1998;116(12):1640–1645.

Environmental Factors

Evidence that environmental factors can also play a role in the etiology of glaucoma arises from studies of twins and analysis of the season of birth of glaucoma patients. If glaucoma is genetically determined, then identical twins should theoretically share this trait more often than fraternal twins. In the Finnish Twin Cohort Study, 3 of 29 monozygotic twin pairs were concordant for POAG, compared with 1 of 79 dizygotic twin pairs. Although a higher percentage of monozygotic twins were concordant for glaucoma, most were not. These data suggest that although genetic factors contribute to the etiology of glaucoma, other factors, such as environmental influences, are important.

Genetic Testing

In the future, the management of some glaucoma patients will involve testing of multiple, and potentially interacting, genetic loci. Although there have been rapid advances in genetic techniques that allow this type of testing, advances in the study of genetic diseases require accurate categorization of individuals and families with specific phenotypes. By appropriately identifying families with strong histories of glaucoma, the practicing clinical ophthalmologist has an opportunity to provide important information to researchers in genetics. The cooperation of the clinician is therefore critical to the advancement of this crucial area of research.

The reader is encouraged to review the literature and to refer to websites such as GeneTests for information on genetic testing and its use in diagnosis, management, and genetic counseling (http://www.ncbi.nlm.nih.gov/sites/GeneTests/?db=GeneTests).

Thorleifsson G, Magnusson KP, Sulem P, et al. Common sequence variants in the *LOXL1* gene confer susceptibility to exfoliation glaucoma. *Science.* 2007;317(5843):1397–1400.

CHAPTER 2

Intraocular Pressure and Aqueous Humor Dynamics

An understanding of *aqueous humor dynamics* is essential for the evaluation and management of glaucoma. As shown in Figure 1-1 in Chapter 1, aqueous humor is produced in the posterior chamber and flows through the pupil into the anterior chamber. Aqueous humor exits the eye by passing through the *trabecular meshwork* and into the *Schlemm canal* before draining into the venous system through a plexus of collector channels, as well as through the uveoscleral pathway, which is proposed to exit through the root of the iris and the ciliary muscle, into the suprachoroidal spaces and through the sclera. The *Goldmann equation* summarizes the relationship between many of these factors and the intraocular pressure (IOP) in the undisturbed eye:

$$P_0 = (F/C) + P_v$$

where P_0 is the IOP in millimeters of mercury (mm Hg), F is the rate of aqueous formation in microliters per minute (µL/min), C is the facility of outflow in microliters per minute per millimeter of mercury (µL/min/mm Hg), and P_v is the episcleral venous pressure in millimeters of mercury. Resistance to outflow (R) is the inverse of facility (C).

Table 2-1 illustrates the impact of reduced outflow facility (C value) of aqueous humor through the trabecular meshwork both in an open angle and in various amounts of angle closure.

Aqueous Humor Formation

Aqueous humor is formed by the *ciliary processes,* each of which is composed of a double layer of epithelium over a core of stroma and a rich supply of fenestrated capillaries (Fig 2-1). Each of the 80 or so processes contains a large number of capillaries, which are supplied mainly by branches of the major arterial circle of the iris. The apical surfaces of both the outer pigmented and the inner nonpigmented layers of epithelium face each other and are joined by tight junctions, which are an important component of the blood–aqueous barrier. The inner nonpigmented epithelial cells, which protrude into the posterior chamber, contain numerous mitochondria and microvilli; these cells are thought to be the actual site of aqueous production. The ciliary processes provide a large surface area for secretion.

Table 2-1 Theoretical Examples of Difference in the Degree to Which the Intraocular Pressure (P) Is Calculated to Be Affected by Changes in Flow (F) and Facility of Outflow (C) in Different Types of Eyes, Assuming Constant Episcleral Venous Pressure (P$_e$ [or P$_v$])

	(mm Hg) P$_e$	+	(μL/min) (F	÷	(μL/min/mm Hg) C)	=	(mm Hg) P
Normal =	9		1.5		0.22		15
	9		2.0 to 2.5		0.22		13 to 17
	9		1.5		0.30		14
Glaucoma =	9		1.5		0.05		39
	9		1 to 2		0.05		29 to 49
	9		1.5		0.10		24
Good baseline C value =	9		1.5		0.30		14
½ angle closed =	9		1.5		0.15		19
¾ angle closed =	9		1.5		0.075		29
Poor normal =	9		1.5		0.15		19
½ angle closed =	9		1.5		0.075		29
¾ angle closed =	9		1.5		0.0375		49

Modified with permission from Epstein DL, Allingham RR, Schuman JS. *Chandler and Grant's Glaucoma.* 4th ed. Baltimore: Williams & Wilkins; 1997:21.

Aqueous humor formation and secretion into the posterior chamber result from the following:

- active secretion, which takes place in the double-layered ciliary epithelium
- ultrafiltration
- simple diffusion

Active secretion, or *transport,* requires energy to move substances against an electrochemical gradient, and it is independent of pressure. The identity of the precise ion or ions transported is not known, but sodium, chloride, and bicarbonate are involved. Active secretion accounts for the majority of aqueous production and involves, at least in part, activity of the enzyme carbonic anhydrase II. *Ultrafiltration* refers to a pressure-dependent movement along a pressure gradient. In the ciliary processes, the hydrostatic pressure difference between capillary pressure and IOP favors fluid movement into the eye, whereas the oncotic gradient between the two resists fluid movement. The relationship between secretion and ultrafiltration is not known. *Diffusion* involves the passive movement of ions, based on charge and concentration, across a membrane.

In humans, aqueous humor has an excess of hydrogen and chloride ions, an excess of ascorbate, and a deficit of bicarbonate relative to plasma. Aqueous humor is essentially protein free (1/200–1/500 of the protein found in plasma), allowing for optical clarity and reflecting the integrity of the blood–aqueous barrier of the normal eye. Albumin accounts for approximately half of the total protein. Other components of aqueous humor include growth factors; several enzymes, such as carbonic anhydrase, lysozyme, diamine oxidase, plasminogen activator, dopamine β-hydroxylase, and phospholipase A$_2$; and prostaglandins, cyclic adenosine monophosphate (cAMP), catecholamines, steroid hormones, and

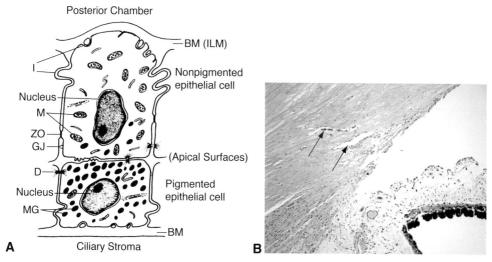

Figure 2-1   A, The 2 layers of the ciliary epithelium showing apical surfaces in apposition to each other. Basement membrane *(BM)* lines the double layer and constitutes the internal limiting membrane *(ILM)* on the inner surface. The nonpigmented epithelium is characterized by large numbers of mitochondria *(M)*, zonula occludens *(ZO)*, and lateral and surface interdigitations *(I)*. The pigmented epithelium contains numerous melanin granules *(MG)*. Additional intercellular junctions include desmosomes *(D)* and gap junctions *(GJ)*. **B,** Light micrograph of the anterior chamber angle shows the Schlemm canal *(black arrow)* adjacent to the trabecular meshwork in the sclera. One of the external collector vessels can be seen *(red arrow)* adjacent to the Schlemm canal. *(Part A reproduced with permission from Shields MB. Textbook of Glaucoma. 3rd ed. Baltimore: Williams & Wilkins; 1992. Part B courtesy of Nasreen A. Syed, MD.)*

hyaluronic acid. Aqueous humor is produced at an average rate of 2.0–2.5 µL/min, and its composition is altered as it flows from the posterior chamber, through the pupil, and into the anterior chamber. This alteration occurs across the hyaloid face of the vitreous, the surface of the lens, the blood vessels of the iris, and the corneal endothelium; and it is secondary to other dilutional exchanges and active processes. See BCSC Section 2, *Fundamentals and Principles of Ophthalmology,* for further discussion of aqueous humor composition and production.

Suppression of Aqueous Formation

The mechanisms of action of the various classes of drugs that suppress aqueous formation—the *carbonic anhydrase inhibitors, β-adrenergic antagonists (β-blockers),* and *α_2-agonists*—are not precisely understood. The role of the enzyme carbonic anhydrase has been debated vigorously. Evidence suggests that the bicarbonate ion is actively secreted in human eyes; thus, the function of the enzyme may be to provide this ion. Carbonic anhydrase may also provide bicarbonate or hydrogen ions for an intracellular buffering system.

Current evidence indicates that β_2-receptors are the most prevalent adrenergic receptors in the ciliary epithelium. The significance of this finding is unclear, but β-adrenergic antagonists may affect active transport by causing a decrease either in the efficiency of the Na^+/K^+ pump or in the number of pump sites. For additional discussion of the sodium pump and the pump–leak mechanism, see BCSC Section 2, *Fundamentals and Principles of Ophthalmology.*

Rate of Aqueous Formation

The most common method used to measure the rate of aqueous formation is *fluorophotometry.* Fluorescein is administered systemically or topically; the subsequent weakening of its concentration in the anterior chamber is measured optically, and this measurement is then used to calculate aqueous flow. As previously noted, the normal flow is approximately 2.0–2.5 μL/min, and the aqueous volume is turned over at a rate of 1% per minute.

The rate of aqueous humor formation varies diurnally and decreases during sleep. It also decreases with age, as does outflow facility. The rate of aqueous formation is affected by a variety of factors, including the following:

- integrity of the blood–aqueous barrier
- blood flow to the ciliary body
- neurohumoral regulation of vascular tissue and the ciliary epithelium

Aqueous humor production may decrease following trauma or intraocular inflammation and following the administration of certain drugs (eg, general anesthetics and some systemic hypotensive agents). Carotid occlusive disease may also decrease aqueous humor production.

Aqueous Humor Outflow

Aqueous humor outflow occurs by 2 major mechanisms: pressure-dependent outflow and pressure-independent outflow. The facility of outflow (*C* in the Goldmann equation; see the beginning of the chapter) varies widely in normal eyes. The mean value reported ranges from 0.22 to 0.30 μL/min/mm Hg. Outflow facility decreases with age and is affected by surgery, trauma, medications, and endocrine factors. Patients with glaucoma and elevated IOP have decreased outflow facility.

Trabecular Outflow

Traditional thought contended that most of the aqueous humor exits the eye by way of the trabecular meshwork–Schlemm canal–venous system. However, evidence questions the exact ratio of trabecular to uveoscleral outflow. As with outflow facility, this ratio is affected by age and by ocular health. The meshwork is classically divided into 3 parts (Fig 2-2). The uveal part is adjacent to the anterior chamber and is arranged in bands that extend from the iris root and the ciliary body to the peripheral cornea. The corneoscleral meshwork consists of sheets of trabeculum that extend from the scleral spur to the lateral wall of the scleral sulcus. The juxtacanalicular meshwork, which is thought to be the major site of outflow resistance, is adjacent to, and actually forms the inner wall of, the Schlemm canal. Aqueous moves both across and between the endothelial cells lining the inner wall of the Schlemm canal.

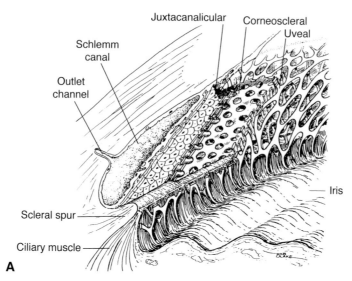

Trabecular Meshwork

Figure 2-2 **A,** Three layers of trabecular meshwork (shown in cutaway views): uveal, corneo-scleral, and juxtacanalicular. **B,** Pars plicata of the ciliary body showing the 2 epithelial layers in the eye of an older person. The unpigmented epithelial cells measure approximately 20 µm high by 12 µm wide. The cuboidal pigmented epithelial cells are approximately 10 µm high. The thickened internal limiting membrane *(a)* is laminated and vesicular; such thickened membranes are a characteristic of older eyes. The cytoplasm of the unpigmented epithelium is character-ized by its numerous mitochondria *(b)* and the cisternae of the rough-surfaced endoplasmic reticulum *(c)*. A poorly developed Golgi apparatus *(d)* and several lysosomes and residual bodies *(e)* are shown. The pigmented epithelium contains many melanin granules, measuring about 1 µm in diameter and located mainly in the apical portion. The basal surface is rather irregular, having many fingerlike processes *(f)*. The basement membrane of the pigmented epithelium *(g)* and a smooth granular material containing vesicles *(i)* and coarse granular particles are seen at the bottom of the figure. The appearance of the basement membrane is typical of older eyes and can be discerned with the light microscope (×5700). *(Part A modified with permission from Shields MB. Textbook of Glaucoma. 3rd ed. Baltimore: Williams & Wilkins; 1992. Part B modified with permission from Hogan MJ, Alvarado JA, Weddell JE. Histology of the Human Eye. Philadelphia: Saunders; 1971:283.)*

(Continued on next page)

The trabecular meshwork is composed of multiple layers, each of which consists of a collagenous connective tissue core covered by a continuous endothelial layer. The trabec-ular meshwork is the site of pressure-dependent outflow. It functions as a one-way valve that permits aqueous to leave the eye by bulk flow but limits flow in the other direction, independent of energy. Its cells are phagocytic, and they may exhibit this function in the presence of inflammation and after laser treatment.

In most eyes of older adults, trabecular cells contain a large number of pigment gran-ules within their cytoplasm that give the entire meshwork a brown or muddy appearance. With age, the number of trabecular cells decreases, and the basement membrane beneath them thickens. There are relatively few trabecular cells—approximately 200,000–300,000 cells per eye. An interesting effect of all types of laser trabeculoplasty is that it induces division of trabecular cells and causes a change in the production of cytokines and other

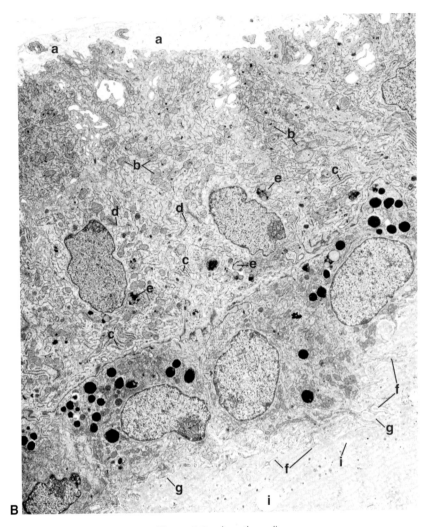

Figure 2-2 *(continued)*

structurally important elements of the extracellular matrix. The extracellular matrix material is found through the dense portions of the trabecular meshwork.

The Schlemm canal is completely lined with an endothelial layer that does not rest on a continuous basement membrane. The canal is a single channel, with an average diameter of approximately 370 μm, and is traversed by tubules. The inner wall of the Schlemm canal contains giant vacuoles that have direct communication with the intertrabecular spaces. The outer wall is actually a single layer of endothelial cells that do not contain pores. A complex system of vessels connects the Schlemm canal to the episcleral veins, which subsequently drain into the anterior ciliary and superior ophthalmic veins. These, in turn, ultimately drain into the cavernous sinus.

When IOP is low, the trabecular meshwork may collapse, or blood may reflux into the Schlemm canal and be visible on gonioscopy.

Uveoscleral Outflow

In the normal eye, any nontrabecular outflow is termed *uveoscleral outflow.* Uveoscleral outflow is also referred to as *pressure-independent outflow.* A variety of mechanisms are likely involved, predominantly aqueous passage from the anterior chamber into the ciliary muscle and then into the supraciliary and suprachoroidal spaces. The fluid then exits the eye through the intact sclera or along the nerves and the vessels that penetrate it. As noted, uveoscleral outflow is largely pressure-independent and is believed to be affected by age. There is evidence that humans have significant outflow via the uveoscleral pathway. Uveoscleral outflow has been estimated to account for 5%–15% of total aqueous outflow, but studies indicate that it may be a higher percentage of total outflow, especially in young, normal eyes. It is increased by cycloplegia, adrenergic agents, prostaglandin analogues, and certain complications of surgery (eg, cyclodialysis) and is decreased by miotics.

Brubaker RF. Measurement of uveoscleral outflow in humans. *J Glaucoma.* 2001;10(5 Suppl 1): S45–S48.

Tonography

Tonography is a method used to measure the facility of aqueous outflow. The clinician can take the measurement by using a Schiøtz tonometer of known weight. The tonometer is placed on the cornea, acutely elevating the IOP. The rate at which the pressure declines with time is related to the ease with which the aqueous leaves the eye. The decline in IOP over time can be used to determine outflow facility in μL/min/mm Hg through a series of mathematical calculations.

Unfortunately, tonography depends on a number of assumptions (eg, the elastic properties of the eye, stability of aqueous formation, and constancy of ocular blood volume) and is subject to many sources of error, such as calibration problems, patient fixation, and eyelid squeezing. These problems reduce the accuracy and reproducibility of tonography for an individual patient. In general, tonography is best used as a research tool for the investigation of pharmacokinetics and is rarely used clinically.

Episcleral Venous Pressure

Episcleral venous pressure is relatively stable, except with sudden alterations in body position and with certain diseases of the orbit, the head, and the neck that obstruct venous return to the heart or shunt blood from the arterial to the venous system. The usual range of values is 8–10 mm Hg. The pressure in the episcleral veins can be measured with specialized equipment. In acute conditions, according to the Goldmann equation, IOP rises approximately 1 mm Hg for every 1 mm Hg increase in episcleral venous pressure. The relationship is more complex and less well understood, however, in chronic conditions. Chronic elevations of episcleral venous pressure may be accompanied by changes in IOP that are of greater or less magnitude than those predicted by the Goldmann equation. In addition, these changes may not vary directly with the episcleral venous pressure.

Abnormally elevated episcleral venous pressure can cause the collapse of the Schlemm canal and an increase in aqueous humor outflow resistance. Episcleral venous pressure is often increased in syndromes with facial hemangiomas (eg, Sturge-Weber) and in thyroid eye disease, and it is partially responsible for the elevated IOP seen in thyroid eye disease.

Intraocular Pressure

Distribution in the Population and Relation to Glaucoma

Pooled data from large Western epidemiologic studies indicate that the mean IOP is approximately 15.5 mm Hg, with a standard deviation of 2.6 mm Hg. However, IOP has a non-Gaussian distribution with a skew toward higher pressures, especially in individuals older than 40 years (Fig 2-3). The value 21 mm Hg (greater than 2 standard deviations above the mean) was traditionally used both to separate normal and abnormal pressures and to define which patients required ocular hypotensive therapy. This division was based on the erroneous clinical assumptions that glaucomatous damage is caused exclusively by pressures that are higher than normal and that normal pressures do not cause damage. An example of the shortcomings created by these assumptions is that screening for glaucoma based solely on IOP greater than 21 mm Hg misses up to half of the people with glaucoma and optic nerve damage in the screened population.

General agreement has been reached that, for the population as a whole, there is no clear IOP level below which IOP can be considered "normal" or safe and above which

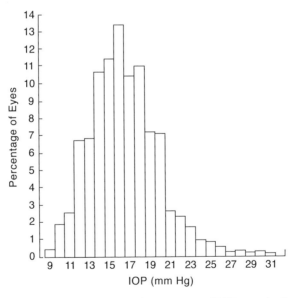

Figure 2-3 Frequency distribution of intraocular pressure: 5220 eyes in the Framingham Eye Study. (*Modified from Colton T, Ederer F. The distribution of intraocular pressures in the general population. Surv Ophthalmol. 1980;25:123–129.*)

IOP can be considered "elevated" or unsafe: some eyes undergo damage at IOPs of 18 mm Hg or less, whereas others tolerate IOPs in the 30s. However, elevation of IOP is still considered a very important risk factor for the development of glaucomatous optic nerve damage. Although other risk factors affect an individual's susceptibility to glaucomatous damage, IOP is the only one that can be effectively altered at this time.

Factors Influencing Intraocular Pressure

Intraocular pressure varies with a number of factors, including the time of day, heartbeat, respiration, exercise, fluid intake, systemic medications, and topical medications (Table 2-2). Alcohol consumption results in a transient decrease in IOP. In most studies, caffeine has not shown an appreciable effect on IOP. Cannabis decreases IOP but has not been proven clinically useful because of its short duration of action and poor side-effect

---

Table 2-2 Factors That Affect Intraocular Pressure

Factors that may increase intraocular pressure
  Elevated episcleral venous pressure
    Valsalva maneuver
    Breath holding
    Playing a wind instrument
    Wearing a tight collar or tight necktie
    Bending over or being in a supine position
    Elevated central venous pressure
    Orbital venous outflow obstruction
    Intubation
  Pressure on the eye
    Blepharospasm
    Squeezing and crying, especially in young children
  Elevated body temperature: associated with increased aqueous humor production
  Hormonal influences
    Hypothyroidism
    Thyroid eye disease
  Drugs unrelated to glaucoma therapy
    Lysergic acid diethylamide (LSD)
    Topiramate
    Corticosteroids
    Anticholinergics: may precipitate angle closure
    Ketamine

Factors that may decrease intraocular pressure
  Aerobic exercise
  Anesthetic drugs
    Depolarizing muscle relaxants such as succinylcholine
  Metabolic or respiratory acidosis: decreases aqueous humor production
  Hormonal influences
    Pregnancy
  Drugs unrelated to glaucoma therapy
    Alcohol consumption
    Heroin
    Marijuana (cannabis)

profile. IOP is higher when an individual is recumbent rather than upright, predominantly because of an increase in the episcleral venous pressure. Some individuals have an exaggerated rise in IOP when they lie down, and this tendency may be important in the pathogenesis of some forms of glaucoma. IOP typically increases with age and is genetically influenced: higher pressures are more common in relatives of patients with primary open-angle glaucoma (POAG) than in the general population.

Diurnal Variation

In individuals without glaucoma, IOP varies 2–6 mm Hg over a 24-hour period, as aqueous humor production and outflow change. Higher IOP is associated with wider fluctuation in pressure, and a diurnal fluctuation of greater than 10 mm Hg is suggestive of glaucoma. The time at which peak IOPs occur in any individual is quite variable; however, many people reach their peak daytime pressures in the morning hours. Such fluctuations can be detected through measurement of ocular pressure at multiple times around the clock. Recent evidence suggests that with around-the-clock IOP measurement performed in individuals in habitual body positions (standing or sitting during the daytime and supine at night), many individuals, those with glaucoma and those without, will show peak pressures in the early-morning hours while they are still in bed. Measurement of IOP during nonoffice hours may be useful for determining why optic nerve damage occurs despite apparently adequately controlled pressure. However, the impact of IOP fluctuations on the optic nerve remains unknown. The relationship between blood pressure and IOP may be important in optic nerve damage: systemic hypotension, especially during sleep, has been suggested as a possible cause of decreased optic nerve perfusion resulting in damage.

Clinical Measurement of Intraocular Pressure

Tonometry is the measurement of IOP. In a clinical setting, this measurement requires a force that flattens (applanates) or indents the eye. *Applanation tonometry,* the most widely used method, is based on the Imbert-Fick principle, which states that the pressure inside an ideal dry, thin-walled sphere equals the force necessary to flatten its surface divided by the area of the flattening:

$$P = F/A$$

where P = pressure, F = force, and A = area. In applanation tonometry, the cornea is flattened, and IOP is determined by measuring the applanating force and the area flattened (Fig 2-4).

The *Goldmann applanation tonometer* measures the force necessary to flatten an area of the cornea of 3.06 mm diameter. At this diameter, the resistance of the cornea to flattening is counterbalanced by the capillary attraction of the tear-film meniscus for the tonometer head. Furthermore, the IOP (in mm Hg) equals the flattening force (in grams) multiplied by 10. A split-image prism allows the examiner to determine the flattened area with great accuracy. To outline the area of flattening, fluorescein dye is instilled in the tear film. The semicircles that are visible through the biprism move with the ocular pulse, and

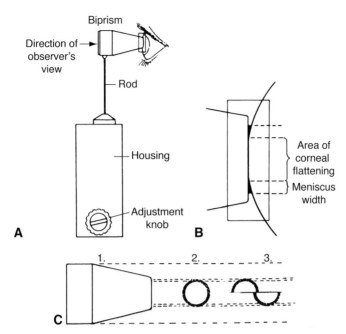

Figure 2-4 Goldmann-type applanation tonometry. **A,** Basic features of tonometer, shown in contact with patient's cornea. **B,** Enlargement shows tear-film meniscus created by contact of biprism and cornea. **C,** View through biprism *(1)* reveals circular meniscus *(2),* which is converted into semicircle *(3)* by prisms. *(Reproduced with permission from Shields MB.* Textbook of Glaucoma. *3rd ed. Baltimore: Williams & Wilkins; 1992.)*

the endpoint is reached when the inner edges of the semicircles touch each other at the midpoint of their excursion (Fig 2-5).

The *Perkins tonometer* is a counterbalanced applanation tonometer that, like the Goldmann tonometer, uses a split-image prism and fluorescein in the tear film. However, it is portable and can be used with the patient either upright or supine.

Applanation measurements are safe, easy to perform, and relatively accurate in most clinical situations. Of the currently available devices, the Goldmann applanation tonometer is the most valid and reliable both in clinical practice and for studies. Because applanation does not displace much fluid (approximately 0.5 µL) or substantially increase the pressure in the eye, this method is relatively unaffected by ocular rigidity.

The accuracy of applanation tonometry is reduced in certain situations, however (see Table 2-3, which lists possible sources of error in tonometry). An excessive amount of fluorescein in the tear film results in wide mires and an artificially high reading, whereas an inadequate amount of fluorescein leads to artificially low readings.

With marked corneal astigmatism, the fluorescein pattern is elliptical. To obtain an accurate reading, the clinician should rotate the prism so the red mark on the prism holder is set at the least-curved meridian of the cornea (along the negative axis). Alternatively, 2 pressure readings taken 90° apart can be averaged.

Corneal edema predisposes to falsely low readings, whereas pressure measurements taken over a corneal scar will be falsely high. Tonometry performed over a soft contact

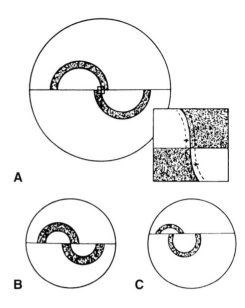

Figure 2-5 Semicircles of Goldmann-type applanation tonometer. **A,** Proper width and position. Enlargement depicts excursions of semicircles caused by ocular pulsations. **B,** Semicircles are too wide. **C,** Improper vertical and horizontal alignment. *(Reproduced with permission from Shields MB. Textbook of Glaucoma. 3rd ed. Baltimore: Williams & Wilkins; 1992.)*

lens gives falsely low values. Alterations in scleral rigidity may compromise the accuracy of measurements; for example, applanation readings that follow scleral buckling procedures may be inaccurately low.

Applanation tonometry measurements are also affected by the central corneal thickness (CCT). Recently, the importance of CCT and its effect on the accuracy of IOP measurement has become better understood. Measurement with the Goldmann tonometer is most accurate when the CCT is 520 μm. Increased CCT may give an artificially high IOP measurement and an artificially low reading. IOP measured after photorefractive keratectomy (PRK) and laser in situ keratomileusis (LASIK) may be reduced because of changes in the corneal thickness induced by these and other refractive procedures.

Table 2-3 Possible Sources of Error in Tonometry

Squeezing of the eyelids
Breath holding or Valsalva maneuver
Pressure on the globe
Extraocular muscle force applied to a restricted globe
Tight collar or tight necktie
Obesity or straining to reach slit lamp
An inaccurately calibrated tonometer
Excessive or inadequate amount of fluorescein
High corneal astigmatism
Central corneal thickness greater or less than normal
Corneal biomechanical properties (eg, rigidity)
Corneal scarring or band keratopathy
Corneal irregularity
Edema
Technician errors
Measurement done over a soft contact lens

The relationship between measured IOP and CCT is not linear, so it is important to remember that any correction factors are only estimates at best. In addition, the biomechanical properties of an individual cornea may vary, such that changes in the relative stiffness or rigidity of the cornea alter IOP measurement. Measurements obtained with the most common types of tonometers (Goldmann, Perkins, pneumatonometer, noncontact tonometer, and Tono-Pen) are affected by CCT. Currently, there is no validated correction factor for the effect of CCT on applanation tonometers; therefore, clinical application of any of the correction methods proposed in the literature should be avoided.

The Ocular Hypertension Treatment Study (OHTS) found that low corneal thickness was a strong predictive factor for the development of glaucoma in subjects with ocular hypertension. Subjects with a corneal thickness of 555 μm or less had a threefold greater risk of developing POAG compared with participants who had a corneal thickness of more than 588 μm. Whether this increased risk of glaucoma is due to underestimating actual IOP in patients with low corneal thickness or whether low corneal thickness is a risk factor independent of IOP measurement has not been completely determined; but OHTS found CCT to be a risk factor for progression independent of IOP level.

Brandt JD. The influence of corneal thickness on the diagnosis and management of glaucoma. *J Glaucoma.* 2001;10(5 Suppl 1):S65–S67.

Doughty MJ, Zaman ML. Human corneal thickness and its impact on intraocular pressure measures: a review and meta-analysis approach. *Surv Ophthalmol.* 2000;44(5):367–408.

Gordon MO, Beiser JA, Brandt JA, et al. The Ocular Hypertension Treatment Study: baseline factors that predict the onset of primary open-angle glaucoma. *Arch Ophthalmol.* 2002;120(6):714–720.

Mills RP. If intraocular pressure measurement is only an estimate—then what? *Ophthalmology.* 2000;107(10):1807–1808.

Shah S. Accurate intraocular pressure measurement—the myth of modern ophthalmology? *Ophthalmology.* 2000;107(10):1805–1807.

Sommer A, Tielsch JM, Katz J, et al. Relationship between intraocular pressure and primary open angle glaucoma among white and black Americans. The Baltimore Eye Survey. *Arch Ophthalmol.* 1991;109(8):1090–1095.

Methods other than Goldmann-type applanation tonometry

With the recognition that the accuracy of applanation tonometry is dependent on many uncontrollable factors, there has been renewed interest in developing novel tonometric methods. In particular, new tonometers aim to lessen the potential inaccuracies in measurement that are secondary to differences in corneal thickness and rigidity. One such technology is the *dynamic contour tonometer (DCT),* a nonapplanation contact tonometer that may be more independent of corneal biomechanical properties and thickness than are older tonometers.

Noncontact (air-puff) tonometers determine IOP, without touching the eye, by measuring the time necessary for a given force of air to flatten a given area of the cornea. Readings obtained with these instruments vary widely, and IOP is often overestimated. Noncontact tonometers are often used in large-scale glaucoma-screening programs or by nonmedical health care providers.

Many of the *portable electronic applanating* devices (eg, Tono-Pen) contain a strain gauge and produce an electrical signal as the tip of the instrument applanates a very small area of the cornea. This device is particularly useful for patients with corneal scars or edema.

The *pneumatic tonometer,* or *pneumotonometer,* has a pressure-sensing device that consists of a gas-filled chamber covered with a silastic diaphragm. The gas in the chamber escapes through an exhaust vent. As the diaphragm touches the cornea, the gas vent decreases in size and the pressure in the chamber rises. Because this instrument applanates only a small area of the cornea, it is especially useful in the presence of corneal scars or edema.

Schiøtz tonometry determines IOP by measuring the indentation of the cornea produced by a known weight. The indentation is read on a linear scale on the instrument and is converted to millimeters of mercury by a calibration table. Because of a number of practical and theoretical problems, however, Schiøtz tonometry is now rarely used.

It is possible to estimate IOP by *digital pressure* on the globe, referred to as *tactile tension.* This test may be used with uncooperative patients, but it may be inaccurate even in very experienced hands. In general, tactile tensions are useful only for detecting large differences between the patient's two eyes.

Infection Control in Clinical Tonometry

Many infectious agents—including the viruses responsible for acquired immunodeficiency syndrome (AIDS), hepatitis, and epidemic keratoconjunctivitis—can be recovered from tears. Tonometers must be cleaned after each use so that transfer of such agents can be prevented:

- The prism head of both Goldmann-type tonometers and the Perkins tonometer should be cleaned immediately after use. The prisms should either be soaked in a 1:10 sodium hypochlorite solution (household bleach), in 3% hydrogen peroxide, or in 70% isopropyl alcohol for 5 minutes, or be thoroughly wiped with an alcohol sponge. If a soaking solution is used, the prism should be rinsed and dried before reuse. If alcohol is employed, it should be allowed to evaporate, or the prism head should be dried before reuse, to prevent damage to the epithelium.
- The front surface of the air-puff tonometer should be wiped with alcohol between uses because the instrument may be contaminated by tears from the patient.
- Portable electronic applanating devices employ a disposable cover, which should be replaced immediately after each use.

For other tonometers, consult the manufacturer's recommendations.

CHAPTER 3

Clinical Evaluation

History and General Examination

Appropriate management of glaucoma depends on the clinician's ability to diagnose the specific form of glaucoma in a given patient, to determine the severity of the condition, to predict the likelihood of progression, and to detect progression when it occurs. Clinical evaluation of the glaucoma patient should include a history of the current complaint, including symptoms, onset, duration, and severity. Past ocular history (medical and surgical) and a general medical history, including the patient's current medications and allergies, should be obtained. On physical examination, prior to biomicroscopy, the patient's pulse and blood pressure should be recorded.

The clinician should inquire about symptoms often associated with glaucoma, such as pain, redness, colored halos around lights, alteration of vision, and loss of vision. Similarly, the general medical history should include specific inquiry about diseases that may have ocular manifestations or that may affect the patient's ability to tolerate medications. Such conditions include diabetes, cardiac and pulmonary disease, hypertension, hemodynamic shock, systemic hypotension, sleep apnea, Raynaud phenomenon, migraine and other neurologic diseases, and renal stones. The clinician should take note of a history of corticosteroid use. See also BCSC Section 1, *Update on General Medicine.*

Refraction

Neutralizing any refractive error is crucial for accurate perimetry with most perimeters, and the clinician should understand how the patient's refractive state could affect the diagnosis. Hyperopic eyes are at increased risk of angle-closure glaucoma and generally have smaller discs. Myopia is associated with disc morphologies that can be clinically confused with glaucoma, and myopic eyes are at increased risk of pigment dispersion.

External Adnexae

Examination and assessment of the external ocular adnexae is useful for determining the presence of a variety of conditions associated with secondary glaucomas as well as external ocular manifestations of glaucoma therapy. The entities described in this section are discussed in greater depth and illustrated in other volumes of the BCSC series; consult the *Master Index.*

An example of an association between adnexal changes and systemic disease is *tuberous sclerosis (Bourneville syndrome)*, in which glaucoma may occur secondary to vitreous hemorrhage, anterior segment neovascularization, or retinal detachment. Typical external and cutaneous signs of tuberous sclerosis include a hypopigmented lesion termed the "ash-leaf sign" and a red-brown papular rash (adenoma sebaceum) that is often found on the face and chin.

Glaucoma is commonly associated with *neurofibromatosis (von Recklinghausen disease)*, likely secondary to developmental abnormalities of the anterior chamber angle. Subcutaneous plexiform neuromas are a hallmark of the type 1 variant of neurofibromatosis. When found in the upper eyelid, the plexiform neuroma can produce a classic S-shaped upper eyelid deformity strongly associated with risk of glaucoma.

In *juvenile xanthogranuloma*, yellow and/or orange papules are commonly found on the skin of the head and neck. Secondary glaucoma may cause acute pain and photophobia and ultimately significant vision loss. *Oculodermal melanocytosis (nevus of Ota)* presents with the key finding of hyperpigmentation of periocular skin. Intraocular pigmentation is also increased, which contributes to a higher incidence of glaucoma and may possibly increase the risk of melanoma. *Axenfeld-Rieger syndrome*, an autosomal dominant disorder with variable penetrance, is associated with microdontia (small, peglike incisors), hypodontia (decreased number of teeth), and anodontia (focal absence of teeth). Maxillary hypoplasia may also be present. Glaucoma occurs in 50% of cases in late childhood or adulthood.

Several entities are associated with signs of increased episcleral venous pressure. The presence of a facial cutaneous angioma (nevus flammeus, or port-wine stain) can indicate *encephalofacial angiomatosis (Sturge-Weber syndrome)*. Hemifacial hypertrophy may also be observed. The cutaneous hemangiomas of the *Klippel-Trénaunay-Weber syndrome* extend over an affected, secondarily hypertrophied limb and may also involve the face.

Orbital varices are associated with secondary glaucoma. Intermittent unilateral proptosis and dilated eyelid veins are key external signs of orbital varices. Carotid cavernous, dural cavernous, and other *arteriovenous fistulae* can produce orbital bruits, restricted ocular motility, proptosis, and pulsating exophthalmos. *Superior vena cava syndrome* can cause proptosis and facial and eyelid edema, as well as conjunctival chemosis. *Thyroid eye disease* and its associated glaucoma are associated with exophthalmos, eyelid retraction, and motility disorders.

Use of prostaglandin analogues may result in trichiasis, hypertrichosis, distichiasis, and growth of facial hair around the eyes, as well as increased skin pigmentation involving the eyelids. Use of glaucoma hypotensive agents may also result in an allergic contact dermatitis. Chapter 7 discusses these agents in detail.

Pupils

Pupil size may be affected by glaucoma therapy, and pupillary responses are one measure of compliance in patients who are on miotic therapy. Testing for a relative afferent pupillary defect may detect asymmetric optic nerve damage. Corectopia, ectropion uveae, and pupillary abnormalities may also be observed in some forms of secondary open-angle glaucoma and angle-closure glaucoma. In some clinical situations, it is not possible to assess the pupils objectively for the presence of a relative afferent defect, and a subjective comparison between the eyes of the perceived brightness of a test light may be helpful. Testing for color vision, extraocular motility, and cranial nerve abnormality may also be indicated.

Biomicroscopy

Biomicroscopy of the anterior segment is performed for signs of underlying or associated ocular disease. BCSC Section 8, *External Disease and Cornea,* discusses slit-lamp technique and the examination of the external eye in greater depth.

Conjunctiva

Eyes with acutely elevated intraocular pressure (IOP) may show conjunctival hyperemia. The chronic elevation of IOP that can occur with arteriovenous fistulae may produce massive episcleral venous dilation. Long-term use of sympathomimetics and prostaglandin analogues may also cause conjunctival hyperemia, and long-term use of epinephrine derivatives may result in black adrenochrome deposits in the conjunctiva. The use of topical antiglaucoma medication can also cause decreased tear production, allergic and hypersensitivity reactions (papillary and follicular conjunctivitis), foreshortening of the conjunctival fornices, and scarring. Prior to filtering surgery, the presence or absence of subconjunctival scarring or other conjunctival abnormalities should be assessed. The presence or absence of any filtering bleb should be noted. If a bleb is present, its size, height, degree of vascularization, and integrity should be noted, and in the situation of postoperative hypotony, a Seidel test performed.

Episclera and sclera

Dilation of the episcleral vessels may indicate elevated episcleral venous pressure, as seen in the secondary glaucomas associated with Sturge-Weber syndrome, arteriovenous fistulae, or thyroid eye disease. Sentinel vessels may be seen in eyes harboring an intraocular tumor. The clinician should note any thinning or staphylomatous areas.

Cornea

Enlargement of the cornea associated with breaks in the Descemet membrane (Haab striae) is commonly found in developmental glaucoma patients. Glaucomas associated with other anterior segment anomalies are described in the following discussions. Punctate epithelial defects, especially in the inferonasal interpalpebral region, are often indicative of medication toxicity. Microcystic epithelial edema is commonly associated with elevated IOP, particularly when the IOP rise is acute. The following corneal endothelial abnormalities can be important clues to underlying associated secondary glaucoma:

- Krukenberg spindle in pigmentary glaucoma
- deposition of exfoliative material in exfoliation syndrome
- keratic precipitates in uveitic glaucoma
- irregular and vesicular lesions in posterior polymorphous dystrophy
- a "beaten bronze" appearance in the iridocorneal endothelial syndrome

An anteriorly displaced Schwalbe line is found in Axenfeld-Rieger syndrome. The clinician should note the presence of traumatic or surgical corneal scars. The central corneal thickness (CCT) of all patients suspected of glaucoma should be assessed by corneal pachymetry, as low central corneal thickness is a risk factor for glaucoma. (See Chapters 2 and 4.)

Anterior chamber

When evaluating the anterior chamber, the examiner should note the uniformity of depth of the chamber and estimate the width of the chamber angle. In the Van Herick method of estimating angle width, the examiner projects a narrow slit beam onto the cornea, just anterior to the limbus. This method may miss narrow angles or angle closure and is not a substitute for gonioscopy, which is discussed in detail later in this chapter (Figs 3-1, 3-2, Table 3-1).

Iris bombé can result in an anterior chamber that is deep centrally and shallow or flat peripherally. Aqueous misdirection and pseudoexfoliation may also be associated with reduced anterior chamber depth and narrow angles. Iris masses, choroidal effusions, or trauma can produce an irregular iris surface contour and nonuniformity or asymmetry in anterior chamber depth. In many circumstances, especially in the assessment of narrow-angle glaucoma, comparing the chamber depth of the 2 eyes is of substantial value. The presence of inflammatory cells, red blood cells, floating pigment, or inflammatory debris (such as fibrin) should be noted. The degree of inflammation (flare and cell) should be determined before instillation of eyedrops.

Iris

Examination should be performed before pupillary dilation. The clinician should note heterochromia, iris atrophy, transillumination defects, ectropion uveae, corectopia, nevi, nodules, and exfoliative material. Early stages of neovascularization of the anterior segment

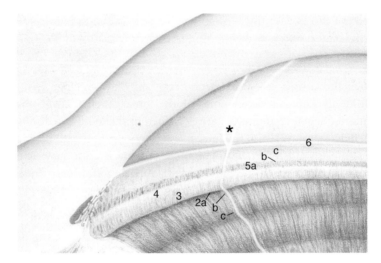

Figure 3-1 Gonioscopic appearance of a normal anterior chamber angle. *2*, Peripheral iris: *a*, insertion; *b*, curvature; *c*, angular approach. *3*, Ciliary body band. *4*, Scleral spur. *5*, Trabecular meshwork: *a*, posterior; *b*, mid; *c*, anterior. *6*, Schwalbe line. *Asterisk*, Corneal optical wedge.

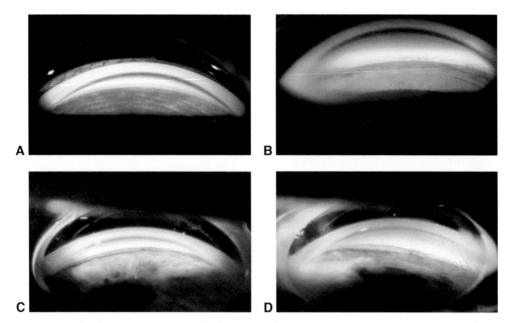

Figure 3-2 **A,** Normal open angle. Gonioscopic photograph shows trace pigmentation of the posterior trabecular meshwork and normal insertion of the iris into a narrow ciliary body band. The Goldmann lens was used. **B,** Normal open angle. This gonioscopic view using the Goldmann lens shows mild pigmentation of the posterior trabecular meshwork. A wide ciliary body band with posterior insertion of the iris can also be seen. **C,** Narrow angle. This gonioscopic view using the Zeiss lens without indentation shows pigment in the inferior angle but poor visualization of angle anatomy. **D,** Narrow angle. Gonioscopy with a Zeiss lens with indentation shows peripheral anterior synechiae in the posterior trabecular meshwork. Pigment deposits on the Schwalbe line can also be seen. This is the same angle as shown in part **C.** *(Courtesy of Elizabeth A. Hodapp, MD.)*

may appear as either fine tufts around the pupillary margin or a fine network of vessels on the surface of the iris. Visualization of neovascular tufts with biomicroscopy may require increased magnification. The clinician should also examine the iris for evidence of trauma, such as sphincter tears or iridodonesis. Iris color should be noted, especially in patients being considered for treatment with a prostaglandin analogue.

Table 3-1 Gonioscopic Examination

Tissue	Features and Pathologic Findings
Posterior cornea	Pigmentation, guttae, corneal endothelium
Schwalbe line	Thickening, anterior displacement
Trabecular meshwork	Pigmentation, peripheral anterior synechiae (PAS), inflammatory or neovascular membranes, keratic precipitates
Scleral spur	Iris processes, presence or absence
Ciliary body band	Width, regularity, cyclodialysis cleft
Iris	Contour, rubeosis, atrophy, cysts, iridodonesis
Pupil and lens	Exfoliation syndrome, posterior synechiae, position and regularity, sphincter rupture, ectropion uveae
Zonular fibers	Pigmentation, rupture

Lens

The clinician should examine the lens both before and after pupillary dilation, evaluating the size, shape, clarity, and stability of the lens. Findings from this examination may help diagnose lens-related glaucomas and guide management. Before the pupil is dilated, phacodonesis, pseudoexfoliation, subluxation, and dislocation should be noted. A posterior subcapsular cataract may be indicative of long-term corticosteroid use. An intraocular foreign body with siderosis and glaucoma may also result in characteristic lens changes. If an intraocular lens is present, the clinician should record its type and position, along with the status of the posterior capsule.

Fundus

A dilated examination allows the clinician to evaluate the vitreous for signs of inflammation, hemorrhage, or ghost cells. Careful stereoscopic evaluation of the optic disc should be performed, followed by examination of the fundus to detect posterior segment pathology such as hemorrhages, effusions, masses, inflammatory lesions, retinovascular occlusions, diabetic retinopathy, or retinal detachments that can be associated with the glaucomas.

Gonioscopy

Gonioscopy is an essential diagnostic tool and examination technique used to visualize the structures of the anterior chamber angle. Figures 3-1 and 3-2 give schematic and clinical views of the angle as seen with gonioscopy. Gonioscopy is required in order to visualize the chamber angle because, under normal conditions, light reflected from the angle structures undergoes total internal reflection at the tear–air interface. At the tear–air interface, the critical angle (approximately 46°) is reached and light is totally reflected back into the corneal stroma. This prevents direct visualization of the angle structures. All gonioscopy lenses eliminate the tear–air interface by placing a plastic or glass surface adjacent to the front surface of the eye. The small space between the lens and cornea is filled by the patient's tears, saline solution, or a clear viscous substance. Depending on the type of lens employed, the angle can be examined with a direct (eg, Koeppe) system or a mirrored indirect (eg, Goldmann or Zeiss) system (Fig 3-3).

Direct and Indirect Gonioscopy

Gonioscopy techniques fall into 1 of 2 broad categories: direct and indirect (see Fig 3-3). Direct gonioscopy is performed with a binocular microscope, a fiber-optic illuminator or slit-pen light, and a direct goniolens, such as the Koeppe, Barkan, Wurst, Swan-Jacob, or Richardson lens. The lens is placed on the eye, and saline solution is used to fill the space between the cornea and the lens. The saline acts as an optical coupler between the 2 surfaces. The lens provides direct visualization of the chamber angle (ie, light reflected directly from the chamber angle is visualized). With direct gonioscopy lenses, the clinician has an erect view of the angle structures, which is essential when performing goniotomies. Direct gonioscopy is most easily performed with the patient in a supine position, and it is commonly used in the operating room for examining the eyes of infants under anesthesia.

Direct gonioscopy

Indirect

Dynamic

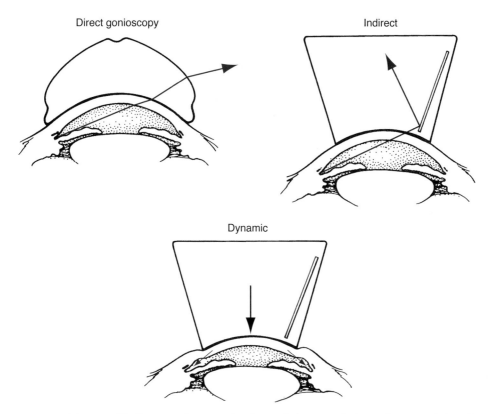

Figure 3-3 Direct and indirect gonioscopy. Gonioscopic lenses eliminate the tear–air interface and total internal reflection. With a direct lens, the light ray reflected from the anterior chamber angle is observed directly, whereas with an indirect lens the light ray is reflected by a mirror within the lens. Posterior pressure with an indirect lens forces open an appositionally closed or narrow anterior chamber angle (dynamic gonioscopy). *(Modified with permission from Wright KW, ed.* Textbook of Ophthalmology. *Baltimore: Williams & Wilkins; 1997.)*

Koeppe-type lenses are also quite useful for performing ophthalmoscopy. When used with a direct ophthalmoscope and a high-plus-power lens, they can provide a good view of the fundus, even through a very small pupil. These lenses are especially helpful for patients with nystagmus or irregular corneas. Inconvenience is the major disadvantage of the direct gonioscopy systems.

Indirect gonioscopy is more frequently used in the clinician's office. Indirect gonioscopy also eliminates the total internal reflection at the surface of the cornea. Light reflected from the chamber angle passes into the indirect gonioscopy lens and is reflected by a mirror within the lens. Indirect gonioscopy may be used with the patient in an upright position, with illumination and magnification provided by a slit lamp. A *goniolens,* which contains a mirror or mirrors, yields an inverted and slightly foreshortened image of the opposite angle. Although the image is inverted with an indirect goniolens, the right–left orientation of a horizontal mirror and the up–down orientation of a vertical mirror remain unchanged. The foreshortening, combined with the upright position of the patient, makes the angle appear a little shallower than it does with direct gonioscopy systems. The

Goldmann-type goniolens requires a viscous fluid such as methylcellulose for optical coupling with the cornea. In lenses with only 1 mirror, the lens must be rotated to view the entire angle. Posterior pressure on the lens, especially if it is tilted, indents the sclera and may falsely narrow the angle. The combination of the lens manipulation and the use of viscous fluid often temporarily reduces the clarity of the cornea and may make subsequent fundus examination, visual field testing, and photography more difficult. These lenses provide the clearest visualization of the anterior chamber angle structures, and they may be modified with antireflective coatings for use during laser procedures.

The Posner, Sussman, and Zeiss 4-mirror goniolenses allow all 4 quadrants of the chamber angle to be visualized without rotation of the lens during examination. They have a smaller area of contact than the Goldmann-type lens and about the same radius of curvature as the cornea; thus, they are optically coupled by the patient's tears. Pressure on the cornea may distort the chamber angle. The examiner can detect this pressure by noting the induced Descemet membrane folds. Although pressure may falsely open the angle, the technique of dynamic gonioscopy is sometimes essential for distinguishing iridocorneal apposition from synechial closure. Many clinicians prefer these lenses because of their ease of use, as well as their ability to perform dynamic gonioscopy.

With dynamic gonioscopy (compression or indentation gonioscopy), gentle pressure is placed on the cornea, and aqueous humor is forced into the chamber angle (see Fig 3-3). The posterior diameter of these goniolenses is smaller than the corneal diameter, and posterior pressure can be used to force open a narrowed angle. In inexperienced hands, dynamic gonioscopy may be misleading, as undue pressure on the anterior surface of the cornea may distort the chamber angle or may give the observer the false impression of an open angle. With all indirect gonioscopy techniques, the observer may manipulate the chamber angle by repositioning the patient's eye (having the patient look toward the mirror) or by applying pressure with the posterior surface of the lens to provide more complete evaluation of the chamber angle. However, caution must be used not to induce artificial opening or closing of the anterior chamber angle with these techniques.

Gonioscopic Assessment and Documentation

In performing both direct and indirect gonioscopy, the clinician must recognize the landmarks of the anterior chamber angle. It is important to perform gonioscopy with dim room light and a thin, short light beam in order to minimize the amount of light entering the pupil. An excessive amount of light could result in increased pupillary constriction and a change in the peripheral angle appearance that could falsely open the angle, thereby preventing the correct identification of a narrow or occluded angle. The scleral spur and the Schwalbe line, two important angle landmarks, are most consistently identified; a convenient gonioscopic technique to determine the exact position of the Schwalbe line is the parallelopiped technique. The parallelopiped, or corneal light wedge, technique allows the observer to determine the exact junction of the cornea and the trabecular meshwork. Using a narrow slit beam and sharp focus, the examiner sees 2 linear reflections, one from the external surface of the cornea and its junction with the sclera and the other from the internal surface of the cornea. The 2 reflections meet at the Schwalbe line (see Fig 3-1).

The scleral spur is a thin, pale stripe between the ciliary face and the pigmented zone of the trabecular meshwork. The inferior portion of the angle is generally wider and is the easiest place in which to locate the landmarks. After verifying the landmarks, the clinician should examine the entire angle in an orderly manner (see Table 3-1).

Proper management of glaucoma requires that the clinician determine not only whether the angle is open or closed, but also whether other pathologic findings, such as angle recession or low peripheral anterior synechiae (PAS), are present. In angle closure, the peripheral iris obstructs the trabecular meshwork—that is, the meshwork is not visible on gonioscopy. The width of the angle is determined by the site of insertion of the iris on the ciliary face, the convexity of the iris, and the prominence of the peripheral iris roll. In many cases, the angle appears to be open but very narrow. It is often difficult to distinguish a narrow but open angle from an angle with partial closure; dynamic gonioscopy is useful in this situation (see Figs 3-2 and 3-3).

The best method for describing the angle is to use a standardized grading system or draw the iris contour, the location of the iris insertion, and the angle between the iris and the trabecular meshwork. A variety of gonioscopic grading systems have been developed, all of which facilitate standardized description of angle structures and abbreviate that description. Keep in mind that, with abbreviated descriptions, some details of the angle structure will be eliminated. The most commonly used gonioscopic grading systems are the Shaffer and Spaeth systems. A quadrant-by-quadrant narrative description of the chamber angle noting localized findings such as neovascular tufts, angle recession, or PAS may also be used to document serial gonioscopic findings. If a grading system is used, the clinician should specify which system is being used.

The *Shaffer system* describes the angle between the trabecular meshwork and the iris as follows:

- *Grade 4:* The angle between the iris and the surface of the trabecular meshwork is 45°.
- *Grade 3:* The angle between the iris and the surface of the trabecular meshwork is greater than 20° but less than 45°.
- *Grade 2:* The angle between the iris and the surface of the trabecular meshwork is 20°. Angle closure is possible.
- *Grade 1:* The angle between the iris and the surface of the trabecular meshwork is 10°. Angle closure is probable in time.
- *Slit:* The angle between the iris and the surface of the trabecular meshwork is less than 10°. Angle closure is very likely.
- *0:* The iris is against the trabecular meshwork. Angle closure is present.

The *Spaeth gonioscopic grading system* expands this system to include a description of the peripheral iris contour, the insertion of the iris root, and the effects of dynamic gonioscopy on the angle configuration (Fig 3-4).

Ordinarily, the Schlemm canal is invisible by gonioscopy. Occasionally during gonioscopy, at times in normal eyes, blood refluxes into the Schlemm canal, where it is seen as a faint red line in the posterior portion of the trabecular meshwork (Fig 3-5). Blood enters the Schlemm canal when episcleral venous pressure exceeds IOP, most commonly because

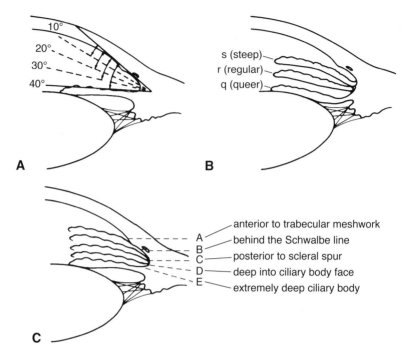

Figure 3-4 The Spaeth gonioscopic classification of the anterior chamber angle, based on 3 variables: **A,** angular width of the angle recess; **B,** configuration of the peripheral iris; and **C,** apparent insertion of the iris root. *(Reproduced with permission from Shields MB.* Textbook of Glaucoma. *3rd ed. Baltimore: Williams & Wilkins; 1992.)*

of compression of the episcleral veins by the lip of the goniolens. Pathologic causes include hypotony and elevated episcleral venous pressure, as in carotid cavernous fistula or Sturge-Weber syndrome.

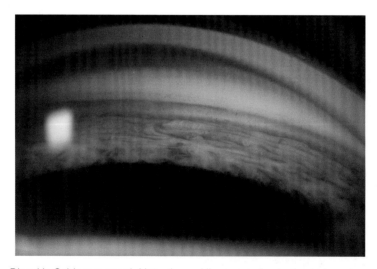

Figure 3-5 Blood in Schlemm canal. Note the red line posterior to the trabecular meshwork in this patient with elevated episcleral venous pressure resulting in blood reflux into the Schlemm canal. *(Courtesy of G. A. Cioffi, MD.)*

Normal blood vessels in the angle include radial iris vessels, portions of the arterial circle of the ciliary body, and vertical branches of the anterior ciliary arteries. Normal vessels are oriented either radially along the iris or circumferentially (in a serpentine manner) in the ciliary body face. Vessels that cross the scleral spur to reach the trabecular meshwork are usually abnormal (Fig 3-6). The vessels seen in Fuchs heterochromic iridocyclitis are fine, branching, unsheathed, and meandering. Patients with neovascular glaucoma have trunklike vessels crossing the ciliary body and scleral spur and arborizing over the trabecular meshwork. Contraction of the myofibroblasts accompanying these vessels leads to PAS formation.

It is important to distinguish PAS from iris processes (the uveal meshwork), which are open and lacy and follow the normal curve of the angle. The angle structures are visible in the open spaces between the processes. Synechiae are more solid or sheetlike (Fig 3-7). They are composed of iris stroma and obliterate the angle recess.

Pigmentation of the trabecular meshwork increases with age and tends to be more marked in individuals with darkly pigmented irides. Pigmentation can be segmental and

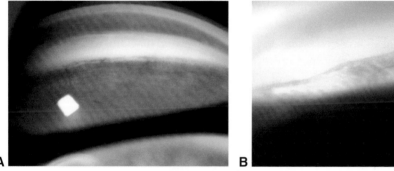

Figure 3-6 Goniophotos of neovascularization of the angle. **A,** Anatomically open angle. **B,** Closed angle. *(Part A courtesy of Keith Barton, MD; part B courtesy of Ronald L. Gross, MD.)*

Figure 3-7 Goniophoto showing both an area of sheetlike PAS *(left)* and an open angle *(right).* *(Courtesy of Louis B. Cantor, MD.)*

is usually most marked in the inferior angle. The pigmentation pattern of an individual angle is dynamic over time, especially in conditions such as pigment dispersion syndrome. Heavy pigmentation of the trabecular meshwork should suggest pigment dispersion or exfoliation syndrome. Exfoliation syndrome may appear clinically similar to pigment dispersion syndrome, with pigment granules on the anterior surface of the iris, increased pigment in the anterior chamber angle, and secondary open-angle glaucoma. Pigmentation of the angle structures is usually patchy in exfoliation syndrome, as compared with the more uniform pigment distribution seen in pigment dispersion syndrome. In addition, a line of pigment deposition anterior to the Schwalbe line is often present in exfoliation syndrome (Sampaolesi line). Other conditions that cause increased anterior chamber angle pigmentation include melanoma, trauma, surgery, inflammation, angle closure, and hyphema.

Posttraumatic angle recession may be associated with monocular open-angle glaucoma. The gonioscopic criteria for diagnosing angle recession include

- an abnormally wide ciliary body band (Fig 3-8)
- increased prominence of the scleral spur
- torn iris processes
- marked variation of ciliary face width and angle depth in different quadrants of the same eye

In evaluating for angle recession, the clinician may find it helpful to compare one part of the angle to other areas in the same eye or to the same area in the fellow eye.

Figure 3-9 illustrates the variety of gonioscopic findings caused by blunt trauma. If the ciliary body separates from the scleral spur (cyclodialysis), it will appear gonioscopically

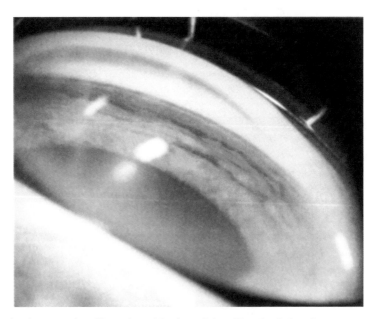

Figure 3-8 Angle recession. Note the widening of the ciliary body band. *(Reprinted with permission from Wright KW, ed.* Textbook of Ophthalmology. *Baltimore: Williams & Wilkins; 1997.)*

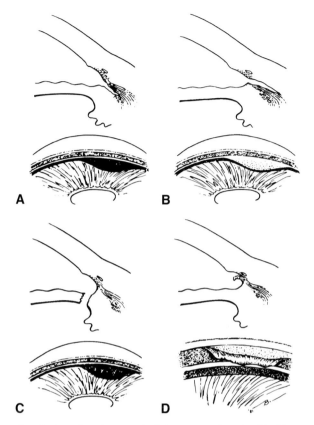

Figure 3-9 Forms of anterior chamber angle injury associated with blunt trauma, showing cross-sectional and corresponding gonioscopic appearance. **A,** Angle recession (tear between longitudinal and circular muscles of ciliary body). **B,** Cyclodialysis (separation of ciliary body from scleral spur) with widening of suprachoroidal space. **C,** Iridodialysis (tear in root of iris). **D,** Trabecular damage (tear in anterior portion of meshwork, creating a flap that is hinged at the scleral spur). *(Reproduced with permission from Shields MB.* Textbook of Glaucoma. *3rd ed. Baltimore: Williams & Wilkins; 1992.)*

as a deep angle recess with a gap between the scleral spur and the ciliary body. Detection of a very small cleft may require ultrasound biomicroscopy.

Other findings that may be visible by gonioscopy are

- microhyphema or hypopyon
- retained anterior chamber foreign body
- iridodialysis
- sclerostomy site
- angle precipitates suggestive of glaucomatocyclitic crisis
- pigmentation of the lens equator
- other peripheral lens abnormalities
- intraocular lens haptics
- ciliary body tumors/cyst

Alward WLM. *Color Atlas of Gonioscopy.* San Francisco: Foundation of the American Academy of Ophthalmology; 2001.

Campbell DG. A comparison of diagnostic techniques in angle-closure glaucoma. *Am J Ophthalmol.* 1979;88(2):197–204.

Fellman RL, Spaeth GL, Starita RJ. Gonioscopy: key to successful management of glaucoma. *Focal Points: Clinical Modules for Ophthalmologists.* San Francisco: American Academy of Ophthalmology; 1984, module 7.

Savage JA. Gonioscopy in the management of glaucoma. *Focal Points: Clinical Modules for Ophthalmologists.* San Francisco: American Academy of Ophthalmology; 2006, module 3.

The Optic Nerve

The entire visual pathway is described and illustrated in BCSC Section 5, *Neuro-Ophthalmology.* For further discussion of retinal involvement in the visual process, see Section 12, *Retina and Vitreous.*

Anatomy and Pathology

The optic nerve is the neural connection between the neurosensory retina and the brain, primarily the lateral geniculate body. An understanding of the normal and pathologic appearance of the optic nerve allows the clinician to detect glaucoma, as well as to follow glaucoma cases. The optic nerve is composed of neural tissue, glial tissue, extracellular matrix, and blood vessels. The human optic nerve consists of approximately 1.2–1.5 million axons of retinal ganglion cells (RGCs), although there is significant individual variability. The cell bodies of the RGCs lie in the ganglion cell layer of the retina. The intraorbital optic nerve is divided into 2 components: the anterior optic nerve and the posterior optic nerve. The anterior optic nerve extends from the retinal surface to the retrolaminar region, just where the nerve exits the posterior aspect of the globe. The average diameter of the optic nerve head is approximately 1.5–1.7 mm as measured with planimetry, but it varies widely among individuals and ethnic groups; the optic nerve expands to approximately 3–4 mm immediately upon exiting the globe. The increase in size is accounted for by axonal myelination, glial tissue, and the beginning of the leptomeninges (optic nerve sheath). The axons are separated into fascicles within the optic nerve, with the intervening spaces occupied by astrocytes.

In primates, there are 3 major RGC types involved in conscious visual perception: magnocellular neurons (M cells), parvocellular neurons (P cells), and koniocellular neurons (bistratified cells). M cells have large-diameter axons, synapse in the magnocellular layer of the lateral geniculate body, are sensitive to luminance changes in dim illumination (scotopic conditions), have the largest dendritic field, primarily process information related to motion perception, and are not responsive to color. In comparison to the M cells, the P cells account for approximately 80% of all ganglion cells; they are concentrated in the central retina; and they have smaller-diameter axons, smaller receptive fields, and slower conduction velocity. They synapse in the parvocellular layers of the lateral geniculate body. P cells subserve color vision, are most active under higher luminance conditions, and discriminate fine detail. The cells are motion-insensitive and process information of high spatial frequency (high resolution). The bistratified cells (koniocellular neurons) process information concerned with blue-yellow color opponency. This system, which is likely preferentially activated by short-wavelength perimetry, is inhibited when red and green cones (yellow) are activated and stimulated when blue cones are activated. Bistratified and large M cells each account for approximately 10% of RGCs.

The distribution of nerve fibers as they enter the optic nerve head is shown in Figure 3-10. The arcuate nerve fibers entering the superior and inferior poles of the disc seem to be more susceptible to glaucomatous damage. This susceptibility explains the frequent occurrence of arcuate nerve fiber bundle visual field defects in glaucoma. The arrangement of the axons in the optic nerve head and their differential susceptibility to damage determine the patterns of visual field loss seen in glaucoma, which are described and illustrated later in this chapter.

The anterior optic nerve can be divided into 4 layers:

- nerve fiber
- prelaminar
- laminar
- retrolaminar

The most anterior zone is the superficial nerve fiber layer region, which is continuous with the *nerve fiber layer* of the retina. This region is primarily composed of the axons of the RGCs in transition from the superficial retina to the neuronal component of the optic

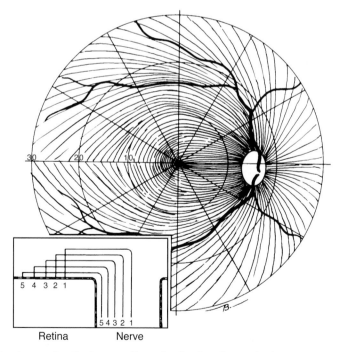

Figure 3-10 Anatomy of retinal nerve fiber distribution. Inset depicts cross-sectional view of axonal arrangement. Peripheral fibers run closer to the choroid and exit in the periphery of the optic nerve, while fibers originating closer to the nerve head are situated closer to the vitreous and occupy a more central portion of the nerve. *(Reproduced with permission from Shields MB.* Textbook of Glaucoma. *3rd ed. Baltimore: Williams & Wilkins; 1992.)*

nerve. The nerve fiber layer can be viewed with the ophthalmoscope when the red-free (green) filter is used. Immediately posterior to the nerve fiber layer is the *prelaminar region,* which lies adjacent to the peripapillary choroid. More posteriorly, the *laminar region* is continuous with the sclera and is composed of the lamina cribrosa, a structure consisting of fenestrated connective tissue lamellae that allow the transit of neural fibers through the scleral coat. Finally, the *retrolaminar region* lies posterior to the lamina cribrosa, is marked by the beginning of axonal myelination, and is surrounded by the leptomeninges of the central nervous system.

The lamina cribrosa is composed of a series of fenestrated sheets of connective tissue and elastic fibers. The lamina cribrosa provides the main support for the optic nerve as it exits the eye, penetrating the scleral coat. The beams of connective tissue are composed primarily of collagen; other extracellular matrix components include elastin, laminin, and fibronectin. Neural components of the optic nerve pass through these connective tissue beams. In addition, relatively large, central fenestrations allow transit of the central retinal artery and central retinal vein. The fenestrations within the lamina have been described histologically as larger superiorly and inferiorly as compared with the temporal and nasal aspects of the optic nerve. It has been suggested that these differences play a role in the development of glaucomatous optic neuropathy. The fenestrations of the lamina cribrosa (laminar dots) may often be seen by ophthalmoscopy at the base of the optic nerve head cup. Between the optic nerve and the adjacent choroidal and scleral tissue lies a rim of connective tissue, the ring of Elschnig. The connective tissue beams of the lamina cribrosa extend from this surrounding connective tissue border and are arranged in a series of parallel, stacked plates.

The vascular anatomy of the anterior optic nerve and peripapillary region has been extensively studied (Fig 3-11). The arterial supply of the anterior optic nerve is derived entirely from branches of the ophthalmic artery via 1 to 5 posterior ciliary arteries. Typically, between 2 and 4 posterior ciliary arteries course anteriorly before dividing into approximately 10–20 short posterior ciliary arteries prior to entering the posterior globe. Often, the posterior ciliary arteries separate into a medial and a lateral group before branching into the short posterior ciliary arteries. The short posterior ciliary arteries penetrate the perineural sclera of the posterior globe to supply the peripapillary choroid, as well as most of the anterior optic nerve. Some short posterior ciliary arteries course, without branching, through the sclera directly into the choroid; others divide within the sclera to provide branches to both the choroid and the optic nerve. Often a noncontinuous arterial circle exists within the perineural sclera, the circle of Zinn-Haller. The central retinal artery, also a posterior orbital branch of the ophthalmic artery, penetrates the optic nerve approximately 10–15 mm behind the globe. The central retinal artery has few, if any, intraneural branches, the exception being an occasional small branch within the retrolaminar region, which may anastomose with the pial system. The central retinal artery courses adjacent to the central retinal vein within the central portion of the optic nerve.

The superficial nerve fiber layer is supplied principally by recurrent retinal arterioles branching from the central retinal artery. These small vessels, originating in the peripapillary nerve fiber layer, run toward the center of the optic nerve head and have been referred to as "epipapillary vessels." The capillary branches from these vessels are continuous with

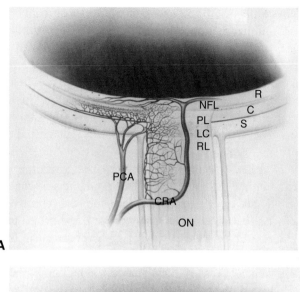

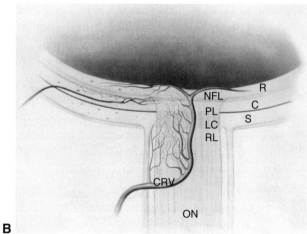

Figure 3-11 Anterior optic nerve vasculature. **A,** Arterial supply to the anterior optic nerve and peripapillary choroid. Lamina cribrosa *(LC)*, superficial nerve fiber layer *(NFL)*, prelamina *(PL)*, retrolamina *(RL)*, central retinal artery *(CRA)*, optic nerve *(ON)*, choroid *(C)*, posterior ciliary artery *(PCA)*, retina *(R)*, sclera *(S)*. **B,** Venous drainage of the anterior optic nerve and peripapillary choroid. Lamina cribrosa *(LC)*, nerve fiber layer *(NFL)*, prelamina *(PL)*, retrolamina *(RL)*, choroid *(C)*, retina *(R)*, sclera *(S)*, optic nerve *(ON)*, central retinal vein *(CRV)*. *(Reprinted with permission from Wright KW, ed. Textbook of Ophthalmology. Baltimore: Williams & Wilkins; 1997:592, Figs 44-2, 44-3. Originally from Ritch R, Shields MB, Krupin T, eds. The Glaucomas. 2nd ed. St Louis: Mosby; 1996:178.)*

the retinal capillaries at the disc margin, but they also have posterior anastomoses with the prelaminar capillaries of the optic nerve. The temporal nerve fiber layer may have an arterial contribution from the cilioretinal artery, when it is present.

The *prelaminar region* is principally supplied by direct branches of the short posterior ciliary arteries and by branches of the circle of Zinn-Haller, when it is present. In eyes with a well-developed circle of Zinn-Haller, arterial branches emerge to supply both the prelaminar and the laminar regions. The lamina cribrosa region also receives its blood supply from branches of the short posterior ciliary arteries or from branches of the circle of Zinn-Haller; this is similar to the prelaminar region. These precapillary branches perforate the outer aspects of the lamina cribrosa before branching into an intraseptal capillary network. Arterioles also branch from the short posterior ciliary arteries and the circle of Zinn-Haller and course posteriorly to supply the pial arteries. These pial arteries often contribute to the laminar region. As in the prelaminar region, the larger vessels of the peripapillary choroid may contribute occasional small arterioles to this region, although there is no connection between the peripapillary choriocapillaris and the capillaries of the optic nerve.

The *retrolaminar region* is also supplied by branches from the short posterior ciliary arteries, as well as by the pial arterial branches coursing adjacent to the retrolaminar optic nerve region. The pial arteries originate from both the central retinal artery, before it pierces the retrobulbar optic nerve, and branches of the short posterior ciliary arteries more anteriorly. The central retinal artery may supply several small intraneural branches in the retrolaminar region.

The rich capillary beds of each of the 4 anatomical regions within the anterior optic nerve are anatomically confluent. The venous drainage of the anterior optic nerve is almost exclusively via a single vein, the central retinal vein. In the nerve fiber layer, blood is drained directly into the retinal veins, which then join to form the central retinal vein. In the prelaminar, laminar, and retrolaminar regions, venous drainage also occurs via the central retinal vein or axial tributaries to the central retinal vein.

Glaucomatous Optic Neuropathy

Glaucomatous optic neuropathy is the sine qua non of all forms of glaucoma (Fig 3-12). Histologically, early glaucomatous cupping consists of loss of axons, blood vessels, and glial cells. The loss of tissue seems to start at the level of the lamina cribrosa and is associated with compaction and fusion of the laminar plates. It is most pronounced at the superior and inferior poles of the disc. Structural optic nerve changes may precede detectable functional loss. Tissue destruction in more advanced glaucoma extends behind the cribriform plate, with posterior neural damage extending to the central visual pathways.

Glaucomatous cupping in infants and children is accompanied by an expansion of the entire scleral ring, which may explain why cupping seems to occur earlier in children and why reversibility of cupping is more prominent with successful treatment in these cases. Cupping may be reversed in adults as well, but such reversal is less frequent and more subtle.

Glaucomatous optic neuropathy is a progressive degeneration of RGCs and their axons, with damage extending from the optic nerve to the major visual centers in the brain, such as the lateral geniculate nucleus. This central visual system degeneration likely results from various factors, which are both intrinsic and extrinsic to the optic nerve. IOP plays a major role in the development of glaucomatous optic neuropathy in most individuals and is considered the most significant risk factor. Unilateral secondary glaucoma, experimental models of glaucoma, and observations of the effect of lowering IOP in

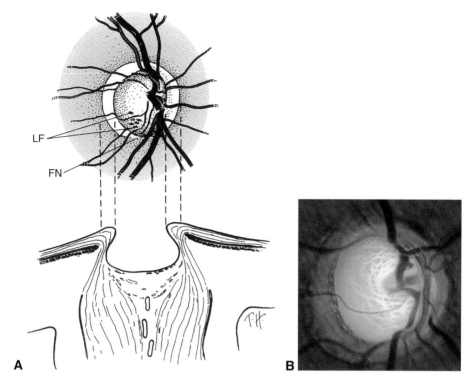

Figure 3-12 **A,** Glaucomatous optic nerve (anterior optic nerve head and transverse view, right eye). Note thinning, undermining, and focal notching *(FN)* of inferior neuroretinal rim; enlarged central cup with visible laminar fenestrations *(LF)*; nasal shift of retinal vessels; and peripapillary atrophy. **B,** Clinical view of glaucomatous optic nerve head demonstrating extensive loss of the neuroretinal rim. *(Part A reprinted with permission from Wright KW, ed. Textbook of Ophthalmology. Baltimore: Williams & Wilkins; 1997. Part B courtesy of Ronald L. Gross, MD.)*

patients all point to this conclusion. However, up to one-third of glaucomatous injury in North America is associated with low IOP. It is clear that factors other than IOP contribute to a given individual's susceptibility to glaucomatous damage.

Damage from direct compression of axonal fibers, with distortion of the lamina cribrosa plates and interruption of axoplasmic flow, may contribute to RGC death. Decreased optic nerve head perfusion and/or disturbance of vascular autoregulation may also contribute to optic nerve damage in glaucoma. Alternatively, changes in systemic hemodynamics may result in perfusion deficits, even at a normal IOP level. Neural degeneration in glaucoma may have a number of triggers. Glutamate excitotoxicity, autoimmunity, and neurotrophic deprivation due to loss of neurons in the lateral geniculate nucleus have all been suggested. Current thinking recognizes that glaucoma is a heterogeneous family of disorders mediated, most likely, by many factors.

Gupta N, Yücel YH. Glaucoma as a neurodegenerative disease. *Curr Opin Ophthalmol.* 2007;18(2):110–114.

Mackenzie PJ, Cioffi GA. Vascular anatomy of the optic nerve head. *Can J Ophthalmol.* 2008;43(3):308–312.

Examination of the Optic Nerve Head

The *optic nerve head,* or *optic disc,* can be examined clinically with a direct ophthalmoscope, an indirect ophthalmoscope, or a slit-lamp biomicroscope combined with a posterior pole lens.

The *direct ophthalmoscope* provides a view of the optic disc through a small pupil. In addition, when used with a red-free filter, it enhances detection of the nerve fiber layer of the posterior pole. The small aperture (5-degree spot) is 1.5 mm in diameter, which is slightly larger than the diameter of the normal optic nerve head. However, the direct ophthalmoscope may not provide sufficient stereoscopic detail to detect subtle changes in optic disc topography.

The *indirect ophthalmoscope* is used for examination of the optic disc in young children, uncooperative patients, individuals with high myopia, and individuals with substantial opacities of the media. With the indirect ophthalmoscope, cupping of the optic nerve can be detected, but, in general, optic nerve cupping and pallor appear less pronounced than with slit-lamp methods, and the magnification is often inadequate for detecting subtle or localized details important in the evaluation of glaucoma. Thus, the indirect ophthalmoscope is not recommended for routine use in examining the optic disc.

The best method of examination for the diagnosis of glaucoma is the *slit lamp* combined with a Hruby lens; a posterior pole contact lens; or a 60, 78, or 90 D lens. The slit beam, rather than diffuse illumination, is useful for determining subtle changes in the contour of the nerve head. This system provides high magnification, excellent illumination, and a stereoscopic view of the disc. This also allows for quantitative measurement of the diameter of the optic disc, by adjusting the height of the slit beam. The disc is viewed through the handheld lens until the height of the slit is the same as the vertical diameter of the disc. The disc diameter can then be calculated by taking into account the lens used. With a 60 D lens, the height of the slit equals the disc diameter in millimeters read directly from the scale. If a 78 D lens is used, the scale reading is multiplied by 1.1, and with a 90 D lens multiplication by 1.3 results in the disc diameter in millimeters. The normal-sized optic disc is approximately 1.5–2.2 mm in diameter.

Slit-lamp techniques require some patient cooperation and moderate pupil size for adequate visibility of the disc.

The optic nerve head is usually round or slightly oval in shape and contains a central *cup.* The tissue between the cup and the disc margin is called the *neural rim* or *neuroretinal rim.* In individuals without glaucoma, the rim has a relatively uniform width and a color that ranges from orange to pink. The size of the physiologic cup is developmentally determined and is related to the size of the disc. For a given number of nerve fibers, the larger the overall disc area, the larger the cup. Cup–disc ratio alone is not an adequate assessment of the optic disc for possible glaucomatous damage. For example, a 0.7 ratio in a large optic disc may be normal, whereas a 0.3 ratio in a very small disc could be pathologic. This shows the importance of assessing the disc size. The size of the cup may increase slightly with age. Nonglaucomatous black individuals, on average, have larger disc areas and larger cup–disc ratios than do whites, although a substantial overlap exists.

Differentiating physiologic or normal cupping from acquired *glaucomatous cupping* of the optic disc can be difficult. The early changes of glaucomatous optic neuropathy are very subtle and include generalized enlargement of the cup, focal rim thinning, superficial disc hemorrhage, nerve fiber loss, asymmetry of cupping, and beta-zone peripapillary atrophy (Table 3-2).

Generalized enlargement of the cup, though difficult to appreciate unless previous photographs or diagrams are available, may be the earliest change detected in glaucoma. Comparing one eye with the fellow eye is helpful, because cup asymmetry is unusual in normal eyes in the absence of disc diameter asymmetry (Fig 3-13). The vertical cup–disc ratio is normally between 0.1 and 0.4, although as many as 5% of individuals without glaucoma will have cup–disc ratios larger than 0.6. Asymmetry of the cup–disc ratio of more than 0.2 occurs in less than 1% of individuals without glaucoma. This asymmetry may be related to disc size asymmetry. Increased size of the physiologic cup may be a familial trait, and it is also seen with high myopia. An oblique insertion of the optic nerve into the globe of individuals with high myopia may also cause a tilted appearance to the optic nerve head. Examination of other family members may clarify whether a large cup is inherited or acquired.

Focal enlargement of the cup appears as localized notching or narrowing of the rim. Focal atrophy most typically occurs at the inferior and superior temporal poles of the optic nerve in early glaucomatous optic neuropathy. *Thinning of the neuroretinal rim* with development of a focal notch or extension of the cup into the neuroretinal rim may be seen. To help identify subtle thinning of the neuroretinal rim, a convention referred to as the *ISNT rule* may be useful. In general, the *I*nferior neuroretinal rim is the thickest, followed by the *S*uperior rim, the *N*asal rim, and finally the *T*emporal rim. However, violation of the

Table 3-2 Ophthalmoscopic Signs of Glaucoma

Generalized	Focal	Less Specific
Large optic cup	Narrowing (notching) of the rim	Exposed lamina cribrosa
Asymmetry of the cups	Vertical elongation of the cup	Nasal displacement of vessels
Progressive enlargement of the cup	Cupping to the rim margin	Baring of circumlinear vessels
	Regional pallor	Peripapillary crescent
	Nerve fiber layer hemorrhage	
	Nerve fiber layer loss	

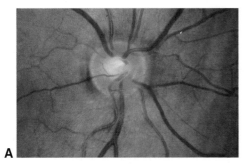 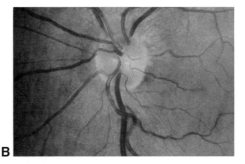

Figure 3-13 Asymmetry of optic nerve cupping. Note the generalized enlargement of the cup in the right eye **(A)** as compared with the left eye **(B)**. Asymmetry of the cup–disc ratio of more than 0.2 occurs in less than 1% of individuals without glaucoma. *(Courtesy of G. A. Cioffi, MD.)*

ISNT rule is not highly specific and may be seen in normal eyes as well. If the rim widths do not follow this progression, there should be increased concern for the presence of focal loss of rim tissue. Deep localized notching, where the lamina cribrosa is visible at the disc margin, is sometimes termed an *acquired optic disc pit.* If notching or acquired pit formation occurs at either the superior or the inferior pole of the disc (or at both poles), the cup becomes vertically oval (Fig 3-14). Even in the normal eye, laminar trabeculations or pores may be seen as grayish dots in the base of the physiologic cup. With glaucomatous optic neuropathy, neural atrophy results in more extensive exposure of the underlying lamina cribrosa and may reveal more laminar pores in the optic nerve cup. Nasalization of the central retinal artery and central retinal vein is often seen as the cup enlarges.

Although *nerve fiber layer hemorrhages* usually appear as a linear red streak on or near the disc surface (Fig 3-15), their appearance is highly variable. One-third of glaucoma patients at some time during the course of their disease may develop hemorrhages, which typically clear over several weeks to months. They are often followed by localized notching of the rim and visual field loss. Some glaucoma patients have repeated episodes of optic disc hemorrhage; others have none. Individuals with normal-tension glaucoma are more likely to have disc hemorrhages. Optic disc hemorrhage is an important prognostic sign

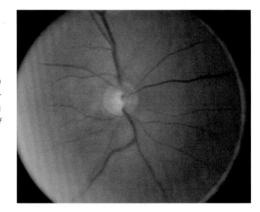

Figure 3-14 Vertical elongation of the cup with localized thinning of the inferior neuroretinal rim in the right eye of a patient with moderately advanced glaucoma. *(Courtesy of Jody Piltz-Seymour, MD.)*

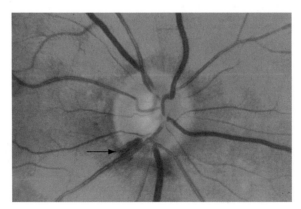

Figure 3-15 Drance hemorrhage *(arrow)* of the right optic nerve at the 7-o'clock position in a patient with early open-angle glaucoma. *(Courtesy of G. A. Cioffi, MD.)*

for the development or progression of visual field loss, and any patient with a disc hemorrhage requires detailed evaluation and follow-up. Disc hemorrhages may also be caused by posterior vitreous detachments, diabetes mellitus, branch retinal vein occlusions, and anticoagulation therapy.

Axons in the nerve fiber layer of the normal eye may best be visualized with red-free illumination. The nerve fiber layer extending from the neuroretinal rim to the surrounding peripapillary retina appears as fine striations created by the bundles of axons. In the healthy eye, the nerve fiber layer bundles have a plush, refractile appearance. With progressive glaucomatous optic neuropathy, the nerve fiber layer thins and becomes less visible. The loss may be diffuse (generalized) or localized to specific bundles (Fig 3-16). *Focal abnormalities* can consist of slitlike grooves or wedge-shaped defects. Slitlike defects can be seen in normal retinal nerve fiber layer anatomy, although they usually do not extend to the disc margin. Early wedge-shaped defects are sometimes visible only at a distance from the optic disc margin. *Diffuse nerve fiber loss* is more common in glaucoma than is focal loss but also more difficult to observe. The nerve fiber layer can be visualized clearly in high-contrast black-and-white photographs, and experienced observers can recognize even early disease if good-quality photographs are available. Both direct ophthalmoscopy and slit-lamp techniques can be successfully employed to observe the retinal nerve fiber layer. The combination of red-free filter, wide slit beam, and posterior pole lens at the slit lamp affords the best view.

In the early stages of nerve fiber loss, often before enlargement of the cup, existing neuroretinal rim tissue can be observed to become more translucent. The clinician can best observe this *neuroretinal rim translucency* by using a lens at the slit-lamp biomicroscope, employing a thin slit beam, and confining the beam to the disc surface.

As the nerve fiber loss continues, the cup may begin to enlarge by progressive posterior collapse and compaction of the remaining viable nerve fibers. In circumstances

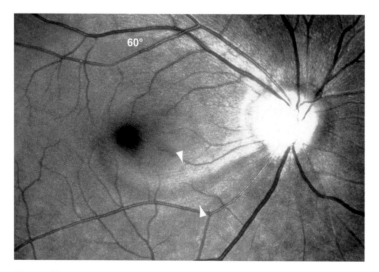

Figure 3-16 Nerve fiber layer photograph shows a nerve fiber bundle defect *(arrowheads)*. *(Courtesy of Louis B. Cantor, MD.)*

where the neuroretinal tissue—but not the overlying nerve head vasculature—has collapsed, blood vessels traverse collapsed neural rim tissue.

Peripapillary atrophy occurs as 2 types. Alpha-zone peripapillary atrophy is the typical temporal crescent often seen in myopia with areas of hyperpigmentation and hypopigmentation; it has no known impact on glaucoma. The second type, *beta-zone peripapillary atrophy,* is seen with greater frequency and is more extensive in eyes with glaucoma than in unaffected eyes. It represents loss of choriocapillaris and retinal pigment epithelium, leaving only large choroidal vessels and sclera and resulting in the characteristic white appearance adjacent to the disc margin. The location of the atrophy often correlates with the position of visual field defects. Other, less specific signs of glaucomatous damage include nasal displacement of the vessels, narrowing of peripapillary retinal vessels, and baring of the circumlinear vessels. With advanced damage, the cup becomes pale and markedly excavated.

It is important to recognize that glaucomatous optic nerve damage is only one type of pathologic change of the optic nerve; other etiologies of optic nerve changes should be considered in the differential diagnosis. Optic discs in which the remaining neuroretinal rim tissue is pale may need to be evaluated for causes of nonglaucomatous optic atrophy (see BCSC Section 5, *Neuro-Ophthalmology*). With rare exceptions, glaucoma results in increased cupping and pallor within the cup, but not pallor of the remaining rim tissue. However, disc pallor may occur following previous episodes of high IOP elevation. In addition, a large cup may be physiologic in a large disc. This can best be assessed following measurement of the disc diameter. The ophthalmologist must also consider drusen or coloboma as possible causes of optic nerve change and visual field loss. Finally, the myopic disc represents a challenge when the ophthalmologist is attempting to assess possible glaucoma damage. The size, tilting, and associated structural changes often preclude the ability to definitively determine the likelihood of glaucoma damage.

Recording of optic nerve findings

It is common practice to grade an optic disc by comparing the diameter of the cup with the diameter of the disc. This ratio is usually expressed as a decimal, for example, 0.2; but such a description poorly conveys the appearance of the nerve head. To clarify the description, the examiner must specify whether the cup is being defined by the change in *contour* between the central area of the disc and the surrounding rim. Furthermore, the examiner must specify what is being measured: the horizontal diameter, the vertical diameter, or the longest diameter. If cup–disc ratios are to be used, the description should include the dimensions of the cup specified by both color and contour criteria in both the vertical and horizontal meridians. The rim, which contains the neural elements, should also be described in detail: color, width, focal thinning or pallor, and slope.

A detailed, annotated diagram of the optic disc topography is preferable to the recording of a simple cup–disc ratio. The diagram must be of adequate size to allow depiction of important topographic landmarks and morphologic features. With annotation, the diagram can convey the cup–disc ratio along all dimensions and serves to document the presence or absence of regions of rim thinning, notching, hemorrhage, rim translucency, vessel overpass, and other findings.

Photography, particularly simultaneous stereophotography, is an excellent method for recording the appearance of the optic nerve for detailed examination and sequential follow-up. This record allows the examiner to compare the present status of the patient with the baseline status without resorting to memory or grading systems. Moreover, photographs allow better evaluation when a patient has changed doctors. Sometimes subtle optic disc changes become apparent when the clinician compares one set of photographs to a previous set. Careful diagrams of the optic nerve head are useful when photography is not possible or available.

Quantitative measurement of the optic nerve head and retinal nerve fiber layer

Since the 1850s, the appearance of the optic nerve head has been recognized as critical in assessing the disease status of glaucoma. However, optic disc assessment can be quite subjective, and interobserver and intraobserver variation is greater than desirable, given the importance of accurate assessments. Thus, the need for reliable and objective measures of optic disc and associated retinal nerve fiber layer morphology is clear. A number of sophisticated image analysis systems have been developed in recent years to evaluate the optic disc and retinal nerve fiber layer. These instruments give quantitative measurements of various anatomical parameters.

Confocal scanning laser ophthalmoscopy (Fig 3-17A) can be used for creation of a 3-dimensional image of the optic nerve head. The optical design of instruments using confocal scanning laser technology allows for a series of tomographic slices, or optical sections, of the structure being imaged. The images acquired by this method are stored as a computer data file and manipulated to reconstruct the 3-dimensional structure, display the image, and perform data analysis. Parameters such as cup area, cup volume, rim volume, cup–disc ratio, and peripapillary nerve fiber layer thickness are then calculated. Software to evaluate the images for the statistical likelihood of glaucoma damage as well as identify areas of possible progression over time are available.

Techniques such as scanning laser polarimetry and optical coherence tomography have been used to acquire images of the retinal nerve fiber layer. The *scanning laser polarimeter* (Fig 3-17B) is basically a scanning laser ophthalmoscope outfitted with a polarization modulator and detector to take advantage of the birefringent properties of the retinal nerve fiber layer arising from the predominantly parallel nature of its microtubule substructure. As light passes through the nerve fiber layer, the polarization state changes. The deeper layers of retinal tissue reflect the light back to the detector, where the degree to which the polarization has been changed is recorded. The acquired data can then be stored, displayed, and manipulated by computer programs, just as with the unmodified confocal scanning laser ophthalmoscope. The fundamental parameter being measured with this instrumentation is *relative* (not absolute) retinal nerve fiber layer thickness. The addition of a variable corneal compensator (VCC) to include analysis of potential anterior segment birefringence has improved the quality of the information available with this technique.

Optical coherence tomography (OCT) (Fig 3-17C) uses interferometry and low-coherence light to obtain a high-resolution cross section of biological structures. Current OCT instruments have an axial resolution of about 10 μm in the human eye, and OCT has the potential to yield an absolute measurement of nerve fiber layer thickness. In vivo OCT

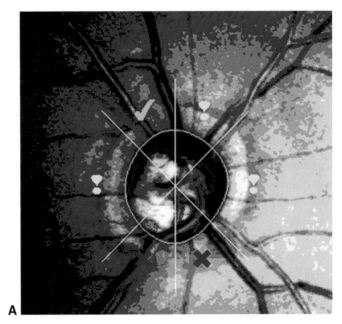

A

Figure 3-17 Commonly used instruments for optic disc and nerve fiber layer imaging in glaucoma. **A,** Optic nerve head analysis with Heidelberg Retina Tomograph (HRT) shows thinning of the inferior neuroretinal rim using Moorfields regression analysis (green check mark = within normal limits; yellow exclamation mark = borderline; red x = abnormal). **B,** Retinal nerve fiber layer analysis with scanning laser polarimetry. *Top,* Deviation map. *Bottom,* Generalized thinning or diffuse loss of the nerve fiber layer in the right eye. **C,** Retinal nerve fiber layer analysis with optical coherence tomography. *Top,* Thinning of the inferior bundle (blunted peak) in the right eye. *Middle,* Thinning of the inferior and nasal nerve fiber layer in the left eye. *Bottom,* Comparison of both eyes. *(Reproduced with permission from Salinas-Van Orman E, Bashford KP, Craven ER. Nerve fiber layer, macula, and optic disc imaging in glaucoma. Focal Points: Clinical Modules for Ophthalmologists. San Francisco: American Academy of Ophthalmology; 2006, module 8.)*

measurements appear to correlate with histologic measurements of the same tissues. With a resolution of 3–5 µm, spectral domain OCT (SD-OCT) provides greatly increased resolution of images and is now clinically available.

Quantitative measurement of the optic disc and retinal nerve fiber layer is a promising nascent science. The instrumentation and techniques used to acquire quantitative imaging and analysis of nerve head and nerve fiber layer anatomical parameters are rapidly evolving. Both for single measurements directed at detecting the presence of glaucoma and, especially, for serial measurements necessary to determine clinical progression of glaucoma, these technologies have great potential. Still, the clinician must remember that no system of measurement and observation is currently more useful or has proven more reliable than good-quality stereophotographs combined with detailed and careful clinical examination.

Chen YY, Chen PP, Xu L, Ernst PK, Wang L, Mills RP. Correlation of peripapillary nerve fiber layer thickness by scanning laser polarimetry with visual field defects in patients with glaucoma. *J Glaucoma.* 1998;7(5):312–316.

Wollstein G, Garway-Heath DF, Hitchings RA. Identification of early glaucoma cases with the scanning laser ophthalmoscope. *Ophthalmology.* 1998;105(8):1557–1563.

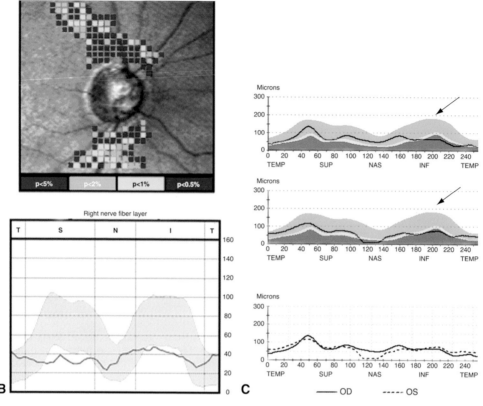

Figure 3-17 *(continued)*

The Visual Field

For many years, the standard method of measuring the visual dysfunction seen with glaucomatous injury has been assessment of the visual field with clinical *perimetry,* which measures differential light sensitivity, or the ability of the subject to distinguish a stimulus from a uniform background. The classic description of the visual field, given by Traquair (1875–1954), is "an island hill of vision in a sea of darkness." The island of vision is usually described as a 3-dimensional graphic representation of differential light sensitivity at different positions in space (Fig 3-18).

Perimetry has traditionally served 2 major purposes in the management of glaucoma:

1. identification and quantification of abnormal fields
2. longitudinal assessment to detect glaucomatous progression

Quantification of visual field sensitivity enables detection of initial loss by comparison with normative data. Regular visual field testing in known cases of disease provides valuable information for helping to differentiate between stability and progressive loss.

Over the past 2 decades, automated static perimetry has become the standard for assessing visual function in glaucoma. With this method, threshold sensitivity measurements are usually performed at a number of test locations using white stimuli on a white

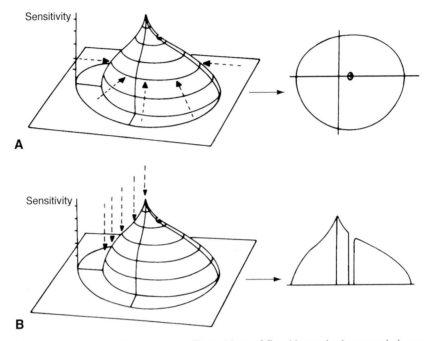

Figure 3-18 **A,** Isopter (kinetic) perimetry. Test object of fixed intensity is moved along several meridians toward fixation. Points where the object is first perceived are plotted in a circle. **B,** Static perimetry. Stationary test object is increased in intensity from below threshold until perceived by the patient. Threshold values yield a graphic profile section. *(Reproduced with permission from Kolker AE, Hetherington J, eds.* Becker-Shaffer's Diagnosis and Therapy of the Glaucomas. *5th ed. St Louis: Mosby; 1983. Modified from Aulhorn E, Harms H. In: Leydhecker W.* Glaucoma. *Tutzing Symposium. Basel: S Karger; 1967.)*

background; this is known as *standard automated perimetry (SAP),* or achromatic automated perimetry. Other technologies have become available that may be useful in evaluating the visual field. According to evidence from detailed investigations using these newer perimetric tests, it is likely that, in individual patients, these different tests show abnormalities at different times in the course of glaucoma. Some methods may be better for identifying defects than for following their progression, and vice versa.

Clinical Perimetry

Two major types of perimetry are in general use today:

- automated static perimetry using a bowl perimeter or video monitor
- manual kinetic and static perimetry using a Goldmann-type bowl perimeter

The following are brief definitions of some of the major perimetric terms:

- *Threshold:* The differential light sensitivity at which a stimulus of a given size and duration of presentation is seen 50% of the time—in practice, the dimmest spot detected during testing.
- *Suprathreshold:* Above the threshold; generally used to mean brighter than the threshold stimulus. A stimulus may also be made suprathreshold by increasing the size or duration of presentation. This is generally used for screening paradigms.

- *Kinetic testing:* Perimetry in which a target is moved from an area where it is not seen toward an area where it is just seen. This is usually performed manually by a perimetrist, who chooses the target, moves it, and records the results.
- *Static testing:* A stationary stimulus is presented at various locations. In theory, the brightness, size, and duration of the stimulus can be varied at each location to determine the threshold. In practice, in a given automated test session, only the brightness is varied. Although static perimetry may be done manually—and is often combined with manual kinetic perimetry—in current practice the term usually refers to automated perimetry.
- *Isopter:* A line on a visual field representation—usually on a 2-dimensional sheet of paper—connecting points with the same threshold.
- *Depression:* A decrease in retinal sensitivity.
- *Scotoma:* An area of decreased retinal sensitivity within the visual field surrounded by an area of greater sensitivity.
- *Decibel (dB):* A 0.1 log unit. This is a relative term used in both kinetic and static perimetry that has no absolute value. Its value depends on the maximum illumination of the perimeter. As usually used, it refers to log units of attenuation of the maximum light intensity available in the perimeter being used.

Variables in Perimetry

Whether automated or manual, perimetry is subject to many variables, including the patient's level of attentiveness, the perimetrist's administration of the test, and the size of the stimulus.

Patient

People vary in their attentiveness and response time from moment to moment and from day to day. Longer tests are more likely to produce fatigue and diminish the ability of the patient to maintain peak performance.

Perimetrist

The individual performing manual perimetry can administer the test slightly differently each time. Different technicians or physicians also vary from one another in how they administer the test. Perimetrist bias is markedly diminished with automated testing. However, the perimetrist can have an effect on test outcome even in automated testing, by monitoring or not monitoring the patient for proper performance and positioning. Most automated instruments can be paused during the test by perimetrist intervention, thereby allowing repositioning or other adjustments to enhance test reliability.

Other variables

Other variables of importance include the following:

- *Fixation:* If the eye is slightly cyclotorted relative to the test bowl, or if the patient's point of fixation is off center, defects may shift locations. Especially in automated static tests (because the test logic does not change), a defect may thus appear and disappear.

- *Background luminance:* The luminance of the surface onto which the perimetric stimulus is projected affects retinal sensitivity and thus the hill of vision. Clinical perimetry is usually performed with a background luminance of 4.0–31.5 apostilbs. Retinal sensitivity is greatest at fixation and falls steadily toward the periphery.
- *Stimulus luminance:* For a given stimulus size and presentation time, the brighter the stimulus, the more visible it is.
- *Size of stimulus:* The larger the stimulus, the more likely it is to be perceived. The sizes of standard stimuli are: $0 = 1/16$ mm^2, I $= 1/4$ mm^2, II $= 1$ mm^2, III $= 4$ mm^2, IV $= 16$ mm^2, and V $= 64$ mm^2. The most common stimuli for automated perimetry are size III.
- *Presentation time:* Up to about 0.5 second, temporal summation occurs. In other words, the longer the presentation time, the more visible a given stimulus. Commercially available static perimeters generally employ a fixed stimulus duration of 0.2 second or less. Comparison of perimetric thresholds between instruments is difficult because different manufacturers use different stimulus durations and background luminances.
- *Patient refraction:* Uncorrected refractive errors cause blurring on the retina and decrease the visibility of stimuli. Thus, proper neutralization of refractive errors is essential for accurate perimetry. In addition, presbyopic patients must have a refractive compensation that focuses fixation at the depth of the perimeter bowl. Care needs to be taken to center the patient close to the correcting lens to avoid a lens rim artifact (see Fig 3-22).
- *Pupil size:* Pupil size affects the amount of light entering the eye, and it should be recorded on each visual field test. Testing with pupils smaller than 2.5 mm in diameter may induce artifacts.
- *Wavelength of background and stimulus:* Color perimetry may yield different results than white-on-white perimetry.
- *Speed of stimulus movement:* Because temporal summation occurs over a period as long as 0.5 second, the area of retina stimulated by a test object is affected by the speed of the stimulus movement. If a kinetic target is moved quickly, by the time the patient responds, the target may have gone well beyond the location at which it was first seen. This period between visualization and response is termed the *latency period* or *visual reaction time*.

Automated Static Perimetry

A computerized perimeter must be able to determine threshold sensitivity at multiple points in the retina, to perform an adequate test in a reasonable amount of time, and to present results in a comprehensible form. The intensity of the stimulus is varied by a system of filters that attenuate the stimulus, usually allowing measurement to approximately 1 dB.

Automated static perimeters have traditionally used staircase algorithms that employ a bracketing approach. These produce more reliable and efficient threshold estimates compared with previous psychophysical test strategies. Any staircase strategy yields threshold estimates that are a compromise between reliability (accuracy and precision) and efficiency (test duration). Threshold estimates from strategies that cross the threshold (reversal) more often or that use smaller staircase intervals are more reliable, but at the expense of requiring a longer test time. The "standard" staircase strategy used by both the Octopus perimeters (Haag-Streit, Mason, OH) and the Humphrey Field Analyzers (HFAs; Carl Zeiss Meditec, Dublin, CA) employs an initial 4-dB step size that decreases to 2 dB on first reversal and continues until a second reversal occurs (Fig 3-19).

General testing categories in common use are as follows:

1. *Threshold:* Threshold testing is the current standard for automated perimetry in glaucoma management. As described earlier, threshold may be determined by a variety of bracketing and statistical strategies.

2. *Efficient threshold strategies:* Full-threshold testing algorithms suffer from patient fatigue, high variability, and generally poor patient acceptance. In an attempt to achieve shorter threshold testing with good accuracy and reproducibility, the *Swedish interactive thresholding algorithm (SITA)* was developed. Unlike staircase strategies, which use discrete intervals to step toward threshold, SITA employs a logical best-guess, or forecasting, approach to threshold estimation. Briefly, the best-guess intensity of SITA's initial stimulus presentation at each test location corresponds to the intensity associated with the highest probability of being seen by an age-matched individual. Depending on the patient's response to this first stimulus, the intensity of each subsequent presentation is modified. This iterative procedure is repeated until the likely threshold measurement error is reduced to below a predetermined level, with at least 1 reversal occurring at every test location. SITA also uses neighborhood comparisons to optimize the best-guess procedure: if adjacent test locations show lower or higher sensitivity than expected, the initial stimulus intensity is altered. SITA monitors the timing of patient responses in order to interactively pace the test. Similar to the SITA test strategy for the HFA, the *tendency-oriented perimeter (TOP)* algorithm was developed for the Octopus perimeter as an alternative to the lengthy staircase threshold procedures. The intent of both of these strategies was to provide a faster, more efficient test procedure that maintained the same degree of accuracy and reliability as the staircase procedures.

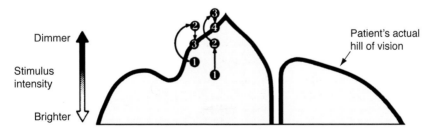

Figure 3-19 Full-threshold strategy determines retinal sensitivity at each tested point by altering the stimulus intensity in 4-dB steps until the threshold is crossed. It then recrosses the threshold, moving in 2-dB steps, in order to check and refine the accuracy of the measurement. *(Reproduced with permission from* The Field Analyzer Primer. *San Leandro, CA: Allergan Humphrey; 1989.)*

Comparisons between SITA testing algorithms and older thresholding algorithms have suggested that the SITA Standard yields visual field results comparable to, though not exactly the same as, full-threshold testing. Both SITA (Standard and Fast) strategies yield marginally higher values for differential light sensitivity compared with other algorithms. The average test time with SITA Standard is approximately 50% of the full-thresholding strategy time, and SITA Fast results in an additional reduction of approximately 30% compared with SITA Standard. The considerably reduced test time with SITA Standard appears to be achieved without a significant reduction in accuracy or an increase in variability or noise levels within the test. *SITA Fast should not be used in the routine evaluation of glaucoma suspects or patients with glaucoma* and should be reserved only for patients who are unable to perform SITA Standard because of mental or physical limitations.

Screening tests

These tests may or may not be threshold-related, and they cover varying areas of the visual field. Suprathreshold tests are not recommended for glaucoma suspects because they do not provide a good reference for future comparison. They may be useful with other conditions causing visual field loss, however.

Threshold tests

The most common programs for glaucoma testing are the central 24° and 30° programs, such as the Octopus 32 and G1 and the Humphrey 24-2 and 30-2 (Fig 3-20). These programs test the central field using a 6° grid. They test points 3° above and 3° below the horizontal midline and facilitate diagnosis of defects that respect this line. For patients with advanced visual field loss that threatens fixation, serial 10-2 or C8 visual fields should be used. These visual fields concentrate on the central 8°–10° of the visual field, and test points every 1°–2°, enabling the ophthalmologist to follow many more test points within the central island and improve the detection of progression.

Although a 30°–60° program is available on most static threshold perimeters, it is rarely performed because the threshold variability is very high in these more peripheral regions.

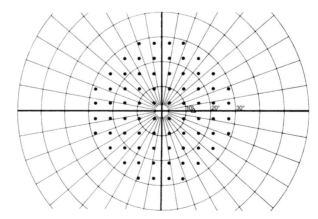

Figure 3-20 Central 30-2 threshold test pattern, right eye. *(Reproduced with permission from The Field Analyzer Primer. San Leandro, CA: Allergan Humphrey; 1989.)*

Interpretation of a Single Visual Field

The clinician should exercise caution when interpreting perimetric results. Even with improved strategies, these remain subjective tests. Therefore, confirmation of a new defect or worsening of an existing defect is usually necessary to validate the clinical implication of the visual field in conjunction with all other pertinent data. Evaluation of the visual field involves the following: 1) assessing the quality or reliability of the visual field; 2) assessing the normality or abnormality; and 3) identifying artifacts.

Quality

The first aspect of the field to be evaluated is its quality or reliability. The percentage of fixation losses, the false-positives and false-negatives, and the fluctuations of doubly determined points are assessed. Damaged areas of the field demonstrate more variability than normal areas. Glaucomatous damage may cause an increase in false-negative responses unrelated to patient reliability. The clinician can evaluate patient reliability by looking at the least-damaged areas in a badly damaged visual field.

Normality or abnormality

The next aspect of the visual field to be assessed is its normality or abnormality. When tested under photopic conditions, the normal visual field demonstrates the greatest sensitivity centrally, with sensitivity falling steadily toward the periphery. A cluster of 2 or more points depressed ≥5 dB compared with surrounding points is suspicious. A single point depressed >10 dB is unusual but is of less value on a single visual field than a cluster, because cluster points confirm one another. Corresponding points above and below the horizontal midline should not vary markedly; normally the superior field is depressed 1–2 dB compared with the inferior field.

To aid the clinician in interpreting the numerical data generated by threshold tests, field indices have been developed by perimeter manufacturers. The mean difference measures average sensitivity loss, and *pattern standard deviation* highlights localized loss.

These corrected indices help distinguish between generalized field depression and localized loss. An abnormal pattern deviation has greater diagnostic specificity than a generalized loss of sensitivity. An abnormally high pattern standard deviation indicates that some points of the visual field are depressed relative to other points in the visual field after correction for the patient's moment-to-moment variability. Such a finding is suggestive of focal damage such as that occurring with glaucoma (and many other conditions). Although a normal pattern standard deviation in an eye with an abnormal visual field indicates a generalized depression of the hill of vision such as that occurring with media opacity, such generalized loss may also occur with diffuse glaucomatous damage.

The Humphrey STATPAC 2 statistical program provides a hemifield analysis. This test is designed only for glaucoma and involves comparison of corresponding clusters of points above and below the horizontal midline (Fig 3-21).

Comparison of various perimetric techniques

As stated earlier, other technologies have recently become available that may be useful in evaluating the visual field. Two of the most commonly used newer techniques are

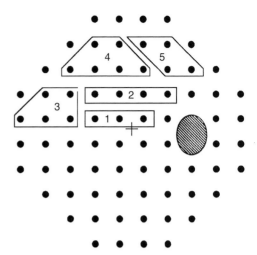

Figure 3-21 Superior visual field zones used in the glaucoma hemifield test. *(Reproduced with permission from* The STATPAC User's Guide. *San Leandro, CA: Allergan Humphrey; 1989.)*

short-wavelength automated perimetry and frequency-doubling technology, both of which are discussed below.

Other measures of the visual field include contrast sensitivity, flicker sensitivity, high-pass resolution perimetry, visually evoked cortical potential, and multifocal electroretinography. However, these tests are not commonly employed in the evaluation of patients with glaucoma. Several of these tests are discussed in greater detail in BCSC Section 12, *Retina and Vitreous.*

With the introduction of these newer perimetric techniques into the clinical arena, clinicians may be asked to derive important clinical information from several perimetric printouts. The association between glaucoma and short-wavelength (blue) color vision deficits has been known for some time. Sensitivity to blue stimuli is believed to be mediated by a small subpopulation of morphologically distinct ganglion cells, the small bistratified ganglion cells, that typically have large receptive fields, little receptive field overlap, and relatively large axon diameters. If early ganglion cell loss in open-angle glaucoma preferentially affects either sparsely represented cell groups or those with larger axons, either scenario may produce reduced short-wavelength sensitivity. If special stimuli and background illumination conditions are used, it is possible to isolate and test the sensitivity of short-wavelength mechanisms throughout the visual field with *short-wavelength automated perimetry (SWAP)*, also known as *blue-yellow perimetry.* Standard perimeters that can project a blue stimulus onto a yellow background are available, and SWAP is available on the HFA II (700 series) and the Octopus 1-2-3. A STATPAC procedure is employed to analyze the data, which are presented in the same layout as that used for standard automated perimetry.

This method is sensitive in the early identification of glaucomatous damage. Several studies suggest that the rate of development of perimetric defects in early glaucoma may be higher with blue-on-yellow testing than with conventional (achromatic) white-on-white visual fields. SWAP is suitable for identifying individuals likely to develop SAP visual field loss. Repeatable visual field loss on SWAP should be carefully monitored. Analyses of local loss such as the Glaucoma Hemifield Test (GHT) and pattern threshold deviations are the best statistical tools to identify glaucomatous SWAP deficits and to separate them from artifacts resulting from media opacities. The availability of SWAP using the SITA testing algorithm (SITA SWAP) has decreased the testing time for SWAP testing, making it much more clinically useful.

Frequency-doubling technology (FDT) perimetry is a visual field testing paradigm that uses a low spatial frequency sinusoidal grating undergoing rapid phase-reversal flicker. Commercially available instruments employ a 0.25 cycle per degree grating, phase-reversed at a rapid 25 Hz. When a low spatial frequency grating is presented in this manner, it appears to have twice as many alternating light and dark bars than are actually present—hence the term *frequency doubling.*

The FDT perimeter was developed to measure contrast detection thresholds for frequency-doubled test targets. The high temporal frequency and low spatial frequency attributes of the stimulus that causes the frequency-doubling stimulus likely preferentially activate the M cells. Whether it is because of the isolation of specific cell populations that are susceptible to early damage in glaucoma or because of the reduced redundancy, visual function tests that employ frequency-doubled stimuli may be useful for detection of early defects in some patients. Because of the small number of areas tested, the original FDT is limited in its usefulness for follow-up of glaucoma patients. The availability of the Humphrey Matrix 24-2 perimeter (Matrix, Carl Zeiss, Dublin, CA), which makes use of frequency-doubling testing with testing areas similar in number to those of SAP 24-2, potentially provides a new method to perform functional assessment in glaucoma.

Agreement between standard perimetry, SWAP, and FDT perimetry is limited. Results obtained with standard perimetry may be abnormal in early disease when those from SWAP and FDT testing are normal. Thus, each of these tests may identify or miss early glaucomatous damage in different patients.

Artifacts

Identification of artifacts is the next step in evaluation of the visual field. The following are common artifacts seen on automated perimetry:

- *Lens rim:* If the patient's corrective lens is decentered or set too far from the eye, the lens rim may project into the central 30° (Fig 3-22).
- *Incorrect corrective lens:* If an incorrect corrective lens is used, the resulting field will be generally depressed. This appears to be less of a problem with FDT perimetry.
- *Cloverleaf visual field:* If a patient stops paying attention and ceases to respond partway through a visual field test, a distinctive visual field pattern may develop. Figure 3-23 shows a cloverleaf visual field, the result of the testing order of the Humphrey 30-2 perimeter, which begins testing with the points circled in this figure and proceeds outward. This pattern may also be seen if a patient is malingering.
- *High false-positive rate:* When a patient responds at a time when no test stimulus is being presented, a false-positive response is recorded. False-positive rates greater than 20% suggest an unreliable test that can mask or minimize an actual scotoma and can, in extreme cases, result in a visual field with impossibly high threshold values (Fig 3-24). Careful instruction of the patient may sometimes resolve this artifact.
- *High false-negative rate:* When a patient fails to respond to a stimulus presented in a location where a dimmer stimulus was previously seen, a false-negative response

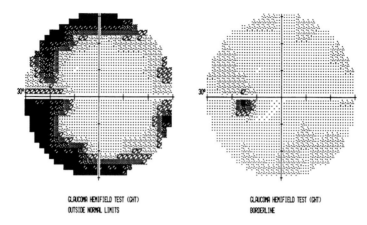

GLAUCOMA HEMIFIELD TEST (GHT)
OUTSIDE NORMAL LIMITS

GLAUCOMA HEMIFIELD TEST (GHT)
BORDERLINE

Figure 3-22 Lens rims artifact. The 2 visual fields shown were obtained 9 days apart. The visual field on the left shows a typical lens rim artifact, whereas the corrective lens was positioned appropriately for the visual field on the right (Humphrey 30-2 program).

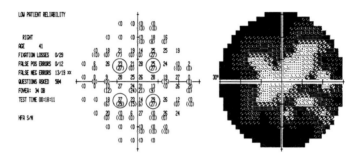

Figure 3-23 Cloverleaf visual field. The Humphrey visual field perimeter test is designed so that 4 circled points are checked initially and the testing in each quadrant proceeds outward from these points. If the patient ceases to respond after only a few points have been tested, the result is some variation of the cloverleaf visual field shown at right (Humphrey 30-2 program).

is recorded. False-negative rates greater than 33% suggest test unreliability. A high false-negative rate should alert the clinician to the likelihood that the patient's actual visual field might not be as depressed as suggested by the test result. However, it should also be noted that patients with significant visual field loss, including scotomata with steep edges, can demonstrate high false-negative rates that do not indicate unreliability. This effect appears to arise from presentation of stimuli at the edges of deep scotomata, where short-term threshold fluctuation can be quite variable.

Interpretation of a Series of Visual Fields

Interpretation of serial visual fields should meet 2 goals:

1. separating real change from ordinary variation
2. using the information from the visual field testing to determine the likelihood that a change is related to glaucomatous progression

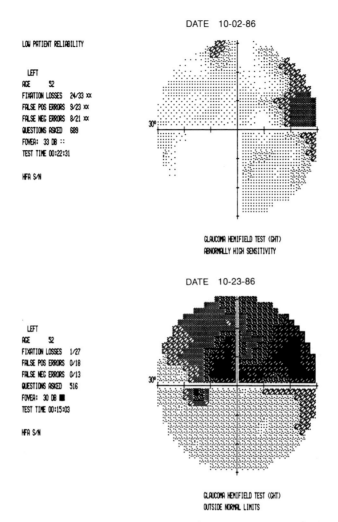

DATE   10-02-86

LOW PATIENT RELIABILITY

LEFT
AGE   52
FIXATION LOSSES   24/33 xx
FALSE POS ERRORS 9/23 xx
FALSE NEG ERRORS 8/21 xx
QUESTIONS ASKED   689
FOVEA: 33 DB ::
TEST TIME 00:22:31

HFA S/N

30°

GLAUCOMA HEMIFIELD TEST (GHT)
ABNORMALLY HIGH SENSITIVITY

DATE   10-23-86

LEFT
AGE   52
FIXATION LOSSES   1/27
FALSE POS ERRORS 0/18
FALSE NEG ERRORS 0/13
QUESTIONS ASKED   516
FOVEA: 30 DB ■
TEST TIME 00:15:03

HFA S/N

30°

GLAUCOMA HEMIFIELD TEST (GHT)
OUTSIDE NORMAL LIMITS

Figure 3-24 High false-positive rate. The top visual field contains characteristic "white scoto-mata," which represent areas of impossibly high retinal sensitivity. Upon return visit 3 weeks later, the patient was carefully instructed to respond only when she saw the light, resulting in the bottom visual field, which shows good reliability and demonstrates the patient's dense superior visual field loss (Humphrey 30-2 program).

A number of methods can be employed to analyze a series of visual fields for glaucoma-tous change. Point-by-point analysis performed with statistical programs available from the major instrument manufacturers (eg, the Humphrey STATPAC 2 or Octopus Delta programs) is a valuable aid in progression analysis. The application of these programs is described clearly in the owner's manual accompanying the program packages. The point-by-point approach is better at identifying regions of change within a visual field.

Another method used in visual field series analysis is comparison of visual field in-dices, which can reveal global trends that may be missed with point-by-point analysis. Raw perimetric data can also be transferred to independent software programs for change analysis. Even when computed statistical methods are employed, however, separating true pathologic progression from normal test-to-test variability remains a difficult challenge. Moreover, the clinician interpreting a series of visual fields must keep in mind that test variability is increased as part of the pathophysiology of glaucoma.

Whatever method the clinician uses, the fundamental requirement for adequate interpretation over time is a good *baseline* visual field. Often the patient experiences a learning effect, and the second visual field may show substantial improvement over the first (Fig 3-25). At least 2 visual fields should be obtained as early as possible in the course of a patient's disease. If they are quite different, a third test should be performed. Subsequent visual fields should be compared with these baseline fields. If a follow-up visual field appears to differ from baseline, the test should be repeated for confirmation.

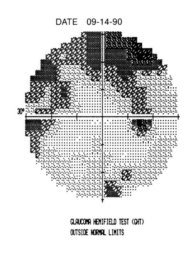

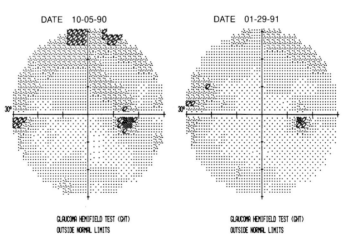

Figure 3-25 Learning effect. These 3 visual fields were obtained within the first 3½ months of diagnosis in a patient with very early, clinically stable glaucoma. They illustrate the learning effect between the first and the second visual fields. The third visual field is similar to the second, and the second and third visual fields provided a baseline for follow-up of the patient (Humphrey 30-2 program).

Progression

No hard-and-fast rules define what determines visual field progression. But, generally, the methods used in the assessment of progression employ regional or global analysis and an event-based or trend-based approach.

Progressive cases such as that shown in Figure 3-26 are easy to recognize. A general decrease in sensitivity may be secondary to glaucoma or may be related to media opacity, and clinical correlation is required, which is often difficult. Two causes of general decline in sensitivity that may confuse interpretation are variable miosis (often related to use of eyedrops) and cataract (Fig 3-27).

Suspected new defects or progression of existing defects should be reproduced on subsequent visual fields to determine their validity. Definitions of progression have varied

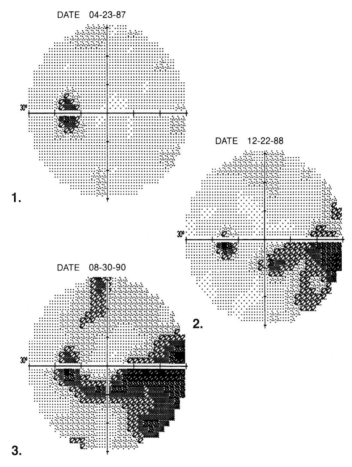

Figure 3-26 Progression of glaucomatous damage. The 3 visual fields shown illustrate the development and advancement of a visual field defect. Between the first and second visual fields, the patient developed a significant inferior nasal step (see the section Patterns of Glaucomatous Nerve Loss). The third visual field illustrates the extension of this defect to the blind spot, as well as the development of superior visual field loss (Humphrey 30-2 program).

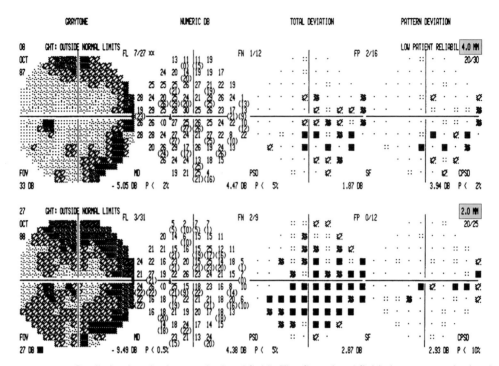

Figure 3-27 Pupil size (marked on each visual field). The first visual field shown was obtained before the patient began pilocarpine therapy. The second visual field was obtained with a miotic pupil (Humphrey 30-2 program).

in clinical trials; these definitions will continue to be refined in the years to come with further improvements in computer software.

The Glaucoma Change Probability (Fig 3-28) uses an event-based analysis, which is based on the analysis performed in the Early Manifest Glaucoma Trial, to provide a sensitive assessment of possible progression. It compares the current visual field with a baseline composed of 2 separate visual field tests. The operator must choose the 2 baseline visual fields. Thus, with this method, if progression occurs, a new baseline must be established for future analysis.

Correlation with the optic disc

It is important to correlate changes in the visual field with those of the optic disc. If such correlation is lacking, the ophthalmologist should consider other causes of vision loss, such as ischemic optic neuropathy, demyelinating or other neurologic disease, pituitary tumor, and so forth. This consideration is especially important in the following situations:

- The patient's optic disc seems less cupped than would be expected for the degree of visual field loss.
- The pallor of the disc is more impressive than the cupping.
- The progression of the visual field loss seems excessive.

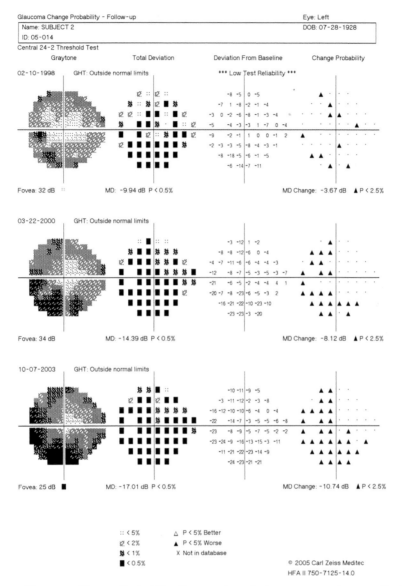

Figure 3-28 Glaucoma Change Probability. Progression of glaucomatous damage. Each of the 3 visual fields shown here demonstrates progressive loss compared with the same baseline. The black triangles designate points with a probability (*P* < .05) that the value is worse than the baseline value. *(Courtesy of Ronald L. Gross, MD.)*

- The pattern of visual field loss is uncharacteristic for glaucoma—for example, it respects the vertical midline.
- The location of the cupping or thinning of the neural rim does not correspond to the proper location of the visual field defect.

Anderson DR, Patella VM. *Automated Static Perimetry.* 2nd ed. St Louis: Mosby; 1999.

Drake MV. A primer on automated perimetry. *Focal Points: Clinical Modules for Ophthalmologists.* San Francisco: American Academy of Ophthalmology; 1993, module 8.

Drance SM, Anderson DR, eds. *Automatic Perimetry in Glaucoma: A Practical Guide.* Orlando, FL: Grune & Stratton; 1985.

Harrington DO, Drake MV. *The Visual Fields: A Textbook and Atlas of Clinical Perimetry.* 6th ed. St Louis: Mosby; 1989.

Lieberman MF. Glaucoma and automated perimetry. *Focal Points: Clinical Modules for Ophthalmologists.* San Francisco: American Academy of Ophthalmology; 1993, module 9.

Spry PGD, Johnson CA. Advances in automated perimetry. *Focal Points: Clinical Modules for Ophthalmologists.* San Francisco: American Academy of Ophthalmology; 2002, module 10.

Walsh TJ, ed. *Visual Fields: Examination and Interpretation.* 2nd ed. Ophthalmology Monograph 3. San Francisco: American Academy of Ophthalmology; 1996.

Patterns of Glaucomatous Nerve Loss

The hallmark defect of glaucoma is the nerve fiber bundle defect that results from damage at the optic nerve head. The pattern of nerve fibers in the retinal area served by the damaged nerve fiber bundle will correspond to the specific defect. The common names for the classic visual field defects are derived from their appearance as plotted on a kinetic visual field chart. In static perimetry, however, the sample points are in a grid pattern, and the representation of visual field defects on a static perimetry chart generally lacks the smooth contours suggested by such terms as *arcuate*.

Glaucomatous visual field defects include the following:

- generalized depression
- paracentral scotoma (Fig 3-29)
- arcuate or Bjerrum scotoma (Fig 3-30)
- nasal step (Fig 3-31)
- altitudinal defect (Fig 3-32)
- temporal wedge

The superior and inferior poles of the optic nerve appear to be most susceptible to glaucomatous damage. However, damage to small, scattered bundles of optic nerve axons commonly produces a generalized decrease in sensitivity, which is harder to recognize than focal defects. Combinations of superior and inferior visual field loss, such as double arcuate scotomata, may occur, resulting in profound peripheral vision loss. Typically, the central island of vision and the inferotemporal visual field are retained until late in the course of glaucomatous optic nerve damage (Fig 3-33).

Manual Perimetry

Since computerized static perimetry has shown itself to be at least as good as the best-quality manual perimetry tests for the detection and quantification of glaucomatous defects, manual perimetry is seldom used today in the management of glaucoma. However, it remains helpful in documenting defects outside the central 30° and in monitoring end-stage visual field loss.

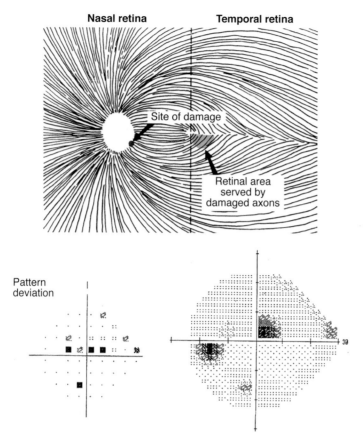

Figure 3-29 A *paracentral scotoma* is an island of relative or absolute vision loss within 10° of fixation. Loss of nerve fibers from the inferior pole, originating from the inferotemporal retina, resulted in the superonasal scotoma shown. Paracentral scotomata may be single, as in this case, or multiple, and they may occur as isolated findings or may be associated with other early defects (Humphrey 24-2 program). *(Visual field courtesy of G. A. Cioffi, MD.)*

Anderson DR. *Perimetry With and Without Automation.* 2nd ed. St Louis: Mosby; 1987.

Other Tests

Several other tests may be helpful in selected patients. Many of these tests are described elsewhere in the BCSC series, and the reader is advised to consult the *Master Index* for the following:

- fluorescein angiography
- corneal pachymetry
- measurement of episcleral venous pressure
- carotid noninvasive vascular studies

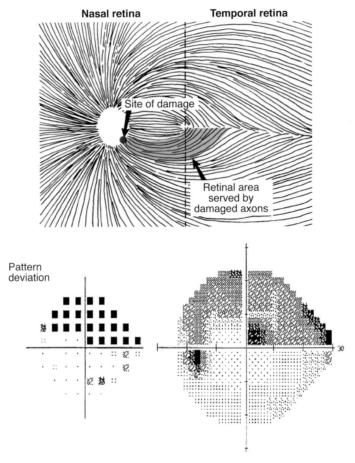

Figure 3-30 An *arcuate scotoma* occurs in the area 10°–20° from fixation. Glaucomatous damage to a nerve fiber bundle containing axons from both the inferonasal and inferotemporal retina resulted in the arcuate defect shown. The scotoma often begins as a single area of relative loss, which then becomes larger, deeper, and multifocal. In its full form an arcuate scotoma arches from the blind spot and ends at the nasal raphe, becoming wider and closer to fixation on the nasal side (Humphrey 24-2 program). *(Visual field courtesy of G. A. Cioffi, MD.)*

- ocular blood-flow measurements
- ultrasonography

Ultrasound biomicroscopy (UBM) may provide information about anterior segment anatomy in several types of glaucoma. The test employs shorter-wavelength sound waves than does conventional ocular ultrasonography, limiting penetration through the sclera but increasing the resolution. UBM allows detailed examination of the anterior segment, the posterior chamber, and the ciliary body (Fig 3-34). Anterior segment optical coherence tomography (AS-OCT) may also provide images of the anterior segment and angle. However, although the resolution of AS-OCT is better than that of UBM, penetration through the sclera is minimal with AS-OCT, reducing its ability to provide images of the ciliary body and adjacent structures.

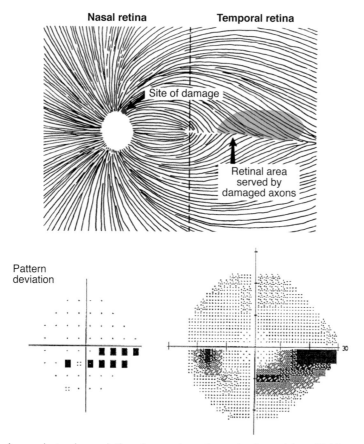

Figure 3-31 A *nasal step* is a relative depression of one horizontal hemifield compared with the other. Damage to superior nerve fibers serving the superotemporal retina beyond the paracentral area resulted in this nasal step. In kinetic perimetry the nasal step is defined as a discontinuity or depression in one or more nasal isopters near the horizontal raphe (Humphrey 24-2 program). *(Visual field courtesy of G. A. Cioffi, MD.)*

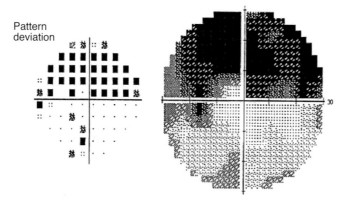

Figure 3-32 Altitudinal defect with near complete loss of the superior visual field, characteristic of moderate to advanced glaucomatous optic neuropathy (left eye). *(Visual field courtesy of G. A. Cioffi, MD.)*

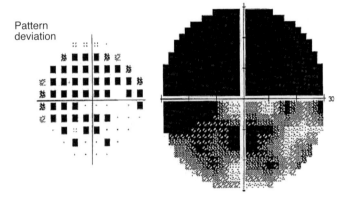

Figure 3-33 Advanced glaucomatous visual field loss with retention of a small central island of vision (foveal threshold: 33 dB) and retention of inferotemporal visual field (right eye). *(Visual field courtesy of G. A. Cioffi, MD.)*

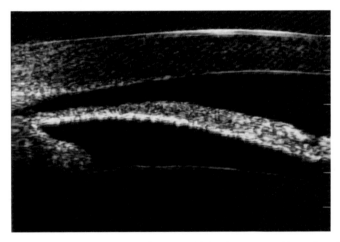

Figure 3-34 Pupillary block as shown by ultrasound biomicroscopy. Note the elevation above the lens of the peripheral iris on the left compared with the central iris on the right. *(Courtesy of Charles J. Pavlin, MD.)*

CHAPTER 4

Open-Angle Glaucoma

Primary Open-Angle Glaucoma

Primary open-angle glaucoma (POAG) is typically a chronic, slowly progressive optic neuropathy with characteristic patterns of optic nerve damage and visual field loss. POAG lacks the identifiable contributing factors of the secondary open-angle glaucomas, such as pigment dispersion in pigmentary glaucoma or the exfoliative material seen in exfoliation syndrome. Elevated intraocular pressure (IOP) is an important risk factor for POAG; other factors, such as lower ocular perfusion pressure, race, low central corneal thickness (CCT), advanced age, and positive family history, also contribute to the risk of developing this disease. POAG is a multifactorial disease process with numerous contributing susceptibility and protective factors that may include abnormalities of axonal or ganglion cell metabolism and disorders of the extracellular matrix of the lamina cribrosa. Unfortunately, we do not yet fully understand the interplay of the multiple factors involved in the development of POAG.

Clinical Features

POAG is usually insidious in onset, slowly progressive, and painless. Though usually bilateral, it can be quite asymmetric. Because central vision is relatively unaffected until late in the disease, visual field loss, as measured by standard automated perimetry, may be severe before symptoms are noted. POAG is diagnosed by assessment of the optic disc appearance and the visual field.

Gonioscopic findings

Prior to establishing a diagnosis of POAG, the clinician must verify that the anterior chamber angle is open. Gonioscopy should be performed in all patients evaluated for glaucoma and should be repeated periodically in patients with established open-angle glaucoma (OAG) to detect possible progressive angle closure caused by miotic therapy or age-related lens changes, especially in patients with hyperopia. Repeated gonioscopy is also indicated when the chamber becomes shallow, when strong miotics are prescribed for any condition, after laser trabeculoplasty or iridotomy is performed, or when IOP rises.

Gonioscopy is discussed in detail in Chapter 3.

Intraocular pressure

Large, population-based epidemiologic studies have revealed a mean IOP of 15.5 mm Hg, with a standard deviation of 2.6 mm Hg. This led to the definition of "normal" IOP as 2 standard deviations within the mean IOP, or approximately 10–21 mm Hg.

Although IOP greater than 21 mm Hg was traditionally defined as "abnormal," this definition has a number of shortcomings. It is known that IOP in the general population is not represented by a Gaussian distribution but is skewed toward higher pressures (see Chapter 2, Fig 2-3). IOPs of 22 mm Hg and above would thus not necessarily represent an abnormality from a statistical standpoint. More importantly, IOP distribution curves in glaucomatous and nonglaucomatous eyes show a great deal of overlap. Several studies have indicated that as many as 30%–50% of individuals in the general population who have glaucomatous optic neuropathy and/or visual field loss have initial screening IOPs below 22 mm Hg. Furthermore, because of diurnal fluctuation, elevations of IOP may occur only intermittently in some glaucomatous eyes, with as many as one-third of the measurements being normal.

The IOP in glaucoma patients may vary widely, by 10 mm Hg or more, over a 24-hour period. Most patients without glaucoma show a diurnal range of 2–6 mm Hg. Patterns of diurnal fluctuation have been broken into several types depending on the time of peak pressure: morning, day, night, or flat (meaning little diurnal variation). Most individuals manifest similar patterns from day to day; however, 10%–20% of patients are "erratic," manifesting different patterns of diurnal IOP fluctuation over time. The shift from upright posture during the day to supine posture at night may be associated with increased nocturnal IOP measurements. Spontaneous asymmetric fluctuations of IOP between fellow eyes occur commonly in individuals without glaucoma and in glaucoma patients.

Thus, single measurements of IOP during office hours do not adequately depict the degree of fluctuation of IOP. Large diurnal IOP fluctuation has been identified as an independent risk factor for progression of glaucoma in some studies but not in others. Regardless of whether IOP fluctuation is an independent risk factor, elevation of IOP is a strong risk factor for glaucoma progression.

As discussed in Chapter 2, corneal thickness affects the measurement of IOP. Thicker corneas resist the indentation inherent in nearly all methods of IOP measurement, resulting in artificially high measurements. The opposite occurs in eyes with low corneal thickness. Average corneal thickness in adults, determined by optical and ultrasonic pachymetry, is 530–545 μm. In populations of persons of African ancestry, mean CCT has been found to be lower than that observed in whites.

Among patients with the condition termed *ocular hypertension (OHT),* which is elevated IOP in the absence of identifiable optic nerve damage or visual field loss, lower CCT has been found to be an important risk factor for progression to glaucoma. Similarly, among patients with OAG (with higher baseline IOPs), lower CCT is a risk factor for disease progression. This increased risk for progression can be explained, in part, by the fact that the true IOP in eyes with lower CCT is higher than that measured by Goldmann tonometry. Lower CCT appears to be an independent risk factor for the development of glaucoma.

Bengtsson B, Leske MC, Hyman L, Heijl A; Early Manifest Glaucoma Trial Group. Fluctuation of intraocular pressure and glaucoma progression in the Early Manifest Glaucoma Trial. *Ophthalmology.* 2007;114(2):205–209.

Bhan A, Browning AC, Shah S, Hamilton R, Dave D, Dua HS. Effect of corneal thickness on intraocular pressure measurements with the pneumotonometer, Goldmann applanation tonometer, and Tono-Pen. *Invest Ophthalmol Vis Sci.* 2002;43(5):1389–1392.

Brandt JD, Beiser JA, Kass MA, Gordon MO. Central corneal thickness in the Ocular Hypertension Treatment Study (OHTS). *Ophthalmology.* 2001;108(10):1779–1788.

Doughty MJ, Zaman ML. Human corneal thickness and its impact on intraocular pressure measures: a review and meta-analysis approach. *Surv Ophthalmol.* 2000;44(5):367–408.

Liu JHK, Kripke DF, Twa MD, et al. Twenty-four-hour pattern of intraocular pressure in the aging population. *Invest Ophthalmol Vis Sci.* 1999;40(12):2912–2917.

Optic disc appearance and visual field loss

Although elevated IOP is a key risk factor for the development of glaucoma, it is not essential to the diagnosis. The diagnosis of POAG is based primarily on the appearance of the optic disc, or optic nerve head, and the assessment of visual function. See Chapter 3 for detailed discussion of the optic nerve head and visual field.

Careful periodic evaluation of the optic disc and visual field is important in the management of glaucoma patients. Stereophotographic documentation of the optic disc or computerized imaging of the disc or retinal nerve fiber layer enhances the clinician's ability to detect subtle changes over time.

Visual field loss should correlate with the appearance of the optic disc. Significant discrepancies in the pattern of field loss and optic nerve damage warrant additional investigation, as noted in Chapter 3.

American Academy of Ophthalmology Glaucoma Panel. Preferred Practice Pattern Guidelines. *Primary Open-Angle Glaucoma.* San Francisco: American Academy of Ophthalmology; 2010. Available at: www.aao.org/ppp.

Jonas JB, Budde WM, Panda-Jonas S. Ophthalmoscopic evaluation of the optic nerve head. *Surv Ophthalmol.* 1999;43(4):293–320.

Risk Factors for POAG Other Than IOP

Advanced age is an important risk factor for the development of POAG and its progression. The Baltimore Eye Survey found that the prevalence of glaucoma increases dramatically with age, particularly among black persons, exceeding 11% in those aged 80 years or older. In the Collaborative Initial Glaucoma Treatment Study (CIGTS) (see Clinical Trial 4-1 at the end of this chapter), visual field defects were 7 times more likely to develop in patients aged 60 years or older than in those younger than 40 years. Although increased IOP with age has been observed in many populations and may account for part of the relationship between age and glaucoma, studies in Japan have shown a relationship between glaucoma and age even with no increase in IOP in the population. Thus, age appears to be an independent risk factor for the development of glaucoma. The Ocular Hypertension Treatment Study (OHTS) (see Clinical Trial 4-2 at the end of this chapter) found an increased risk of progression to OAG with age (per decade), of 43% in the univariate analysis and 22% in the multivariate analysis.

Race is another important risk factor for POAG. The prevalence of POAG is 3 to 4 times greater in black persons and Hispanic persons than in non-Hispanic white individuals. Blindness from glaucoma is at least 4 times more common in blacks than in whites. Glaucoma is more likely to be diagnosed at a younger age and likely to be at a more advanced stage at the time of diagnosis in black patients than in white patients. In OHTS, black patients were 59% more likely than white patients to develop glaucoma in a univariate analysis, but this relationship was not present after corneal thickness and baseline vertical cup–disc ratio were factored into the multivariate analysis (black patients had lower corneal thickness and larger baseline vertical cup–disc ratios on average).

A *positive family history* is also a risk factor for POAG. The Baltimore Eye Survey found that the relative risk of POAG is increased approximately 3.7-fold for individuals who have a sibling with POAG. The Finnish Twin Cohort Study showed a 13% inheritance for chronic OAG.

Varma R, Ying-Lai M, Francis BA, et al. Prevalence of open-angle glaucoma and ocular hypertension in Latinos: the Los Angeles Latino Eye Study. *Ophthalmology.* 2004;111(8): 1439–1448.

Wilson MR, Martone JF. Epidemiology of chronic open-angle glaucoma. In: Ritch R, Shields MB, Krupin T. *The Glaucomas.* 2nd ed. St Louis: Mosby; 1996:753–768.

Associated Disorders

Myopia

The preponderance of evidence supports an association between POAG and myopia. For example, population-based data from the Beaver Dam Eye Study showed that myopia (≤–1 D spherical equivalent) was a significant risk factor for glaucoma prevalence. In addition, in the Rotterdam follow-up study, high myopia (≤–4 D spherical equivalent) was associated with a hazard ratio of 2.31 for the development of incident glaucoma. An association between myopia and the development of glaucoma was not observed in OHTS.

The concurrence of POAG and myopia may complicate both diagnosis and management. Evaluation of the optic disc is particularly complicated in highly myopic eyes that have tilted discs or posterior staphylomas. In addition, the magnification of the disc associated with the myopic refractive error interferes with optic disc evaluation.

Myopia-related retinal anomalies can cause visual field abnormalities apart from any glaucomatous process. High refractive error may also make it difficult to perform accurate perimetric measurement and to interpret visual field abnormalities.

Wong TY, Klein BE, Klein R, Knudtson M, Lee KE. Refractive errors, intraocular pressure, and glaucoma in a white population. *Ophthalmology.* 2003;110(1):211–217.

Diabetes mellitus

There is controversy as to whether diabetes is a risk factor for glaucoma. The Beaver Dam Eye Study, the Blue Mountains Eye Study, and the Los Angeles Latino Eye Study found an association between diabetes and OAG. However, the Framingham Study, the Baltimore Eye Survey, the Barbados Eye Study, and a revised analysis of the Rotterdam Study did not find a significant association. Further, the Rotterdam Study and the Barbados Eye

Study, which were large longitudinal population-based studies, did not identify diabetes as a risk factor for the development of incident glaucoma. OHTS found that diabetes was not associated with an increased risk of glaucoma development, although patients with retinopathy were not enrolled in the trial.

de Voogd S, Ikram MK, Wolfs RC, et al. Is diabetes mellitus a risk factor for open-angle glaucoma? The Rotterdam Study. *Ophthalmology.* 2006;113(10):1827–1831.

Blood pressure

The Baltimore Eye Survey found that systemic hypertension was associated with a lower risk of the presence of glaucoma in younger (<65 years) subjects and with an increased risk in older subjects. The hypothesis is that, in younger individuals, higher blood pressure is associated with improved perfusion of the optic nerve; but with advancing age, the adverse effects of chronic hypertension on the optic nerve microcirculation may increase the nerve's susceptibility to the development of glaucomatous optic neuropathy. Conversely, results of the Barbados Eye Studies showed that the relative risk of the development of incident glaucoma among subjects with systemic hypertension was <1.0 in all age groups, including those 70 years of age and older.

Extensive evidence demonstrates that lower ocular perfusion pressure is a strong risk factor for the development of glaucoma, independent of IOP alone. In various studies, *ocular perfusion pressure* has been defined as blood pressure (systolic, diastolic, or mean arterial) minus IOP. Although this is an extreme simplification of actual ocular blood flow in light of the autoregulatory mechanisms at play in central nervous system perfusion and in light of other factors, the associations between these estimates of ocular perfusion pressure and the risk of the presence of glaucoma and the development of incident glaucoma are compelling. The overtreatment of systemic hypertension may be a contributing factor to glaucoma progression in some cases and should be avoided.

Leske MC, Wu SY, Hennis A, Honkanen R, Nemesure B; BESs Study Group. Risk factors for incident open-angle glaucoma: the Barbados Eye Studies. *Ophthalmology.* 2008; 115(1):85–93.

Retinal vein occlusion

Patients with central retinal vein occlusion (CRVO) may present with elevated IOP and glaucoma. They may have preexisting POAG or other types of glaucoma. After CRVO, patients may develop angle-closure glaucoma or, at a later stage, neovascular glaucoma. Glaucoma and OHT are risk factors for the development of CRVO. In susceptible individuals, eyes with elevated IOP are at risk of developing CRVO. In OHTS, the occurrence of vein occlusions was higher in the observation group than in the treatment group; however, the difference did not reach statistical significance. OHTS was insufficiently powered to detect a treatment effect, given the apparent relative risk and low incidence of CRVO. Thus, consideration should be given to treating elevated IOP in patients with a history of CRVO, the aim being to reduce the risk of CRVO in the fellow eye. As the pathophysiology of hemicentral retinal vein occlusion is similar to that of CRVO, the association with glaucoma in these 2 conditions should be similar.

Other associated conditions

Sleep apnea, thyroid disorders, hypercholesterolemia, migraine, and Raynaud phenomenon have variously been identified as risk factors for the development of glaucoma in some studies. Further research is required in order to clarify the significance of these systemic conditions in patients with POAG and their relationship to glaucoma, if any.

Prognosis

Most patients with POAG will retain useful vision for their entire lives. The prevalence of bilateral blindness among persons with OAG has been estimated at 8% in black persons and 4% in white persons. The patients who are at greatest risk of blindness have visual field loss at the time of diagnosis of glaucoma.

Treatment with medication, laser surgery, or incisional surgery to lower IOP has been shown to significantly reduce the risk of progression of the disease. Many clinical trials have compared various treatments at different points in the clinical course and have confirmed the efficacy of IOP reduction. In the Early Manifest Glaucoma Trial (EMGT), a 25% reduction in IOP reduced the risk of progression of OAG from 62% to 45% of patients at 6 years' follow-up. In the CIGTS, initial medical therapy and initial surgical therapy for OAG resulted in relatively equivalent outcomes after 5 years, with significant visual field progression in only 10%–13% of participants. For further details, see Clinical Trials 4-1 through 4-4 at the end of this chapter.

The AGIS Investigators. Advanced Glaucoma Intervention Study (AGIS): 4. Comparison of treatment outcomes within race: seven-year results. *Ophthalmology.* 1998;105(7):1146–1164.

The AGIS Investigators. Advanced Glaucoma Intervention Study (AGIS): 7. The relationship between control of intraocular pressure and visual field deterioration. *Am J Ophthalmol.* 2000;130(4):429–440.

American Academy of Ophthalmology Glaucoma Panel. Preferred Practice Pattern Guidelines. *Primary Open-Angle Glaucoma.* San Francisco: American Academy of Ophthalmology; 2010. Available at: www.aao.org/ppp.

Leske MC, Heijl A, Hyman L, Bengtsson B, Dong L, Yang Z; EMGT Group. Predictors of long-term progression in the Early Manifest Glaucoma Trial. *Ophthalmology.* 2007;114(11):1965–1972.

Oliver JE, Hattenhauer MG, Herman D, et al. Blindness and glaucoma: a comparison of patients progressing to blindness from glaucoma with patients maintaining vision. *Am J Ophthalmol.* 2002;133(6):764–772.

Quigley HA, Vitale S. Models of open-angle glaucoma prevalence and incidence in the United States. *Invest Ophthalmol Vis Sci.* 1997;38(1):83–91.

Wilson MR, Brandt JD. Update on glaucoma clinical trials. *Focal Points: Clinical Modules for Ophthalmologists.* San Francisco: American Academy of Ophthalmology; 2003, module 9.

Open-Angle Glaucoma Without Elevated IOP (Normal-Tension Glaucoma, Low-Tension Glaucoma)

Controversy remains about whether normal-tension glaucoma represents a distinct disease entity or whether it is simply POAG with IOP within the average range. Because glaucoma can develop at any IOP level within the range of pressures observed in the general population, IOP is a continuous risk factor for the development of glaucoma, and any cut-off between "normal" and "abnormal" IOP is arbitrary. Accordingly, many authorities believe the terms *low-tension glaucoma* and *normal-tension glaucoma* should be abandoned.

Clinical Features

As previously emphasized, glaucoma is a multifactorial disease process for which elevated IOP is just one of several risk factors. The other risk factors may play a more important role in normal-tension glaucoma than they do in POAG with higher IOPs. Many authorities have hypothesized that local vascular factors may have a significant part in the development of this disorder. Some studies have suggested that patients with normal-tension glaucoma show a higher prevalence of vasospastic disorders such as migraine headache and Raynaud phenomenon, ischemic vascular diseases, autoimmune diseases, and coagulopathies compared with patients who have high-tension glaucoma. However, these findings have not been consistent. Vascular autoregulatory defects have also been described in studies of eyes with normal-tension glaucoma.

The condition is characteristically bilateral but often asymmetric. Studies have indicated that in glaucomatous eyes with normal but asymmetric IOP, worse damage usually occurs in the eye with the higher IOP.

Optic disc hemorrhages are more common among patients with normal-tension glaucoma, compared to those with POAG and higher IOPs. Some authorities have separated normal-tension glaucoma into 2 groups based on disc appearance:

- a *senile sclerotic group* with shallow, pale sloping of the neuroretinal rim (primarily seen in older patients with vascular disease)
- a *focal ischemic group* with deep, focal notching of the neuroretinal rim

The visual field defects in normal-tension glaucoma tend to be more focal, deeper, and closer to fixation, especially early in the course of the disease, compared with those commonly seen in POAG. A dense paracentral scotoma encroaching on fixation is not an unusual finding as the initial defect. Although many reports have described these differences between groups of patients with normal-tension glaucoma and those with POAG, others have failed to confirm them. In any individual patient, there is no characteristic abnormality of the optic disc or visual field that distinguishes normal-tension glaucoma from POAG with higher IOPs.

Cartwright MJ, Anderson DR. Correlation of asymmetric damage with asymmetric intraocular pressure in normal-tension glaucoma (low-tension glaucoma). *Arch Ophthalmol.* 1988;106(7):898–900.

Collaborative Normal-Tension Glaucoma Study Group. Comparison of glaucomatous progression between untreated patients with normal-tension glaucoma and patients with therapeutically reduced intraocular pressures. *Am J Ophthalmol.* 1998;126(4):487–497.

Differential Diagnosis

Normal-tension glaucoma can be mimicked by many conditions, as summarized in Table 4-1. Several of these conditions can cause visual field defects similar to those seen in glaucoma, and some may be progressive. Great care must be taken to distinguish

Table 4-1 Differential Diagnosis of Normal-Tension Glaucoma

Undetected high-tension glaucoma
  Primary open-angle glaucoma with diurnal IOP variation
  Intermittent IOP elevation
    Angle-closure glaucoma
    Glaucomatocyclitic crisis
  Previously elevated IOP
    Past secondary glaucoma (eg, corticosteroid-induced glaucoma, uveitic glaucoma,
      pigmentary glaucoma, previous trauma)
    Normalized IOP in an eye with previously elevated IOP
  Use of medication that may cause IOP lowering (systemic β-blocker)
  Tonometry error (low corneal thickness, reduced scleral rigidity)

Nonglaucomatous optic nerve disease
  Congenital anomalies (coloboma, optic nerve pits)
  Compressive lesions of optic nerve and chiasm
  Shock optic neuropathy
  Anterior ischemic optic neuropathy
  Retinal disorders (ie, retinal detachment, retinoschisis, vascular occlusions, chorioretinitis,
    syphilis)
  Optic nerve drusen
  Toxic/nutritional optic neuropathy (eg, methanol)

normal-tension glaucoma from a nonglaucomatous optic neuropathy, angle-closure glaucoma, optic disc anomalies, and retinal disease because appropriate treatment may vary greatly.

Diurnal IOP measurement is useful to determine peak IOP, which also aids in determining the target IOP. Elevated IOP can be obscured in patients taking systemic medication, particularly systemic β-blockers. Some patients with apparent normal-tension glaucoma may have artifactually low tonometry readings caused by, for example, reduced scleral rigidity or low CCT. Decreased corneal thickness in patients who have undergone refractive surgery may be associated with underestimation of IOP and an erroneous diagnosis of normal-tension glaucoma in these patients. From a clinical standpoint, for eyes with normal-tension glaucoma and a low CCT, the clinical management should be unchanged in that the ophthalmologist should carefully determine the baseline IOP prior to initiation of therapy, with a typical target pressure 30% below baseline, to be adjusted as necessary based on the patient's unique circumstances.

Many patients with myopia may have anomalous discs or myopic visual field changes, further complicating the diagnosis of glaucoma. Other conditions to consider in the differential diagnosis include normalized IOP in an eye with previously elevated IOP and previous corticosteroid-induced or other secondary glaucoma.

Diagnostic Evaluation

It is difficult to know how often glaucomatous damage occurs with IOP in the normal range. Population-based epidemiologic studies have suggested that as many as 30%–50% of eyes with POAG may have IOP below 21 mm Hg on a single reading. Repeated testing would undoubtedly have detected elevated IOP in many of these eyes. The prevalence of normal-tension glaucoma appears to vary among different populations. Studies have suggested that among Japanese patients, a particularly high proportion of OAG occurs with IOP in the normal range.

Before making a diagnosis of normal-tension glaucoma, the clinician should measure the patient's IOP by applanation tonometry at various times during the day. Gonioscopy should be performed to rule out angle closure, angle recession, or evidence of previous intraocular inflammation or pigment dispersion. Careful stereoscopic disc evaluation is essential to rule out other congenital or acquired disc anomalies, such as optic nerve coloboma, drusen, and physiologically enlarged cups. The clinician must also consider the patient's medical history, particularly any record of cardiovascular disease and low blood pressure caused by hemorrhage, myocardial infarction, or shock. Visual field loss consistent with glaucoma has been noted after a decrease in blood pressure following a hypotensive crisis. However, damage secondary to such a specific precipitating event tends to be stable and does not progress once the underlying problem has been corrected. Similarly, a previous episode of prolonged, elevated IOP, such as that related to the use of topical steroids in susceptible individuals, may result in optic nerve damage that later mimics normal-tension glaucoma but is not progressive.

In the setting of atypical findings such as unilateral disease, decreased central vision, dyschromatopsia, young age, the presence of a relative afferent pupillary defect, neuroretinal rim pallor, or visual field loss not consistent with the optic disc appearance, additional medical and neurological evaluation should be considered, including tests for anemia, carotid artery insufficiency, syphilis, certain vitamin deficiencies, and temporal arteritis or other causes of systemic vasculitis. Auscultation and palpation of the carotid arteries should be performed, and noninvasive tests of carotid circulation may be helpful. Evaluation of the optic nerve and chiasm with computed tomography or magnetic resonance imaging may be warranted in some cases to rule out compressive lesions, especially if the visual field loss is at all suggestive of a neurological defect (see also BCSC Section 5, *Neuro-Ophthalmology*).

Greenfield DS, Siatkowski RM, Glaser JS, Schatz NJ, Parrish RK II. The cupped disc. Who needs neuroimaging? *Ophthalmology.* 1998;105(10):1866–1874.

Prognosis and Therapy

The Collaborative Normal-Tension Glaucoma Study (CNTGS) found that lowering IOP by at least 30% reduced the 5-year risk of visual field progression from 35% to 12%, confirming that IOP has a clear role in this disease. However, because some patients did progress despite the reduction in IOP, other factors may be operative as well. It should be noted that the protective effect of IOP reduction was evident only after adjusting for the effect of cataracts, which were more frequent in the treated group.

Based on the findings of the CNTGS, treatment of normal-tension glaucoma is generally initiated unless the optic neuropathy is determined to be stable. This study demonstrated that in some patients (65%), the glaucoma did not progress over the length of the study despite the lack of treatment, whereas in others (12%) the disease progressed despite successful IOP reduction. The rate of visual field progression was highly variable but slow in the majority of those with visual field progression. Treatment benefit was lower among patients with a baseline history of disc hemorrhage. The potential role of neuroprotective agents is experimental and remains under investigation.

The goal of therapy should be to use currently available treatments to achieve an IOP level that is approximately 30% below a carefully determined baseline, with appropriate adjustments of the target pressure that take into account the baseline severity of the optic nerve damage, the risks of therapy, and other relevant factors, such as life expectancy and comorbid conditions.

As with POAG, topical medical therapy is the most common initial approach in the management of normal-tension glaucoma. In addition to their IOP-lowering effect, some glaucoma medications may have neuroprotective properties or may improve ocular circulation. These potential benefits have not been proven clinically, however.

Medications, laser trabeculoplasty, and glaucoma filtering surgery may be indicated in an attempt to achieve the target IOP range. An antifibrotic agent, either mitomycin C or 5-fluorouracil, may be used to improve the success rate of filtering surgery. In the EMGT, the combination of betaxolol and argon laser trabeculoplasty (ALT) had little pressure-lowering effect on eyes with baseline IOPs of 15 mm Hg or lower, suggesting that in such eyes incisional surgery and medications other than β-blockers are more likely to be beneficial. (See Chapter 8.)

Bhandari A, Crabb DP, Poinoosawmy D, Fitzke FW, Hitchings RA, Noureddin BN. Effect of surgery on visual field progression in normal-tension glaucoma. *Ophthalmology.* 1997;104(7):1131–1137.

Collaborative Normal-Tension Glaucoma Study Group. Comparison of glaucomatous progression between untreated patients with normal-tension glaucoma and patients with therapeutically reduced intraocular pressures. *Am J Ophthalmol.* 1998;126(4):487–497.

Collaborative Normal-Tension Glaucoma Study Group. The effectiveness of intraocular pressure reduction in the treatment of normal-tension glaucoma. *Am J Ophthalmol.* 1998;126(4):498–505.

Mikelberg FS. Normal tension glaucoma. *Focal Points: Clinical Modules for Ophthalmologists.* San Francisco: American Academy of Ophthalmology; 2000, module 12.

The Glaucoma Suspect

A glaucoma suspect is defined as an individual who has an optic nerve or nerve fiber layer defect suggestive of glaucoma (enlarged cup–disc ratio, asymmetric cup–disc ratio, notching or narrowing of the neuroretinal rim, a disc hemorrhage, or suspicious alteration in the nerve fiber layer) in the absence of an abnormality in visual function as determined by perimetry; or who has a visual field abnormality consistent with glaucoma in the absence of a corresponding glaucomatous optic disc abnormality. Patients with such findings are typically monitored for the development of glaucoma with periodic evaluation of the optic nerve, retinal nerve fiber layer, and visual field. The increasing use of short-wavelength automated perimetry (SWAP) and frequency-doubling technology (FDT) perimetry, as well as assessment of the pattern electroretinogram, may improve the ophthalmologist's ability to recognize early glaucomatous visual function loss in patients considered to be glaucoma suspects because of a suspicious optic disc appearance (see Chapter 3). If signs of optic nerve damage are present, the diagnosis of early POAG should be considered and treatment initiated. However, in uncertain cases, the ophthalmologist should not hesitate to closely monitor patients without therapy to confirm either initial findings or progressive change, with the aim of better establishing the diagnosis prior to initiating therapy. It may be difficult to classify a glaucoma suspect who has elevated IOP and structural or functional findings that are suggestive but not firmly diagnostic of glaucomatous optic neuropathy. Such patients do not fit neatly into one diagnostic category.

Ocular Hypertension

Some authors consider patients with OHT to be glaucoma suspects. In this book, we define OHT as a condition in which the IOP is elevated above an arbitrary cutoff value, typically 21 mm Hg, in the absence of optic disc, retinal nerve fiber layer, or visual field abnormalities. Estimates of the prevalence of OHT vary considerably; some authorities believe the prevalence of OHT may be as high as 8 times that of definite POAG. Analysis of studies that have observed individuals with elevated IOP for variable periods indicates that the higher the baseline IOP, the greater the risk of developing glaucoma. However, it is important to note that even among individuals with elevated IOP, the majority never develop glaucoma.

Differentiating between diagnoses of OHT and early POAG is often difficult. The ophthalmologist must look carefully for signs of early damage to the optic nerve, such as focal notching, asymmetry of cupping, optic disc hemorrhage, nerve fiber layer defects, or subtle visual field defects.

There is no clear consensus about whether elevated IOP should be treated in the absence of signs of early damage. Some clinicians, after assessing all risk factors, select and treat those individuals thought to be at greatest risk of developing glaucoma. In OHTS, patients 40–80 years of age with IOP between 24 and 32 mm Hg were randomized to observation or to the reduction of IOP by topical medications (Fig 4-1; see Clinical Trial 4-2 at the end of this chapter). In this study, 4.4% of patients treated (with topical glaucoma medications to reduce IOP 20%) progressed to glaucoma during a 5-year period, based on the development of optic nerve or visual field damage. More than twice as many of the untreated observation group, or 9.5%, progressed. Thus, topical medications were definitively shown to reduce the risk of progression to glaucoma in patients with OHT; however, most untreated patients did not get worse over a 5-year period. Each millimeter of mercury of elevated baseline IOP increased the risk of glaucomatous change by 10%. For each 0.1 increment in vertical cup–disc ratio, the risk was increased by 32%.

OHTS identified older age, higher IOP, lower CCT, higher pattern standard deviation on standard automated perimetry, and higher cup–disc ratio at baseline as important risk factors for the development of POAG. Data from OHTS and the European Glaucoma Prevention Study were combined to create a risk calculation model to predict the 5-year risk of conversion from OHT to glaucoma based on these risk factors.

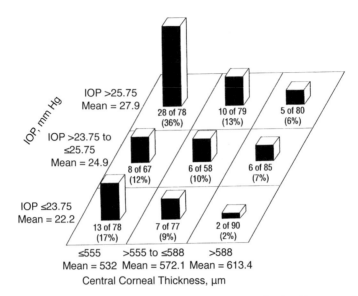

IOP, mm Hg

IOP >25.75
Mean = 27.9

28 of 78
(36%)

10 of 79
(13%)

5 of 80
(6%)

IOP >23.75 to
≤25.75
Mean = 24.9

8 of 67
(12%)

6 of 58
(10%)

6 of 85
(7%)

IOP ≤23.75
Mean = 22.2

13 of 78
(17%)

7 of 77
(9%)

2 of 90
(2%)

≤555   >555 to ≤588   >588
Mean = 532 Mean = 572.1 Mean = 613.4
Central Corneal Thickness, μm

Figure 4-1 The number and percentage of participants in the Ocular Hypertension Treatment Study observation group that developed primary open-angle glaucoma (POAG) as a function of baseline intraocular pressure (IOP) and central corneal thickness (CCT). *(Reprinted with permission from Gordon MO, Beiser JA, Brandt JD, et al. The Ocular Hypertension Treatment Study: baseline factors that predict the onset of primary open-angle glaucoma.* Arch Ophthalmol. *2002;120:718, Fig 1. Copyrighted 2002, American Medical Association.)*

It has been recognized that variations in CCT affect the IOP measurement. For example, a thicker cornea resists indentation by applanation, resulting in a higher IOP reading. But the increased risk of progression attributed to lower CCT in OHTS was not fully explained by the estimated artifactual error in measured IOP. It is therefore hypothesized that lower CCT may be a marker for other susceptibility factors. Other potential risk factors, such as myopia, diabetes mellitus, positive family history, migraine, and high or low blood pressure, were not confirmed in OHTS to be significant risk factors in the univariate or multivariate analysis. As mentioned previously, black race was found to increase the risk of glaucoma development in the univariate but not in the multivariate analysis, presumably because the increased risk in this population is attributable to the presence of lower CCT and higher cup–disc ratios.

That family history was not identified as a significant risk factor in OHTS is widely thought to be due to inadequate assessment of this information. Clinicians should still consider the patient's family history when evaluating the patient's risk of developing glaucoma, if this information is believed to be accurate.

Based on the findings of the examination and the results of OHTS, an assessment of the patient's risk of developing glaucoma can be derived. The clinician and the patient can decide together whether this risk warrants the inconvenience, cost, and potential side effects of therapy. Care must be taken that the risks and morbidity of therapy do not exceed the risks of the disease. Additional factors that may affect the decision to start ocular hypotensive therapy include the desires of the patient, patient compliance and availability for follow-up visits, reliability of visual fields, and ability to examine the optic disc.

The initial reports from OHTS clearly demonstrated that treatment reduced the risk of progression to glaucoma; however, the incremental structural or functional change that constituted a progression endpoint would not have been associated with the development of symptomatic vision loss. Therefore, the question remained whether delaying treatment was associated with poorer outcomes compared to early initiation of IOP-lowering therapy.

To help answer this question, subjects in the OHTS control arm, after a median of 7.5 years of observation without treatment, received IOP-lowering therapy. Subjects in both groups were monitored for an additional median follow-up period of 5.5 years, during which time all subjects were receiving treatment to lower IOP. At the conclusion of the median follow-up period of 13 years, 16% and 22% of subjects in the initial- and late-treatment groups, respectively, progressed. Although the two groups diverged with respect to the development of glaucoma during the original study period (when the observation group did not receive treatment), there was no further divergence in the Kaplan-Meier curves after both groups received IOP-lowering treatment. This result suggests that clinicians may safely consider delaying the treatment of OHT, particularly among patients with a lower risk of conversion to glaucoma.

American Academy of Ophthalmology Glaucoma Panel. Preferred Practice Pattern Guidelines. *Primary Open-Angle Glaucoma Suspect.* San Francisco: American Academy of Ophthalmology; 2010. Available at: www.aao.org/ppp.

Gordon MO, Beiser JA, Brandt JD, et al. The Ocular Hypertension Treatment Study: baseline factors that predict the onset of primary open-angle glaucoma. *Arch Ophthalmol.* 2002; 120(6):714–720.

Kass MA, Gordon MO, Gao F, et al. Delaying treatment of ocular hypertension: the Ocular Hypertension Treatment Study. *Arch Ophthalmol.* 2010;128(3):276–287.

Kass MA, Heuer DK, Higginbotham EJ, et al. The Ocular Hypertension Treatment Study: a randomized trial determines that topical ocular hypotensive medication delays or prevents the onset of primary open-angle glaucoma. *Arch Ophthalmol.* 2002;120(6):701–713.

Wilson MR, Brandt JD. Update on glaucoma clinical trials. *Focal Points: Clinical Modules for Ophthalmologists.* American Academy of Ophthalmology; 2003, module 9.

Secondary Open-Angle Glaucoma

Exfoliation Syndrome

Exfoliation syndrome (pseudoexfoliation) is characterized by the deposition of a distinctive fibrillar material in the anterior segment of the eye. Histologically, this material has been found in and on the lens epithelium and capsule, pupillary margin, ciliary epithelium, iris pigment epithelium, iris stroma, iris blood vessels, and subconjunctival tissue. The material has also been identified in other parts of the body. Mutations in a single gene, *LOXL1*, seem to be present in nearly all cases of exfoliation syndrome and exfoliation glaucoma; however, these disease-associated mutations are also common in the population without glaucoma, suggesting that the disorder is multifactorial. The exact mechanism by which *LOXL1* mutations are related to the development of glaucoma is unclear, but it likely involves the reduced or abnormal synthesis of elastin fibers. The IOP elevation associated with exfoliation syndrome is thought to be caused by the fibrillar material obstructing flow through, and causing damage to, the trabecular meshwork or the uveoscleral pathway. Since elastin is an important component of the lamina cribrosa, exfoliation syndrome may increase the susceptibility of the optic nerve to injury. This may explain why the presence of exfoliation syndrome was shown to be an independent risk factor for progression of OHT in the European Glaucoma Prevention Study (EGPS) and for progression of OAG in the EMGT.

The deposits occur in a targetlike pattern on the anterior lens capsule, and they are best seen after pupillary dilation. A central area and a peripheral zone of deposition are usually separated by an intermediate clear area, where iris movement presumably rubs the material from the lens (Fig 4-2). The material is often visible on the iris, at the edge of the pupil. Deposits also occur on the zonular fibers of the lens, ciliary processes, inferior anterior chamber angle, and corneal endothelium (Fig 4-3). In aphakic individuals, these deposits may be seen on the anterior hyaloid as well.

The chamber angle is often characterized by a trabecular meshwork that is heavily pigmented with brown pigment, usually in a variegated fashion. An inferior pigmented deposition, scalloped in nature, is often present anterior to the Schwalbe line. This pigmented line is often referred to as the *Sampaolesi line* (Fig 4-4). The chamber angle may be narrow, presumably as a result of the anterior movement of the lens–iris interface, which can occur because of zonular weakness.

In addition to the typical deposits and pigmentation, other anterior segment abnormalities are noted. Fine pigment deposits often appear on the iris surface, and peripupillary atrophy with transillumination of the pupillary margin is common. A more scattered, diffuse depigmentation may also occur, with transillumination defects over the entire sphincter region. The pupil often dilates poorly. Phacodonesis and iridodonesis are not

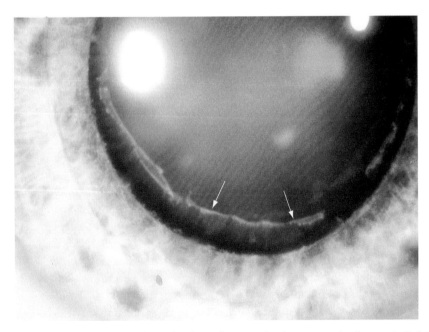

Figure 4-2 Exfoliative material deposited on the anterior lens capsule *(arrows)*. Exfoliative material may also be deposited on other structures within the anterior segment, including the iris, ciliary processes, peripheral retina, and conjunctiva.

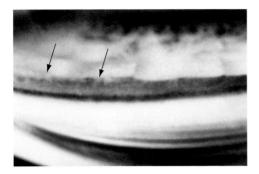

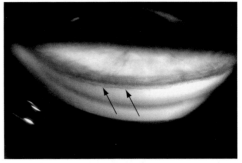

Figure 4-3 Exfoliative debris *(arrows)* collecting on iris processes in inferior anterior chamber angle. *(Courtesy of Steven T. Simmons, MD.)*

Figure 4-4 The Sampaolesi line *(arrows)* in the inferior anterior chamber angle of a patient with exfoliation syndrome. *(Courtesy of L. J. Katz, MD.)*

uncommon; they are related to zonular weakness, which may predispose affected eyes to zonular dehiscence, vitreous loss, and other complications (including lens dislocation) during and after cataract surgery (see also BCSC Section 11, *Lens and Cataract*). Iris angiography has shown abnormalities of the iris vessels with fluorescein leakage.

Exfoliation syndrome may be unilateral or bilateral with varying degrees of asymmetry. Often the disorder is clinically apparent in only 1 eye, although the uninvolved fellow eye often develops the syndrome at a later time. Exfoliation syndrome is associated with OAG in all populations, but the prevalence varies considerably. In Scandinavian countries, exfoliation syndrome accounts for more than 50% of cases of OAG. The odds of the exfoliation syndrome leading to glaucoma vary widely, and range up to 40% over a 10-year period. This syndrome is strongly age-related: it is rarely seen in persons younger than 50 years and occurs most commonly in individuals older than 70 years.

Exfoliation glaucoma differs from POAG in often presenting unilaterally and in showing greater pigmentation of the trabecular meshwork. In addition, the IOP is often higher, with greater diurnal fluctuations than occurs in POAG, and the overall prognosis is worse. Laser trabeculoplasty can be very effective, but the response in exfoliation glaucoma may not last as long as that in POAG. Lens extraction does not alleviate the condition.

Ritch R. Exfoliation syndrome. In: Ritch R, Shields MB, Krupin T, eds. *The Glaucomas.* 2nd ed. St Louis: Mosby; 1996:993–1022.

Schlötzer-Schrehardt U, Naumann GO. Ocular and systemic pseudoexfoliation syndrome. *Am J Ophthalmol.* 2006;141(5):921–937.

Thorleifsson G, Magnusson KP, Sulem P, et al. Common sequence variants in the *LOXL1* gene confer susceptibility to exfoliation glaucoma. *Science.* 2007;317(5843):1397–1400.

Pigmentary Glaucoma

The *pigment dispersion syndrome* consists of pigment deposition on the corneal endothelium in a vertical spindle pattern (Krukenberg spindle; Fig 4-5), in the trabecular meshwork, and on the lens periphery. Typically, peripheral iris transillumination defects are also present. The spindle pattern on the posterior cornea is caused by the aqueous convection currents and subsequent phagocytosis of pigment by the corneal endothelium.

The presence of Krukenberg spindles is not absolutely necessary to make the diagnosis of pigment dispersion syndrome, and it may occur in other diseases, such as exfoliation syndrome. Characteristic spokelike loss of the iris pigment epithelium occurs, manifesting as transillumination defects in the iris midperiphery (Fig 4-6). The peripheral iris transillumination defects appear in front of the lens zonular fibers.

Gonioscopy reveals a homogeneous, densely pigmented trabecular meshwork with speckled pigment at or anterior to the Schwalbe line (Fig 4-7), often forming a Sampaolesi line. The midperipheral iris is often concave in appearance, bowing posteriorly, toward the zonular fibers. When the eye is dilated, pigment deposits can be seen on the zonular fibers, the anterior hyaloid, and the lens capsule near the equator of the lens (Zentmayer line; Fig 4-8).

This syndrome does not universally lead to glaucoma. An individual with pigment dispersion syndrome may never develop elevated IOP, and various studies have suggested

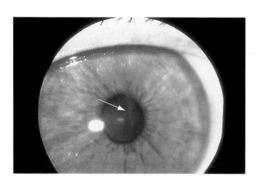

Figure 4-5 Krukenberg spindle *(arrow)*. *(Courtesy of L. J. Katz, MD.)*

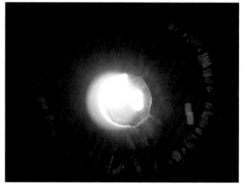

Figure 4-6 Classic spokelike iris transillumination defects seen in pigment dispersion syndrome. *(Courtesy of Angelo P. Tanna, MD.)*

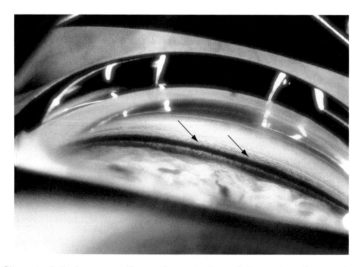

Figure 4-7 Characteristic heavy, uniform pigmentation of the trabecular meshwork *(arrows)* seen in the pigment dispersion syndrome and pigmentary glaucoma. *(Courtesy of M. Roy Wilson, MD.)*

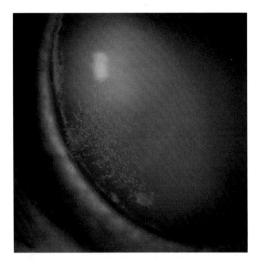

Figure 4-8 In pigment dispersion syndrome, pigment deposits can be seen on the equatorial region of the lens capsule (Zentmayer line) and on the zonules. *(Courtesy of Angelo P. Tanna, MD.)*

that the risk of an affected individual developing glaucoma is approximately 25%–50%. Pigmentary glaucoma occurs most commonly in white males who have myopia and who are between the ages of 20 and 50 years.

Pigmentary glaucoma is characterized by wide fluctuations in IOP, which can exceed 50 mm Hg in untreated eyes. High IOP often occurs when pigment is released into the aqueous humor, such as following exercise or pupillary dilation. Symptoms may include halos, intermittent visual blurring, and ocular pain.

Posterior bowing of the iris with "reverse pupillary block" configuration is noted in many eyes that have pigmentary glaucoma. This iris configuration results in greater contact of the zonular fibers with the posterior iris surface, with subsequent pigment release. Laser iridotomy has been proposed as a means of minimizing posterior bowing of the iris (Fig 4-9). However, its effectiveness in treating pigmentary glaucoma has not been established.

With age, the signs and symptoms of pigment dispersion may decrease in some individuals, possibly as a result of normal growth of the lens and an increase in physiologic pupillary block, moving the iris forward, away from contact with the zonular fibers. Loss of accommodation may also be a factor. As pigment dispersion is reduced, the deposited pigment may fade from the trabecular meshwork, anterior iris surface, and corneal endothelium. Transillumination defects may also gradually disappear.

Medical treatment is often successful in reducing the IOP. Patients respond reasonably well to laser trabeculoplasty, although the effect may be short-lived. The heavy trabecular pigmentation allows increased absorption of laser energy, in turn allowing lower energy levels for trabeculoplasty. Spikes in IOP may be seen more frequently with higher energy settings in pigment dispersion syndrome following laser trabeculoplasty. Filtering surgery is usually successful; however, extra care is warranted, because young patients with myopia may be at increased risk of hypotony maculopathy.

Liebmann JM. Pigmentary glaucoma: new insights. *Focal Points: Clinical Modules for Ophthalmologists.* San Francisco: American Academy of Ophthalmology; 1998, module 2.

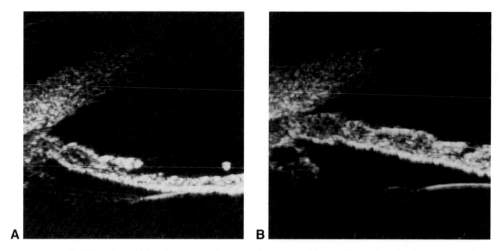

Figure 4-9 **A,** Ultrasound biomicroscopy image of concave iris configuration in pigmentary glaucoma, before laser treatment. **B,** Same eye, after laser treatment. *(Courtesy of Charles J. Pavlin, MD.)*

Reistad CE, Shields MB, Campbell DG, Ritch R, Wang JC, Wand M; American Glaucoma Society Pigmentary Glaucoma Iridotomy Study Group. The influence of peripheral iridotomy on the intraocular pressure course in patients with pigmentary glaucoma. *J Glaucoma.* 2005;14(4):255–259.

Yang JW, Sakiyalak D, Krupin T. Pigmentary glaucoma. *J Glaucoma.* 2001;10(5 Suppl 1): S30–S32.

Lens-Induced Glaucoma

The lens may cause both open-angle and angle-closure glaucomas. These are listed in Table 4-2. The open-angle, lens-induced glaucomas are divided into 3 clinical entities:

- phacolytic glaucoma
- lens particle glaucoma
- phacoantigenic glaucoma

See also BCSC Section 9, *Intraocular Inflammation and Uveitis,* and Section 11, *Lens and Cataract.*

Phacolytic glaucoma

Phacolytic glaucoma is an inflammatory glaucoma caused by the leakage of lens protein through the capsule of a mature or hypermature cataract (Fig 4-10). As the lens ages, its protein composition becomes altered, with an increased concentration of high-molecular-weight lens protein. In a mature or hypermature cataract, these proteins are released

---

Table 4-2 Lens-Induced Glaucomas

Open-angle	Angle-closure (see Chapter 5)
Phacolytic glaucoma	Phacomorphic glaucoma
Lens particle glaucoma	Ectopia lentis
Phacoantigenic glaucoma	

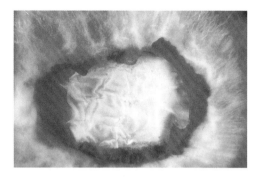

Figure 4-10 Characteristic appearance of hypermature cataract with wrinkling of the anterior lens capsule, which results from loss of cortical volume. Extensive posterior synechiae are present, and they confirm the presence of previous inflammation. *(Courtesy of Steven T. Simmons, MD.)*

through microscopic openings in the lens capsule. The proteins precipitate a secondary glaucoma as they, along with phagocytizing macrophages and other inflammatory debris, obstruct the trabecular meshwork.

The clinical picture usually involves an elderly patient with a history of poor vision who has sudden onset of pain, conjunctival hyperemia, and worsening vision. Examination reveals a markedly elevated IOP, microcystic corneal edema, prominent cell and flare reaction without keratic precipitates (KP), and an open anterior chamber angle (Fig 4-11). The lack of KP helps distinguish phacolytic glaucoma from phacoantigenic glaucoma. Cellular debris may be seen layered in the anterior chamber angle, and a pseudohypopyon may be present. Large white particles (clumps of lens protein) may also be seen in the anterior chamber. A mature or hypermature (morgagnian) cataract is present, often with wrinkling of the anterior lens capsule representing loss of volume and the release of lens material (see Fig 4-10). Although medications to control the IOP should be used immediately, definitive therapy requires cataract extraction.

Lens particle glaucoma

Lens particle glaucoma occurs when lens cortex particles obstruct the trabecular meshwork following cataract extraction, capsulotomy, or ocular trauma. The severity of IOP elevation depends on the quantity of lens material released, the degree of inflammation,

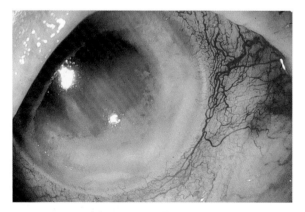

Figure 4-11 Phacolytic glaucoma. The typical presentation of phacolytic glaucoma is conjunctival hyperemia, microcystic corneal edema, mature cataract, and prominent anterior chamber reaction, as demonstrated in this photograph. Note lens protein deposits on endothelium and layering in the angle, creating a pseudohypopyon. *(Courtesy of George A. Cioffi, MD.)*

the ability of the trabecular meshwork to clear the lens material, and the functional status of the ciliary body, which is often altered following surgery or trauma.

Lens particle glaucoma usually occurs within weeks of the initial surgery or trauma, but it may occur months or years later (Fig 4-12). Clinical findings include free cortical material in the anterior chamber, elevated IOP, moderate anterior chamber reaction, microcystic corneal edema, and, with time, the development of posterior synechiae and peripheral anterior synechiae.

If possible, medical therapy should be initiated to control the IOP while the residual lens material resorbs. Appropriate therapy includes medications to decrease aqueous formation, mydriatics to inhibit posterior synechiae formation, and topical corticosteroids to reduce inflammation. If the IOP cannot be controlled, surgical removal of the lens material is necessary.

Phacoantigenic glaucoma

Phacoantigenic glaucoma (previously known as *phacoanaphylaxis*) is a rare entity in which patients become sensitized to their own lens protein following surgery or penetrating trauma, resulting in a granulomatous inflammation. The clinical picture is quite variable, but most patients present with a moderate anterior chamber reaction with KP on both the corneal endothelium and the anterior lens surface. In addition, a low-grade vitritis, synechial formation, and residual lens material in the anterior chamber may be found. Glaucomatous optic neuropathy, although it may occur, is not common in eyes with phacoantigenic glaucoma. Phacoantigenic glaucoma is treated medically with corticosteroids and aqueous suppressants, which are used to reduce inflammation and IOP. If medical treatment is unsuccessful, residual lens material should be removed.

Intraocular Tumors

A variety of tumors can cause unilateral chronic glaucoma. Many of the tumors described in this section are discussed in greater detail in BCSC Section 4, *Ophthalmic Pathology and Intraocular Tumors*. The glaucoma can result from several different mechanisms, depending on the size, type, and location of the tumor:

- direct tumor invasion of the anterior chamber angle
- angle closure by rotation of the ciliary body or by anterior displacement of the lens–iris interface (see Chapter 5)

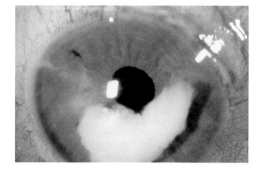

Figure 4-12 Lens particle glaucoma. Despite the large amount of lens cortex remaining in the anterior chamber following cataract surgery, this eye is relatively quiet; the IOP remained normal. *(Courtesy of the Wills Eye Hospital slide collection, 1986.)*

- intraocular hemorrhage
- neovascularization of the angle
- deposition of tumor cells, inflammatory cells, and cellular debris within the trabecular meshwork

Choroidal melanomas and other choroidal and retinal tumors tend to cause secondary angle-closure glaucoma as the result of a forward shift in the lens–iris interface and closure of the anterior chamber angle. Inflammation caused by necrotic tumors may cause posterior synechiae, which can exacerbate this angle closure through a pupillary block mechanism. Choroidal melanomas, medulloepitheliomas, and retinoblastomas can also cause anterior segment neovascularization, which can result in angle closure.

The most common cause of glaucoma in primary or metastatic tumors of the ciliary body is direct invasion of the anterior chamber angle. This glaucoma can be exacerbated by anterior segment hemorrhage and inflammation, which further obstruct outflow. Necrotic tumor and tumor-filled macrophages may cause obstruction of the trabecular meshwork and result in a secondary OAG. Tumors causing glaucoma in adults include uveal melanoma, metastatic carcinoma, lymphomas, and leukemia. Glaucoma in children is associated with retinoblastoma, juvenile xanthogranuloma, and medulloepithelioma.

Grostern RJ, Brown SVL. Glaucoma associated with intraocular tumors. In: Higginbotham E, Lee D, eds. *Management of Difficult Glaucomas.* Boston: Butterworth Heinemann; 2004: 343–351.

Shields CL, Materin MA, Shields JA, Gershenbaum E, Singh AD, Smith A. Factors associated with elevated intraocular pressure in eyes with iris melanoma. *Br J Ophthalmol.* 2001;85(6): 666–669.

Ocular Inflammation and Secondary Glaucoma

Inflammatory glaucoma is a secondary glaucoma that often combines components of open-angle and angle-closure disease. In uveitis, elevated IOP occurs when the trabecular dysfunction exceeds the ciliary body hyposecretion seen with acute inflammation. Often the ocular inflammation is nonspecific. When the inflammation is accompanied by increased IOP, the physician's dilemma is whether the cause of the increased IOP is the active inflammation and insufficient anti-inflammatory therapy, chronic structural damage to the outflow pathway related to the underlying inflammation, or corticosteroid therapy.

Inflammatory glaucoma may be caused by a variety of mechanisms:

- edema of the trabecular meshwork
- trabecular meshwork endothelial cell dysfunction
- blockage of the trabecular meshwork by fibrin and inflammatory cells
- prostaglandin-mediated breakdown of the blood–aqueous barrier
- the presence of peripheral anterior synechiae
- blockage of the Schlemm canal by inflammatory cells
- steroid-induced reduction in aqueous outflow through the trabecular meshwork

Most cases of anterior uveitis are idiopathic, but uveitides commonly associated with open-angle inflammatory glaucoma include Fuchs heterochromic iridocyclitis, herpes zoster iridocyclitis, herpes simplex keratouveitis, toxoplasmosis, juvenile idiopathic arthritis, and pars planitis. See also BCSC Section 9, *Intraocular Inflammation and Uveitis.*

The presence of KP suggests iritis as the cause of IOP elevation. Gonioscopic evaluation may reveal subtle trabecular meshwork precipitates. Sometimes, peripheral anterior synechiae (PAS) or posterior synechiae with iris bombé may develop, resulting in angle closure. The treatment of inflammatory glaucoma is complicated by the fact that corticosteroid therapy may increase IOP, either by reducing inflammation and improving aqueous production or by decreasing outflow. Miotic agents should be avoided in patients with iritis, because they may aggravate the inflammation and cause posterior synechiae. Prostaglandin analogues may exacerbate inflammation in some eyes with uveitis and herpetic keratitis; however, studies have demonstrated their ocular hypotensive efficacy in eyes with anterior uveitis. In uveitic glaucomas, inadequately controlled inflammation with elevated IOP is often mistaken for steroid-induced glaucoma. In the face of active inflammation, elevated IOP should be presumed to be inflammation-related rather than steroid-induced.

Glaucomatocyclitic crisis

Glaucomatocyclitic crisis (Posner-Schlossman syndrome), an uncommon form of open-angle inflammatory glaucoma, is characterized by recurrent bouts of markedly increased IOP and low-grade anterior chamber inflammation. First described by Posner and Schlossman in 1948, the condition most frequently affects middle-aged patients and usually presents with unilateral blurred vision and mild eye pain. The iritis is mild, with few KP that are small, discrete, and round in nature and that usually resolve spontaneously within a few weeks. KP may be seen on the trabecular meshwork on gonioscopy, suggesting a "trabeculitis." The IOP is usually markedly elevated, in the 40–50 mm Hg range, and corneal edema may be present. In between bouts, the IOP usually returns to normal, but, with increasing numbers of attacks, a chronic secondary glaucoma may develop, resulting in vision loss. The etiology of the disease remains unknown, but infection with herpes simplex virus has been implicated. There is no evidence that long-term suppressive therapy with topical nonsteroidal anti-inflammatory agents or mild steroids is effective in preventing attacks. Recurrent attacks of acute angle-closure glaucoma have been mistaken for this condition. In some cases in which glaucomatocyclitic crisis was initially diagnosed, cytomegalovirus DNA was subsequently detected in the aqueous humor by polymerase chain reaction (see BCSC Section 9, *Intraocular Inflammation and Uveitis*). Distinguishing glaucomatocyclitic crisis from cytomegalovirus is important, because specific antiviral therapy for cytomegalovirus is available.

Fuchs heterochromic iridocyclitis

Fuchs heterochromic iridocyclitis, a relatively rare, chronic form of iridocyclitis, is characterized by iris heterochromia with loss of iris pigment in the affected eye; low-grade anterior chamber reaction with small, stellate, pancorneal KP; posterior subcapsular cataracts; and secondary OAG. The condition is insidious and unilateral, affecting the hypochromic eye (in patients with blue irides, the affected eye may appear hyperchromic), and presents equally in middle-aged men and women. The secondary OAG occurs in approximately 15% of the cases. Gonioscopy reveals multiple fine vessels that cross the trabecular meshwork (Fig 4-13). These vessels, unlike those in iris neovascularization, do not appear to be

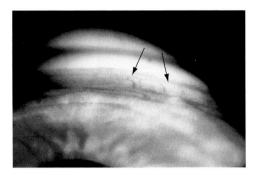

Figure 4-13 Fuchs heterochromic iridocyclitis. Fine vessels *(arrows)* are seen crossing the trabecular meshwork. This neovascularization is not accompanied by a fibrovascular membrane and does not result in peripheral anterior synechiae formation and secondary angle closure. *(Courtesy of Steven T. Simmons, MD.)*

associated with a fibrous membrane and usually do not lead to PAS and secondary angle closure, although in rare cases the neovascularization may be progressive. These vessels are fragile and may cause an anterior chamber hemorrhage, either spontaneously or with trauma, including cataract or glaucoma surgery.

The IOP does not correspond to the degree of inflammation and may be difficult to control. Corticosteroids are generally not effective in treating this condition and could potentially cause a steroid-induced IOP elevation. Medical therapy starts with aqueous suppressants, which are often effective in controlling IOP. Recent evidence suggests that rubella virus infection may be the underlying cause of this condition.

Birnbaum AD, Tessler HH, Schultz KL, et al. Epidemiologic relationship between Fuchs heterochromic iridocyclitis and the United States rubella vaccination program. *Am J Ophthalmol.* 2007;144(3):424–428.

Elevated Episcleral Venous Pressure

Episcleral venous pressure is an important factor in the regulation of IOP. Normal episcleral venous pressure is 8–10 mm Hg, but it can be raised by a variety of clinical entities that either obstruct venous outflow or involve arteriovenous malformations. A list of entities that increase episcleral venous pressure is presented in Table 4-3.

Patients may note a chronic red eye without discomfort or allergic symptoms. Occasionally, a distant history of significant head trauma may suggest the cause of a carotid cavernous sinus or dural fistula. However, most cases are idiopathic, often without

Table 4-3 Causes of Elevated Episcleral Pressure

Arteriovenous malformations
  Arteriovenous fistula
    Dural
    Carotid cavernous sinus
  Orbital varix
  Sturge-Weber syndrome
Venous obstruction
  Retrobulbar tumor
  Thyroid eye disease
Superior vena cava syndrome
Idiopathic (may be familial)

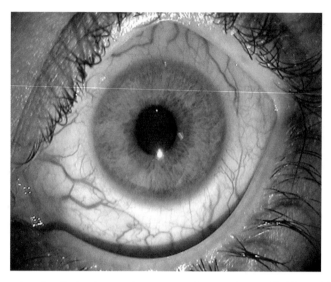

Figure 4-14 Prominent episcleral vessels are seen in a patient with idiopathic elevated episcleral venous pressure. *(Courtesy of Keith Barton, MD.)*

angiographic abnormalities, and may be familial. Clinically, patients with elevated episcleral venous pressure present with tortuous, dilated episcleral veins (Fig 4-14). These vascular abnormalities may be unilateral or bilateral. Gonioscopy often discloses blood in the Schlemm canal (see Chapter 3, Fig 3-5). In rare instances, signs of ocular ischemia or venous stasis may be present. Sudden, severe carotid-cavernous fistulas may be accompanied by proptosis and other orbital or neurological signs. These cases may require neuroradiologic intervention.

Prostaglandin analogues and medications that reduce aqueous humor formation may be effective in some patients. Laser trabeculoplasty is not effective. Glaucoma filtering surgery may be complicated by ciliochoroidal effusion or suprachoroidal hemorrhage.

Accidental and Surgical Trauma

Nonpenetrating, or blunt, trauma to the eye causes a variety of anterior segment injuries:

- hyphema
- angle recession
- iridodialysis
- iris sphincter tear
- cyclodialysis
- lens subluxation

A combination of posttraumatic inflammation, presence of blood, and direct injury to the trabecular meshwork often results in elevated IOP initially after trauma. This elevation tends to be short in duration but may be protracted, with the risk of corneal blood staining (Fig 4-15) and glaucomatous optic nerve damage.

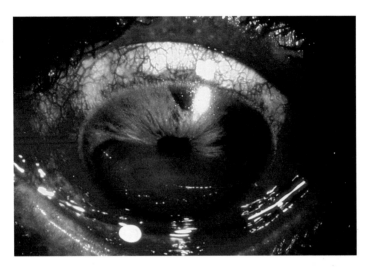

Figure 4-15 Corneal blood staining following trauma. *(Courtesy of Steven T. Simmons, MD.)*

OAG is one of the long-term sequelae of *siderosis* or *chalcosis* from a retained intraocular metallic foreign body in penetrating or perforating injuries. Chemical injuries, particularly alkali, may cause acute secondary glaucoma as a result of inflammation, shrinkage of scleral collagen, release of chemical mediators such as prostaglandins, direct damage to the chamber angle, or compromise of the anterior uveal circulation. Trabecular damage or inflammation may cause glaucoma to develop months or years after a chemical injury.

Hyphema

Elevated IOP may result from hyphema through several mechanisms (Fig 4-16). Increased IOP is more common following recurrent hemorrhage or rebleeding following a traumatic hyphema. The reported frequency of rebleeding following hyphema varies considerably in

Figure 4-16 A small hyphema seen gonioscopically in the inferior chamber angle, with layering of blood on the trabecular meshwork. *(Courtesy of Steven T. Simmons, MD.)*

the literature, probably because of differences in study populations, with an average incidence of 5%–10%. Rebleeding usually occurs within 3–7 days of the initial hyphema and may be related to normal clot retraction and lysis. In general, the larger the hyphema, the higher the incidence of increased IOP, although small hemorrhages may also be associated with marked elevation of IOP, especially in the already compromised angle. Increased IOP is a result of obstruction of the trabecular meshwork with red blood cells (RBCs), inflammatory cells, debris, and fibrin, and of direct injury to the trabecular meshwork from the blunt trauma.

Individuals with sickle cell hemoglobinopathies have an increased incidence of elevated IOP following hyphema and are more susceptible to the development of optic neuropathy. Normal RBCs generally pass through the trabecular meshwork without difficulty. However, in the sickle cell hemoglobinopathies (including sickle trait), the RBCs tend to sickle in the anterior chamber, because of the low pH of aqueous humor. These more rigid cells tend to become trapped in the trabecular meshwork. Even small amounts of blood in the anterior chamber may therefore result in marked elevations of IOP. In addition, the optic nerves of patients with sickle cell disease are much more sensitive to elevated IOP and are prone to developing anterior ischemic optic neuropathy and central retinal artery occlusion, as a result of compromised microvascular perfusion.

In general, the patient with an uncomplicated hyphema should be managed conservatively, with an eye shield, limited activity, and head elevation. Topical and systemic corticosteroids may reduce associated inflammation, although their effect on rebleeding is debatable. If significant ciliary spasm or photophobia occurs, cycloplegic agents may be helpful, but they have no proven benefit for prevention of rebleeding. Systemic administration of aminocaproic acid has been shown to reduce rebleeding in some studies. However, this has not been confirmed in all studies, and systemic adverse effects, such as hypotension, syncope, abdominal pain, and nausea, can be significant. Also, discontinuation of aminocaproic acid may be associated with clot lysis and with additional IOP elevation. Patching and bed rest are advocated by some authors, although these precautions are of unproven value.

If the IOP is elevated, aqueous suppressants and hyperosmotic agents are recommended. It has been suggested that patients with sickle cell hemoglobinopathies avoid carbonic anhydrase inhibitors, because these agents may increase the sickling tendency in the anterior chamber by further lowering the pH; however, this relationship has not been firmly established. Physicians should be aware of the potential of systemic carbonic anhydrase inhibitors and hyperosmotic agents to induce sickle crises in susceptible individuals who are significantly dehydrated. Both classes of drugs may enhance sickling, as each may exacerbate dehydration. Adrenergic agonists with significant α_1-agonist effects (apraclonidine, dipivefrin, epinephrine) should also be avoided in sickle cell disease because of concerns regarding anterior segment vasoconstriction. Parasympathomimetic agents should be avoided in all patients with hyphemas.

Clinicians should have a lower threshold for surgical intervention in sickle cell patients, given the increased risk of optic atrophy from elevated IOP. If the hyphema or corneal staining significantly obstructs vision, the possibility of amblyopia may justify early surgical intervention in very young children. If surgery for elevated IOP becomes necessary, an anterior chamber irrigation or washout procedure is commonly performed first. If a total hyphema is present, pupillary block may occur, and an iridectomy is helpful at the time of the washout. If the IOP remains uncontrolled, incisional surgery may be required. Some surgeons prefer to perform incisional glaucoma surgery as the initial surgical procedure with the anterior chamber washout in order to obtain immediate control of IOP and relief of any pupillary block.

> Campagna JA. Traumatic hyphema: current strategies. *Focal Points: Clinical Modules for Ophthalmologists.* San Francisco: American Academy of Ophthalmology; 2007, module 10.

Hemolytic and ghost cell glaucoma

Hemolytic and/or ghost cell glaucoma may develop after a vitreous hemorrhage. In *hemolytic glaucoma,* hemoglobin-laden macrophages block the trabecular outflow channels. Red-tinged cells are seen floating in the anterior chamber, and a reddish brown discoloration of the trabecular meshwork is often present.

Ghost cell glaucoma is a secondary OAG caused by degenerated RBCs (ghost cells) blocking the trabecular meshwork. Ghost cells are RBCs that have lost their intracellular hemoglobin and appear as small, khaki-colored cells. They are less pliable than normal RBCs (Fig 4-17); thus, they obstruct the trabecular meshwork, causing IOP elevation. RBCs degenerate within 1–3 months of a vitreous hemorrhage. They gain access to the anterior chamber through a disrupted hyaloid face, which can occur from previous surgery (pars plana vitrectomy, cataract extraction, or capsulotomy), from trauma, or spontaneously.

Clinically, patients present with elevated IOP and a history of vitreous hemorrhage resulting from trauma, surgery, or preexisting retinal disease. The IOP may be markedly elevated, causing corneal edema. The anterior chamber is filled with small, circulating, tan-colored cells (see Fig 4-17). The cellular reaction appears out of proportion to the

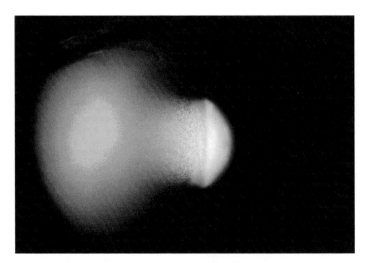

Figure 4-17 Ghost cell glaucoma: the classic appearance of ghost cells in the anterior chamber. These khaki-colored cells are small and can become layered, as is seen in a hyphema and hypopyon. *(Courtesy of Ron Gross, MD.)*

aqueous flare, and the conjunctiva tends not to be inflamed unless the IOP is markedly elevated. On gonioscopy, the angle appears normal except for the layering of ghost cells over the trabecular meshwork inferiorly. A long-standing vitreous hemorrhage is present, with characteristic khaki coloration and clumps of extracellular pigmentation from degenerated hemoglobin.

Both hemolytic and ghost cell glaucoma generally resolve once the hemorrhage has cleared. Medical therapy with aqueous suppressants is the preferred initial approach. If medical therapy fails to control the IOP, some patients may require irrigation of the anterior chamber, pars plana vitrectomy, and/or incisional glaucoma surgery. When a collection of RBCs or ghost cells is present in the vitreous, a pars plana vitrectomy is usually required for IOP control.

Traumatic, or angle-recession, glaucoma

Angle recession is due to a tear in the ciliary body, usually between the longitudinal and circular muscle fibers. Angle recession is often associated with injury to the trabecular meshwork as well. Angle-recession glaucoma is a chronic, unilateral secondary OAG that may occur soon after ocular trauma or may develop months to years later. It resembles POAG in presentation and clinical course but can usually be distinguished by its classic gonioscopic findings (Figs 4-18, 4-19):

- brown-colored, broad angle recess
- absent or torn iris processes
- white, glistening scleral spur
- depression in the overlying trabecular meshwork
- PAS at the border of the recession

The degree of angle involvement is an important factor in determining whether a secondary glaucoma will develop. A significant proportion (up to 50%) of fellow eyes may

Figure 4-18 Angle recession occurs when the ciliary body is torn, usually between the longitudinal and circular fibers of the ciliary body. There is a deepened angle recess as a result of a tear in the ciliary body *(arrows)*. *(Courtesy of Joseph Krug, MD.)*

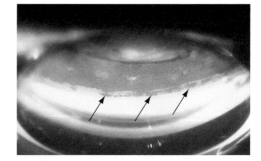

Figure 4-19 Typical angle appearance of an angle recession. Torn iris processes *(arrows)*, a whitened and increasingly visible scleral spur, and a localized depression in the trabecular meshwork are seen. *(Courtesy of Steven T. Simmons, MD.)*

develop elevated IOP, suggesting that many eyes with angle-recession glaucoma may have been predisposed to OAG.

Angle-recession glaucoma should be considered in a patient presenting with unilateral IOP elevation. The patient's history may reveal the contributing incident; however, often this has been forgotten. Examination may show findings consistent with previous trauma, such as corneal scars, iris injury, changes in the angle as mentioned previously, focal anterior subcapsular cataracts, and phacodonesis. Comparing gonioscopic findings in the affected eye with those in the fellow eye may help the clinician identify areas of recession.

A greater extent of angle recession is associated with a greater risk of glaucoma. However, even with substantial angle recession, this risk is not high. Regardless, all eyes with angle recession must be observed because it is not possible to predict which eyes will develop glaucoma. Although the risk of developing glaucoma decreases appreciably after several years, it is still present even 25 years or more following injury. These eyes should continue to be examined annually.

The treatment of angle-recession glaucoma is often initiated with aqueous suppressants, prostaglandin analogues, and α_2-adrenergic agonists. Miotics may be useful, but paradoxical responses with increased IOP may occur. Laser trabeculoplasty has a limited role and a reduced chance of success. Incisional glaucoma surgery may be required in order to control the IOP in patients not responding to medical therapy.

Surgical trauma

Surgical procedures such as cataract extraction, filtering surgery, and corneal transplantation may be followed by an increase in IOP. Similarly, laser surgery—including trabeculoplasty, iridotomy, and posterior capsulotomy—may be complicated by posttreatment IOP elevation. Although the IOP may rise as high as 50 mm Hg or more, these elevations are usually transient, lasting from a few hours to a few days. The exact mechanism is not always known. However, pigment release; presence of inflammatory cells, RBCs, and debris; mechanical deformation of the trabecular meshwork; and angle closure may all be implicated.

In addition, agents used as adjuncts to intraocular surgery may cause secondary IOP elevations. For example, the injection of viscoelastic substances such as sodium hyaluronate into the anterior chamber may result in a transient and possibly severe postoperative increase in IOP. Dispersive viscoelastics, especially in higher-molecular-weight forms, may be more likely to cause IOP increases than retentive viscoelastic agents (chondroitin sulfate).

Such postoperative pressure elevation can cause considerable damage to the optic nerve of a susceptible individual, even in a short time. Eyes with preexisting glaucoma are at particular risk of further damage. Elevated IOP may increase the risk of retinal and optic nerve ischemia. It is therefore important to measure IOP soon after surgery or laser treatment. If a substantial rise in IOP does occur, therapy may be required. Usually, use of β-adrenergic antagonists, α_2-adrenergic agonists, or carbonic anhydrase inhibitors is adequate. However, hyperosmotic agents, and even paracentesis, are sometimes necessary. Persistent elevation of IOP may require filtering surgery.

The implantation of an intraocular lens (IOL) can lead to a variety of secondary glaucomas:

- uveitis-glaucoma-hyphema syndrome
- secondary pigmentary glaucoma
- pseudophakic pupillary block (see Chapter 5)

Uveitis-glaucoma-hyphema (UGH) syndrome is a form of secondary inflammatory glaucoma caused by chronic irritation that is usually the result of a malpositioned or rotating anterior chamber IOL. Characterized by chronic inflammation, cystoid macular edema, secondary iris neovascularization, and recurrent hyphemas, this condition often results in an intractable glaucoma following the chafing of the iris by the IOL or erosion of the lens haptics through the iris or ciliary body. UGH syndrome may also occur following implantation of a posterior chamber or suture-fixated IOL. Gonioscopy and ultrasound biomicroscopy may be helpful in revealing the IOL's exact relation to the iris and ciliary body. Persistent or recurrent cases often require lens repositioning or lens exchange, which can be technically challenging because many of these eyes may have synechiae and/or an open posterior capsule. This syndrome may be mimicked in patients with neovascularization of the internal lip of a corneoscleral wound. These patients may have recurrent spontaneous hyphemas, which can lead to elevated IOP. Argon laser ablation of the vessels may successfully resolve these cases.

Jarstad JS, Hardwig PW. Intraocular hemorrhage from wound neovascularization years after anterior segment surgery (Swan syndrome). *Can J Ophthalmol.* 1987;22(5):271–275.

Glaucoma and penetrating keratoplasty

Secondary glaucoma is a common complication of penetrating keratoplasty, and it occurs with increased frequency in the aphakic/pseudophakic patient and with a second graft. Wound distortion of the trabecular meshwork and a progressive angle closure are the most common causes of long-standing glaucoma, and attempts to minimize these secondary glaucomas with different-sized donor grafts, peripheral iridectomies, and surgical repair of the iris sphincter have been only partially successful. Alternative procedures, such as lamellar stromal or endothelial grafts, may be associated with a lower percentage of patients having elevated IOP. BCSC Section 8, *External Disease and Cornea,* discusses penetrating keratoplasty in detail.

Schwartz Syndrome (Schwartz-Matsuo Syndrome)

Rhegmatogenous retinal detachments typically lower IOP, presumably as a result of increased outflow by active pumping of fluid through the exposed retinal pigment epithelium. Schwartz first described elevated IOP in association with a rhegmatogenous retinal detachment, and Matsuo later demonstrated photoreceptor outer segments in the aqueous humor in a group of similar patients. The postulated mechanism of IOP elevation is a chronic rhegmatogenous retinal detachment that leads to the liberation of photoreceptor outer segments, which, migrating through the retinal tear, reach the anterior chamber and impede aqueous outflow through the trabecular meshwork. The photoreceptor segments may be mistaken for an anterior chamber inflammatory reaction or pigment. The IOP tends to normalize after successful retinal reattachment.

Drugs and Glaucoma

Corticosteroid-induced glaucoma is an OAG caused by prolonged use of topical, periocular, intravitreal, inhaled, or systemic corticosteroids. It mimics POAG in its presentation and clinical course. Approximately one-third of all patients demonstrate some responsiveness to corticosteroids, but only a small percentage will have a clinically significant elevation in IOP. The type and potency of the agent, the means and frequency of its administration, and the susceptibility of the patient all affect not only the length of time before the IOP rises but also the extent of this rise. A high percentage of patients with POAG demonstrate this response to topical corticosteroids. Systemic administration of corticosteroids may also raise IOP in some individuals, though less frequently than does topical administration. The elevated IOP is a result of an increased resistance to aqueous outflow in the trabecular meshwork. See also BCSC Section 9, *Intraocular Inflammation and Uveitis,* for a discussion of corticosteroids.

Corticosteroid-induced glaucoma may develop at any time during long-term corticosteroid administration. IOP thus needs to be monitored regularly in patients receiving corticosteroid treatment. In general, the potency of the anti-inflammatory glucocorticoid activity of a particular drug parallels its ocular hypertensive potency. For example, some corticosteroid preparations, such as fluorometholone, rimexolone, medrysone, or loteprednol, are less likely to raise IOP than are prednisolone, dexamethasone, or difluprednate. However, even weaker corticosteroids or lower concentrations of stronger drugs can raise IOP in susceptible individuals.

A corticosteroid-induced rise in pressure may cause glaucomatous optic nerve damage in some patients. This condition can mimic POAG in patients of any age.

The cause of the elevation in IOP is not always related to the use of a corticosteroid and may instead be related to underlying ocular disease such as anterior uveitis. After the corticosteroid is discontinued, the IOP usually decreases with a time course similar to or slightly longer than that of the onset of elevation. However, unmasked POAG or secondary open-angle inflammatory glaucoma may remain.

Patients with excessive levels of endogenous corticosteroids (eg, Cushing syndrome) can also develop increased IOP. When the corticosteroid-producing tumor or hyperplastic tissue is excised, IOP generally returns to normal.

After treatment with periocular injection of corticosteroid, patients may develop increased IOP. Medical therapy may be used to lower the IOP. Although many patients respond to medical therapy, some may require excision of the depot of corticosteroid or filtering surgery.

Intravitreal corticosteroid injection may be associated with transient elevation of IOP in more than 50% of patients. Up to 25% of these patients may require topical medications to control IOP, and 1%–2% may require incisional glaucoma surgery. In contrast, intravitreal implants that release corticosteroid are frequently associated with elevated IOP, often requiring patients to undergo incisional glaucoma surgery as therapy. In patients with corticosteroid-induced IOP elevation unresponsive to medical therapy, surgical treatment has a high success rate. Some studies suggest that laser trabeculoplasty may be effective in lowering IOP in such eyes as well.

Cycloplegic drugs can increase IOP in individuals with open angles. Routine dilation for ophthalmoscopy may increase IOP; those at greater risk include patients with POAG, exfoliation syndrome, or pigment dispersion syndrome, as well as those on miotic therapy.

Epstein DL, Allingham RR, Schuman JS, eds. *Chandler and Grant's Glaucoma.* 4th ed. Baltimore: Williams & Wilkins; 1997.

Shields MB. *Shields' Textbook of Glaucoma.* 5th ed. Philadelphia: Lippincott Williams & Wilkins; 2005.

CLINICAL TRIAL 4-1

Collaborative Initial Glaucoma Treatment Study Essentials

Purpose: To determine whether patients with newly diagnosed open-angle glaucoma (OAG) are better treated by initial treatment with medications or by immediate filtering surgery.

Participants: 607 patients with OAG (primary, pigmentary, or pseudoexfoliative) recruited between 1993 and 1997.

Study design: Multicenter randomized controlled clinical trial comparing initial medical with initial surgical therapy for OAG.

Results: Although IOP was lower in the surgery group, initial medical and initial surgical therapy resulted in similar visual field outcomes after up to 9 years of follow-up. Early visual acuity loss was greater in the surgery group, but the differences between groups converged over time. At the 8-year follow-up examination, substantial worsening ($\geq$3 dB) of mean deviation from baseline was found in 21.3% and 25.5% of the initial surgery and initial medicine groups, respectively. Patients with worse baseline visual fields were less likely to progress if treated with trabeculectomy first. Patients with diabetes were more likely to progress if treated with surgery first.

The quality of life (QOL) impact reported by the 2 treatment groups was very similar. The most persistent QOL finding was the increased impact of local eye symptoms reported by the surgery group compared with the medical group.

The overall rate of progression of OAG in CIGTS was lower than in many clinical trials, potentially the result of more aggressive IOP goals and the stage of the disease. Individualized target IOPs were determined according to a formula that accounted for baseline IOP and visual field loss. Over the course of follow-up, IOP in the medical therapy group averaged 17–18 mm Hg (IOP reduction of approximately 38%), whereas IOP in the surgery group averaged 14–15 mm Hg (IOP reduction of approximately 46%). The rate of cataract removal was greater in the surgically treated group.

CLINICAL TRIAL 4-2

Ocular Hypertension Treatment Study Essentials

Purpose: To evaluate the safety and efficacy of topical ocular hypotensive medications in preventing or delaying the onset of visual field loss and/ or optic nerve damage in subjects with ocular hypertension.

Participants: 1637 patients with ocular hypertension recruited between 1994 and 1996.

Study design: Multicenter randomized controlled clinical trial comparing observation with medical therapy for ocular hypertension.

Results 2002: Topical ocular hypotensive medication was effective in delaying or preventing the onset of POAG: a 22.5% decrease in IOP in the treatment group (vs 4.0% in controls) was associated with a reduction of the development of POAG from 9.5% in controls to 4.4% in treated patients at 60 months' follow-up. Topical medications were generally well tolerated.

Increased risk of the onset of POAG was associated with increased age (10 years: 22% increase in relative risk), vertical and horizontal cup–disc ratio (0.1 increase: 32% and 27% increases in relative risk, respectively), pattern standard deviation (0.2 dB increase: 22% increase in relative risk), and IOP at baseline (1 mm Hg increase: 10% increase in relative risk). Central corneal thickness (CCT) was found to be a powerful predictor for the development of POAG (the relative risk of POAG increased 81% for every 40 μm thinner).

The corneas of OHTS subjects were thicker than those of the general population. Black subjects had lower corneal thickness than white subjects had in the study. The effect of CCT may influence the accuracy of applanation tonometry in the diagnosis, screening, and management of patients with glaucoma and ocular hypertension.

Results 2007: The same predictors for the development of POAG were identified independently in both the OHTS observation group and the European Glaucoma Prevention Study (EGPS) placebo group, including baseline age, IOP, CCT, cup–disc ratio, and Humphrey visual field pattern standard deviation. The OHTS prediction model was validated in the EGPS placebo group.

Results 2010: Subjects in the original observation group received medical treatment for a median of 5.5 years after a median period of observation without treatment of 7.5 years. Subjects in the original treatment group continued to receive medical therapy for a median of 13 years. The proportion of subjects who developed POAG was 0.22 in the original observation group and 0.16 in the original medication group. The primary purpose of the follow-up study was to determine whether delaying treatment resulted in a persistently increased risk of conversion to glaucoma,

(Continued on next page)

(continued)
even after the initiation of therapy. Although the two groups diverged with respect to the development of glaucoma during the original study period (when the observation group did not receive treatment), there was no further divergence in the Kaplan-Meier curves after both groups received IOP-lowering treatment.

CLINICAL TRIAL 4-3

Early Manifest Glaucoma Trial Essentials

Purpose: To compare immediate lowering of IOP with observation in the progression of newly detected open-angle glaucoma (OAG).

Participants: Newly diagnosed patients who were 50 to 80 years of age and had early glaucomatous visual field defects were identified mainly from a population-based screening of more than 44,000 residents of Malmö and Helsingborg, Sweden. Exclusion criteria were advanced visual field loss; mean IOP greater than 30 mm Hg or any IOP greater than 35 mm Hg; visual acuity less than 0.5 (20/40). Two hundred fifty-five patients were randomized between 1993 and 1997.

Study design: Multicenter randomized controlled clinical trial comparing observation with betaxolol and argon laser trabeculoplasty for OAG.

Results: At 6 years, 62% of untreated patients showed progression, whereas 45% of treated patients progressed. Treatment reduced IOP by 25%. In a univariate analysis, risk factors for progression included no treatment, age, higher IOP, exfoliation, more-severe visual field defect, and bilateral glaucoma. In multivariate analyses, the progression risk was halved by treatment (HR = 0.50; 95% CI, 0.35–0.71). The progression risk decreased by approximately 10% with each millimeter of mercury of IOP reduction from baseline to the first follow-up visit. The percentage of patient follow-up visits with disc hemorrhages was also related to progression (HR = 1.02 per percent higher; 95% CI, 1.01–1.03).

Baseline risk factors for progression included higher IOP, exfoliation, older age, lower systolic perfusion pressure (systolic BP – IOP), and lower CCT among patients with higher, but not lower, baseline IOPs. During the course of follow-up, higher mean IOP and the occurrence of disc hemorrhages were risk factors for progression; however, IOP fluctuation was not.

In the control group, the rate of visual field progression was fastest in the subgroup of patients with exfoliation and slowest in those with normal IOPs at baseline.

CLINICAL TRIAL 4-4

Advanced Glaucoma Intervention Study (AGIS) Essentials

Purpose: To compare the clinical outcomes of 2 treatment sequences: argon laser trabeculoplasty–trabeculectomy–trabeculectomy (ATT) and trabeculectomy–argon laser trabeculoplasty–trabeculectomy (TAT).

Participants: 789 eyes of 591 patients with medically uncontrolled OAG recruited from 1988 to 1992.

Study design: Multicenter randomized controlled clinical trial comparing 2 treatment sequences (ATT and TAT) for patients with OAG uncontrolled by medical therapy.

Results

AGIS 4 and AGIS 13: Black patients had less combined visual acuity and visual field loss if treated with the ATT sequence. White patients had less combined visual acuity and visual field loss at 7 years if treated with the TAT sequence. In the first years of follow-up in the white patients, the TAT group had greater visual acuity loss than the ATT group, but by 7 years the groups' acuities were equivalent.

AGIS 5: Encapsulated blebs were slightly more common in patients with prior argon laser trabeculoplasty (ALT), but this difference was not statistically significant. The 4-week postoperative mean IOP was higher in eyes with encapsulated blebs than in those without; with resumption of medical therapy, eyes with and without encapsulated blebs had similar IOP after 1 year.

AGIS 6: Visual function scores improved after cataract surgery. Adjustment for cataract did not alter the findings of previous AGIS studies.

AGIS 7: Lower IOP was associated with less visual field loss. Eyes with average IOP of 14 mm Hg or less during the first 18 months after the first surgical intervention, or eyes with IOP of 18 mm Hg or less at all visits throughout the study had significantly less visual field loss.

AGIS 8: Approximately half of the study patients developed cataract in the first 5 years of follow-up. Trabeculectomy increases the relative risk of cataract formation by 78%.

AGIS 9: Trabeculectomy retards the progression of glaucoma more effectively in white patients than in black patients. ALT was slightly more effective in blacks than in whites.

AGIS 10: Assessment of optic nerve findings showed good intraobserver but poor interobserver agreement.

(Continued on next page)

(continued)

AGIS 11: ALT failure is associated with younger age and higher IOP. Trabeculectomy failure was associated with younger age, higher IOP, diabetes, and postoperative complications such as particularly elevated IOP and marked inflammation.

AGIS 12: Risk factors for sustained decrease of visual field included better baseline visual fields, male sex, worse baseline visual acuity, and diabetes. Risk factors for sustained decrease of visual acuity included better baseline visual acuity, older age, and less formal education.

AGIS 14: In patients with worsening of the visual field, 1 confirmatory test within 6 months has a 72% probability of indicating a persistent defect. When the number of confirmatory tests is increased from 1 to 2, the percentage of eyes that show a persistent defect increases from 72% to 84%.

2009 AGIS Report: IOP fluctuation was an independent predictor of progression of OAG in eyes with lower baseline IOPs.

CHAPTER 5

Angle-Closure Glaucoma

Introduction

Of the nearly 67 million patients with glaucoma worldwide, it has been estimated that one-half are of Asian descent. The prevalence of angle-closure glaucoma (ACG), much of which is primary angle closure, has been shown to be higher than that of other types of glaucoma among Asian persons. Population studies have determined that the ratio of open-angle glaucoma (OAG) to ACG in Chinese individuals ranges from 1:1 to 2.6:1. Primary ACG (PACG) is more common than previously recognized and is a leading cause of bilateral blindness worldwide. For example, PACG is responsible for 91% of the bilateral blindness in China, affecting more than 1.5 million Chinese persons.

In 1920, Curran proposed the mechanism of pupillary block and the importance of an iridectomy in breaking this impeded aqueous flow. Curran's observations and theories on PACG were finally accepted in 1951 following papers by Haas, Scheie, and Chandler, confirming the principle of "relative pupillary block." Advances in gonioscopy prior to 1940, by Barkan, Trantas, Koeppe, Salzmann, and Troncoso, further helped define and distinguish the ACGs. The development of the Goldmann lens in 1938 allowed more universal use of gonioscopy, further advancing our knowledge and understanding of the anterior chamber angle.

In primary OAG, while the resistance to aqueous outflow is known to be increased, structures proximal to the trabecular meshwork do not add to the resistance to aqueous outflow and the pathologic resistance to outflow resides in the meshwork itself. Conversely, in ACG, the primary pathology is anatomical, proximal to the trabecular meshwork. Specifically, in such cases, the peripheral iris impedes the access of aqueous to the trabecular meshwork. The meshwork itself may be anatomically and functionally normal.

The ACGs are a diverse group of diseases. While the various forms of angle closure are unified by the presence of peripheral anterior synechiae (PAS) and/or iridotrabecular apposition, the mechanism of iris apposition or synechiae formation is varied. Moreover, the clinical presentation of angle closure varies from the abrupt and dramatic onset of acute ACG (20%–30% of cases) to the insidious and asymptomatic presentation of chronic ACG (70%–80% of cases).

In either presentation, acute or chronic, the physician must identify the anatomical changes within the angle and the underlying pathophysiology that has precipitated these changes in order to initiate the appropriate therapy. Early diagnosis and treatment of most forms of ACG can be invaluable, and sometimes curative. Accordingly, understanding the pathophysiology is essential if proper treatment is to be initiated. Also, screening patients at greatest risk for angle closure can be beneficial in reducing the number of patients who develop these diseases and in reducing the risk of blindness.

Traditionally, the ACGs are divided into 2 main categories: primary and secondary angle closure. Each category is subdivided by the symptomatology, etiology, and duration of each of the diseases.

In *primary* angle closure, there is no identifiable underlying pathology; there is only an anatomical predisposition to pupillary block. In *secondary* angle closure, an identifiable pathologic cause, such as an intumescent lens, iris neovascularization, chronic inflammation, corneal endothelial migration, or epithelial ingrowth, initiates the angle closure.

Lowe RF. A history of primary angle-closure glaucoma. *Surv Ophthalmol.* 1995;40(2): 163–170.

Yip JL, Foster PJ. Ethnic differences in primary angle-closure glaucoma. *Curr Opin Ophthalmol.* 2006;17(2):175–180.

Pathogenesis and Pathophysiology of Angle Closure

The hallmark of angle closure is the apposition or adhesion of the peripheral iris to the trabecular meshwork. The portion of the anterior chamber angle affected by such apposition is "closed," and drainage of aqueous humor through the angle is reduced as a result. Such closure may be transient and intermittent (appositional) or permanent (synechial). The intraocular pressure (IOP) becomes elevated as a result of the reduced aqueous outflow through the trabecular meshwork. Apposition of the iris to the trabecular meshwork is abnormal and requires further assessment.

Conceptually, the mechanism of angle closure falls into 2 categories (Table 5-1):

- mechanisms that push the iris forward from behind
- mechanisms that pull the iris forward into contact with the trabecular meshwork

In addition to these traditional descriptions of angle closure, more recent work has suggested that the dynamic changes in iris volume and water content normally occurring in the human eye are dysfunctional in patients with ACG and may play an important role in the pathogenesis of angle closure. Indeed, there is mounting evidence that dynamic features of the eye rather than its static anatomy contribute to ACG.

Pupillary Block

Pupillary block is the most frequent cause of angle closure and is the underlying cause of most cases of *primary* angle closure. The flow of aqueous from the posterior chamber through the pupil is impeded at the level of the lens–iris interface, and this obstruction creates a pressure gradient between the posterior and anterior chambers, causing the peripheral iris to bow forward against the trabecular meshwork (Fig 5-1). Pupillary block is maximal when the pupil is in the mid-dilated position. In most cases of PACG, pupillary block results from anatomical factors at the lens–iris interface. Though rare, absolute pupillary block occurs when there is no movement of aqueous through the pupil as a result of 360° of posterior synechiae (secluded pupil). These posterior synechiae can form between

Table 5-1 Underlying Mechanisms of Angle Closure

Iris pushed forward from behind, into the angle:
- pupillary block
- aqueous misdirection (malignant glaucoma)
- ciliary body swelling, inflammation, or cysts
- anteriorly located ciliary processes (plateau iris configuration/syndrome)
- choroidal swelling, serous or hemorrhagic choroidal detachments or effusions
- posterior segment tumors or space-occupying lesions (silicone oil, gas bubble)
- contracting retrolental tissue (persistent fetal vasculature, retinopathy of prematurity)
- anteriorly displaced lens
- encircling retinal bands/buckles

Iris pulled forward into contact with the trabecular meshwork:
- contraction of inflammatory membrane or fibrovascular tissue
- migration of corneal endothelium (iridocorneal endothelial [ICE] syndrome)
- fibrous ingrowth
- epithelial ingrowth
- iris incarceration in traumatic wound or surgical incision

the iris and the crystalline lens, an intraocular lens, capsular remnants, and/or the vitreous face. Pupillary block occurs when there is restricted movement of aqueous through the pupil because of iris contact with the lens, intraocular lens, capsular remnants, anterior hyaloid, or vitreous space–occupying substance (air, silicone oil). Pupillary block may be broken by an unobstructed peripheral iridectomy.

Angle Closure Without Pupillary Block

Angle closure may occur without pupillary block. Iridotrabecular apposition or synechiae can result from the iris and/or lens being pushed, rotated, or pulled forward for a variety of reasons, as outlined in Table 5-1. Each of these underlying mechanisms can usually be identified by a comprehensive examination, including gonioscopy. Many patients may present with multiple underlying causes for their angle closure.

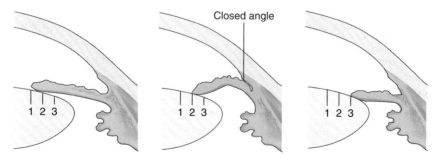

Figure 5-1 *1,* The pupil is constricted and the angle is open. *2,* The pupil is in the mid-dilated position. Pupillary block is maximal in this position and as a result the iris is bowed anteriorly and the angle narrows. *3,* The pupil is more completely dilated and the pupillary block is diminished, with a return to a flatter iris configuration. If full-blown angle closure occurs, the iris may stay in the mid-dilated position until the angle-closure attack is broken. *(Redrawn with permission from Quigley HA, Friedman DS, Congdon NG. Possible mechanisms of primary angle-closure and malignant glaucoma. J Glaucoma. 2003;12:171. © 2003 Lippincott Williams & Wilkins, Inc. Illustration by Cyndie C. H. Wooley.)*

Lens-Induced Angle-Closure Glaucoma

Intumescent or dislocated lenses (complete zonular dehiscence) may increase pupillary block and cause angle closure. Angle closure from an unusually large or intumescent lens is often referred to as *phacomorphic glaucoma*. With lens subluxation (partial zonular dehiscence), as in Marfan syndrome, exfoliation syndrome, or homocystinuria, pupillary block from the lens or vitreous may occur. Lens block describes an underlying mechanism of primary angle closure, in which the lens's increased anterior-posterior excursion is due to weakened or lax zonular fibers. This zonular laxity allows the lens to move forward, increasing the relative resistance to aqueous flow through the pupil, which aggravates the pupillary block, inciting angle closure. The prone position may aggravate the tendency of the lens to move forward.

Iris-Induced Angle Closure

Iris-induced angle closure occurs when the peripheral iris, either directly or indirectly, is the cause of the iridotrabecular apposition. This can occur directly with developmental anomalies such as anterior cleavage abnormalities, in which the iris insertion is more anterior into the scleral spur or meshwork; a thick peripheral iris, which on dilatation "rolls" into the trabecular meshwork; and/or anteriorly displaced ciliary processes, which may secondarily rotate the peripheral iris forward (plateau iris) into the meshwork. Another example of iris-induced angle closure is seen in aniridia, where the rudimentary iris leaflets rotate into the angle, resulting in secondary angle closure.

Primary Angle Closure

Primary angle closure is a complex disease entity that is a leading cause of glaucoma worldwide. Although the pathophysiology is complex and not completely understood, pupillary block is considered to be at least partially involved as the underlying cause in most cases of primary angle closure. Eyes with shorter axial lengths are at risk for PACG. Recent research suggests that regulation of iris volume may also play an important role in the pathogenesis of PACG. Whereas most eyes show a loss of iris volume with dilation of the pupil, eyes at risk for angle closure may have less ability to rid the iris stroma of water upon dilation. The retention of water within the stroma results in greater iris volume as the pupil dilates, crowding the angle and closing it in susceptible individuals. This *dynamic* feature of iris physiology may explain why only certain eyes with anatomically narrow angles develop overt angle closure.

Risk Factors for Developing Primary Angle Closure

Race

The prevalence of PACG in patients older than 40 years varies greatly depending on race: 0.1%–0.6% in whites, 0.1%–0.2% in blacks, 2.1%–5.0% in the Inuit, 0.4%–1.4% in East Asians, 0.3% in the Japanese, and 2.3% in a mixed ethnic group in South Africa. Some of these differences can be explained by the difference in the biometric parameters (anterior chamber depth, axial length) of the different white and Inuit populations, whereas the increased incidence in the Chinese and East Asian populations cannot be explained by biometric parameters alone. In addition, some races present more commonly with acute forms (whites), whereas Africans and Asians present more frequently with asymptomatic chronic disease. It has become increasingly clear that the burden of ACG is greater in Asian countries.

Bonomi L, Marchini G, Marraffa M, et al. Epidemiology of angle-closure glaucoma: prevalence, clinical types, and association with peripheral anterior chamber depth in the Egna-Neumarket Glaucoma Study. *Ophthalmology.* 2000;107(5):998–1003.

Dandona L, Dandona R, Mandal P, et al. Angle-closure glaucoma in an urban population in southern India: the Andhra Pradesh Eye Disease Study. *Ophthalmology.* 2000;107(9): 1710–1716.

Foster PJ, Oen FT, Machin D, et al. The prevalence of glaucoma in Chinese residents of Singapore: a cross-sectional population survey of the Tanjong Pagar district. *Arch Ophthalmol.* 2000;118(8):1105–1111.

Quigley HA. Angle-closure glaucoma—simpler answers to complex mechanisms: LXVI Edward Jackson Memorial Lecture. *Am J Ophthalmol.* 2009;148(5):657–669.

Quigley HA. The iris is a sponge: a cause of angle closure. *Ophthalmology.* 2010;117(1):1–2.

Quigley HA, Broman AT. The number of people with glaucoma worldwide in 2010 and 2020. *Br J Ophthalmol.* 2006;90(3):262–267.

Ocular biometrics

Patients who develop primary angle closure have small, "crowded" anterior segments and short axial lengths (ALs). The most important factors predisposing an eye to angle closure are a shallow anterior chamber, a thick lens, increased anterior curvature of the lens, a short AL, and a small corneal diameter and radius of curvature. An anterior chamber depth (ACD) of less than 2.5 mm predisposes patients to primary angle closure, whereas most patients with primary angle closure have an ACD of less than 2.1 mm. With improvements in biometry techniques, a clear association between ACD and PAS has been demonstrated. While primary PAS seem to be uncommon with an ACD of greater than 2.4 mm, there is a strong correlation of increasing PAS formation with an ACD shallower than 2.4 mm. However, despite these generalizations, angle closure still occurs with deep anterior chambers in some cases.

The prevalence of ACG increases with each decade after 40 years of age. This increased prevalence has been explained by the increasing thickness and forward movement of the lens with age, and the resultant increase in iridolenticular contact. PACG is rare in persons younger than 40 years, and the etiology of angle closure in young individuals is most often related to structural or developmental anomalies rather than pupillary block.

Aung T, Nolan WP, Machin D, et al. Anterior chamber depth and the risk of primary angle closure in 2 East Asian populations. *Arch Ophthalmol.* 2005;123(4):527–532.

Devereux JG, Foster PJ, Baasanhu J, et al. Anterior chamber depth measurement as a screening tool for primary angle-closure glaucoma in an East Asian population. *Arch Ophthalmol.* 2000;118(2):257–263.

Ritch R, Chang BM, Liebmann JM. Angle closure in younger patients. *Ophthalmology.* 2003;110(10):1880–1889.

Gender

Primary angle closure has been reported 2 to 4 times more commonly in women than in men, irrespective of race. In studies assessing ocular biometry, women tend to have smaller anterior segments and ALs than do men. This difference does not appear to be large enough to explain this gender predilection.

Family history

The incidence of primary angle closure is increased in first-degree relatives of affected individuals. In whites, the prevalence of primary angle closure in first-degree relatives has been reported to be between 1% and 12%, whereas results from a survey in a Chinese population showed that the risk was 6 times greater in patients with any family history. In the Inuit, the relative risk in patients with a family history is increased 3.5 times compared with the general Inuit population. Although such familial associations support a genetic influence in ACG, the specific gene responsible for this type of glaucoma has not been identified.

Refraction

Primary angle closure occurs more commonly in patients with hyperopia, irrespective of race. Increasing rates of myopia, especially in Asia, have influenced the prevalence of this disease. Angle closure occurring in a patient with significant myopia should alert the clinician to search for secondary mechanisms such as microspherophakia, plateau iris configuration, or phacomorphic closure related to nuclear sclerotic cataract.

Acute Primary Angle Closure

Acute primary angle closure (PAC) occurs when IOP rises rapidly as a result of relatively sudden blockage of the trabecular meshwork by the iris. It is typically manifested by ocular pain, headache, blurred vision, and rainbow-colored halos around lights. Acute systemic distress may result in nausea and vomiting. The rise in IOP to relatively high levels causes corneal epithelial edema, which is responsible for the visual symptoms. Signs of acute angle closure include

- high IOP
- mid-dilated, sluggish, and irregularly shaped pupil
- corneal epithelial edema
- congested episcleral and conjunctival blood vessels
- shallow anterior chamber
- mild amount of aqueous flare and cells

Definitive diagnosis depends on the gonioscopic verification of angle closure. Gonioscopy should be possible in almost all cases of acute angle closure, although medical treatment of elevated IOP and clearing of corneal edema with topical glycerin may be necessary to enable visualization of the chamber angle. Dynamic gonioscopy may help the physician determine whether the iris–trabecular meshwork blockage is reversible (appositional closure) or irreversible (synechial closure), and it may also be therapeutic in breaking the attack of acute angle closure. Gonioscopy of the fellow eye in a patient with PAC usually reveals a narrow, occludable angle. The presence of a deep angle in the fellow eye should alert the clinician to search for alternative causes of elevated IOP. When performing gonioscopy, the clinician should observe the effect that the examination light has on the angle recess. For example, the pupillary constriction stimulated by the slit-lamp beam itself may open the angle and the narrow recess may go unrecognized (Fig 5-2).

During an acute attack, the IOP may be high enough to cause glaucomatous optic nerve damage, ischemic nerve damage, and/or retinal vascular occlusion. PAS can form rapidly, and IOP-induced ischemia may produce sector atrophy of the iris. Such atrophy releases pigment and causes pigmentary dusting of the iris surface and corneal endothelium. Iris ischemia, specifically of the iris sphincter muscle, may cause the pupil to become permanently fixed and dilated. *Glaukomflecken,* characteristic small anterior subcapsular lens opacities, may also develop as a result of ischemia. These findings are helpful in the detection of previous episodes of acute ACG.

The definitive treatment for acute angle closure is a laser iridotomy or, much less commonly, a surgical iridectomy; these procedures are discussed in detail in Chapter 8. Lensectomy is also a viable treatment option, although laser iridotomy may be more easily accomplished in the acute setting, especially if the eye is inflamed. Mild attacks may be broken by cholinergic agents (pilocarpine 1%–2%), which induce miosis that pulls the peripheral iris away from the trabecular meshwork. Stronger miotics should be avoided, as they may increase the vascular congestion of the iris or rotate the lens–iris interface more anteriorly, increasing the pupillary block. Moreover, when the IOP is markedly elevated (eg, above 40–50 mm Hg), the pupillary sphincter may be ischemic and unresponsive to

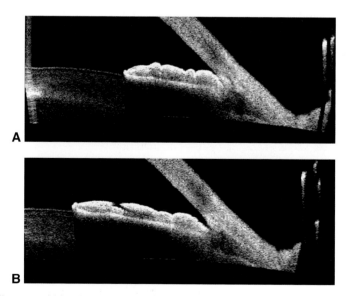

A

B

Figure 5-2 Ultrasound biomicroscopy (UBM) of a narrow angle. **A,** Angle closure is evident when the angle is imaged with lights off. **B,** The same angle is much more open when imaged with lights on. *(Courtesy of Yaniv Barkana, MD.)*

miotic agents alone. In this case, the patient should be treated with other agents, such as β-adrenergic antagonists; $α_2$-adrenergic agonists; prostaglandin analogues; and oral, topical, or intravenous carbonic anhydrase inhibitors. When necessary, a hyperosmotic agent may be administered orally or intravenously. Such treatment is used to reduce IOP to the point where the miotic agent will constrict the pupil and open the angle. Globe compression and dynamic gonioscopy have also been described to treat acute ACG. Nonselective adrenergic agonists or medications with significant $α_1$-adrenergic activity (apraclonidine) should be avoided to prevent further pupillary dilation and iris ischemia.

In most cases of PACG, the fellow eye shares the anatomical predisposition for increased pupillary block and is at high risk of developing acute angle closure. This is especially true if the inciting mechanism included a systemic sympathomimetic agent such as a nasal decongestant or an anticholinergic agent. In addition, the pain and emotional upset resulting from the involvement of the first eye may increase sympathetic flow to the fellow eye and produce pupillary dilation. It is recommended that a peripheral iridotomy be performed in the other eye if a similar angle configuration is present. If the contralateral eye has a significantly different angle configuration, secondary ACGs must be strongly considered in the differential diagnosis. In general, PAC is a bilateral disease, and its occurrence in a patient whose fellow eye has a deep chamber angle raises the possibility of a secondary cause, such as a posterior segment mass, zonular insufficiency, or the iridocorneal endothelial (ICE) syndrome.

Laser iridotomy is the treatment of choice for PAC due to pupillary block. Surgical iridectomy or lensectomy with or without goniosynechialysis is indicated when laser iridotomy cannot be accomplished. Once an iridotomy or iridectomy has been performed, the pupillary block is relieved and the pressure gradient between the posterior and anterior chambers is normalized, which in most cases allows the iris to fall away from the trabecular meshwork. As a result, the anterior chamber deepens and the angle opens. If a laser iridotomy cannot be performed, the acute attack may be broken in 1 of 2 ways: the peripheral iris may be flattened with a laser iridoplasty or the pupillary block may be relieved with a laser pupilloplasty. In such cases, a peripheral iridectomy should be accomplished once the attack is broken and the cornea is of adequate clarity. Following resolution of the acute attack, it is important to reevaluate the angle by gonioscopy to assess the degree of residual synechial angle closure and to confirm the reopening of at least part of the angle.

Improved IOP does not necessarily mean that the angle has opened. Because of ciliary body ischemia and reduced aqueous production, the IOP may remain low for weeks following acute angle closure. Thus, IOP may be a poor indicator of angle function or anatomy. A second gonioscopy or serial gonioscopy is therefore essential for follow-up of the patient to be certain that the angle has adequately opened.

Lam DS, Leung DY, Tham CC, et al. Randomized trial of early phacoemulsification versus peripheral iridotomy to prevent intraocular pressure rise after acute primary angle closure. *Ophthalmology.* 2008;115(7):1134–1140.

Seah SK, Foster PJ, Chew PT, et al. Incidence of acute primary angle-closure glaucoma in Singapore: an island-wide survey. *Arch Ophthalmol.* 1997;115(11):1436–1440.

Subacute or Intermittent Angle Closure

Subacute or intermittent angle closure is a condition characterized by episodes of blurred vision, halos, and mild pain caused by elevated IOP. These symptoms resolve spontaneously, especially during sleep-induced miosis, and IOP is usually normal between the episodes, which occur periodically over days, weeks, or months. These episodes are often confused with headaches or migraines. The correct diagnosis can be made only with a high index of suspicion and gonioscopy. The typical history and the gonioscopic appearance of a narrow chamber angle with or without PAS help establish the diagnosis. Such episodes may occur in the absence of symptoms as well, identified by measurement of increased IOP or by identification of PAS in the setting of a narrow angle.

Laser iridotomy is the treatment of choice in subacute angle closure unless significant lens opacity is present, in which case lensectomy is typically curative. This condition can progress to chronic angle closure or to an acute attack that does not resolve spontaneously. With improvements in phacoemulsification, especially in terms of anterior chamber stabilization and fluidic control, primary lensectomy is increasingly recognized as an effective treatment for this disorder. In cases of significant synechial closure, goniosynechialysis may be performed in conjunction with lensectomy to help open the angle and improve trabecular outflow. Such treatment is more definitive than iridotomy but also introduces the additional risks inherent in intraocular surgery.

Chronic Angle Closure

Chronic angle closure may develop after acute angle closure in which synechial closure persists. It may also develop when the chamber angle closes gradually and IOP rises slowly as angle function progressively becomes compromised. The latter form of chronic angle closure, in which there is gradual asymptomatic angle closure, is the most common. Because of the asymptomatic nature of this condition, vision loss may be the presenting complaint. Accordingly, this disease tends to be diagnosed in its later stages and is a major cause of blindness in Asia. Chronic PAC is often referred to as *creeping angle closure* because of the slow formation of PAS, which advance circumferentially. The cause of the phenomenon is uncertain, but evidence suggests that multiple mechanisms are involved, including pupillary block, abnormalities in iris thickness and position, and plateau iris configuration.

In chronic ACG, permanent PAS are present, as determined by dynamic gonioscopy. The clinical course resembles that of OAG in its lack of symptoms, modest elevation of IOP, progressive glaucomatous optic nerve damage, and characteristic visual field loss. The diagnosis of chronic ACG is frequently overlooked, and it is commonly confused with chronic OAG. Gonioscopic examination of all glaucoma patients is important for accurate diagnosis.

Even if miotics and other agents lower the IOP, an iridectomy is necessary to relieve the pupillary block component and reduce the potential for further permanent synechial angle closure. Without an iridectomy, the closure of the angle usually progresses and makes the glaucoma more difficult to control. Even with a patent peripheral iridectomy, progressive angle closure can occur, and repeated periodic gonioscopy is imperative. An iridectomy with or without long-term use of ocular hypotensive medication will control the disease in most patients with chronic ACG. Others may require iridoplasty or lensectomy with or without goniosynechialysis. If these measures fail to lower the IOP, subsequent filtering surgery may be necessary.

Alsagoff Z, Aung T, Ang LP, Chew PT. Long-term clinical course of primary angle-closure glaucoma in an Asian population. *Ophthalmology.* 2000;107(12):2300–2304.

Ritch R, Lowe RF. Angle closure glaucoma: clinical types. In: Ritch R, Shields MB, Krupin T, eds. *The Glaucomas.* 2nd ed. St Louis: Mosby; 1996:821–840.

Ritch R, Lowe RF. Angle closure glaucoma: mechanisms and epidemiology. In: Ritch R, Shields MB, Krupin T, eds. *The Glaucomas.* 2nd ed. St Louis: Mosby; 1996:801–819.

The Occludable, or Narrow, Anterior Chamber Angle

The nomenclature pertaining to the narrow anterior chamber angle may be somewhat misleading. For example, a narrow angle is not synonymous with a diagnosis of glaucoma, but rather an anatomical description. Only a small percentage of patients with shallow anterior chambers develop ACG. Unfortunately, even when performed by experienced clinicians, gonioscopy has relatively poor predictive value for determining which susceptible patients will develop overt angle closure. Many clinicians have attempted to predict which asymptomatic patients with normal IOP will develop angle closure by performing a variety of provocative tests. These tests are designed to precipitate a limited form of angle closure, which can then be detected by gonioscopy and IOP measurement. The methods commonly used include pharmacologic pupillary dilation and the darkroom prone-position test. An IOP increase of 8 mm Hg or more, in conjunction with gonioscopic evidence of appositional angle closure in at least a portion of the angle, is considered a positive result. An asymmetric pressure rise between the 2 eyes with a corresponding degree of angle closure is also considered a positive result. Provocative testing has not been validated in a prospective study; thus, it is rarely used.

The decision to treat an asymptomatic patient with narrow angles rests on the clinical judgment of the ophthalmologist and the accurate assessment of the anterior chamber angle. Any patient with narrow angles, regardless of the results of provocative testing, should be advised of the symptoms of angle closure, of the need for immediate ophthalmic attention if symptoms occur, and of the value of long-term periodic follow-up. An iridotomy is not necessary in all patients with a suspicious or borderline narrow angle. If a patient with a narrow angle has documented appositional or near-appositional closure, PAS, increased segmental trabecular meshwork pigmentation, a history of previous angle closure, a positive provocative test result, or a significant risk of angle closure (ACD of less than 2.0 mm, strong family history), then the ophthalmologist should consider performing an iridotomy. The status of the lens and the benefit of cataract surgery should also be considered in the decision.

Various factors that cause pupillary dilation may induce angle closure. These factors include a variety of drugs, as well as pain, emotional upset, or fright. In predisposed eyes with shallow anterior chambers, either mydriatic or miotic agents can precipitate acute angle closure. Mydriatic agents include not only dilating drops but also systemic medications with sympathomimetic or anticholinergic activity that may cause pupillary dilation.

The effect of miotics is to pull the peripheral iris away from the chamber angle. However, strong miotics may also cause the zonular fibers of the lens to relax, allowing the lens–iris interface to move forward. Furthermore, their use results in an increase in the amount of iris–lens contact, thus potentially increasing pupillary block. For these reasons, miotics, especially the cholinesterase inhibitors, may induce or aggravate angle closure. Gonioscopy should be repeated soon after miotic drugs are administered to patients with narrow angles.

Because of their potential for precipitating angle closure in susceptible individuals, a number of systemic medications that possess adrenergic (sympathomimetic) or anticholinergic (parasympatholytic) activity carry warnings against use by patients with glaucoma; these include allergy and cold medications, antidepressants, and some urological drugs. Although systemic administration generally does not raise intraocular drug levels to the same degree as does topical administration, even slight mydriasis in a patient with a critically narrow chamber angle can induce angle closure. When such drugs are administered to patients with potentially occludable angles, the ophthalmologist should consider informing the patients of this risk and performing iridotomy.

Dapiprazole and thymoxamine are α-receptor blockers that reverse pharmacologic dilation more rapidly than does placebo. Although the use of dapiprazole following pupillary dilation does not eliminate the possibility of precipitating angle closure, it does reduce the overall time that the pupil is dilated, as well as the critical period when the pupil is mid-dilated.

Foster PJ, Devereux JG, Alsbirk PH, et al. Detection of gonioscopically occludable angles and primary angle-closure glaucoma by estimation of limbal chamber depth in Asians: modified grading scheme. *Br J Ophthalmol.* 2000;84(2):186–192.

Plateau Iris

Plateau iris represents an atypical configuration of the anterior chamber angle that may result in acute or chronic ACG. Angle closure in plateau iris is most often caused by anteriorly positioned ciliary processes that critically narrow the anterior chamber recess by pushing the peripheral iris forward. More recent evidence suggests that plateau iris configuration may result from a more anterior junction of the iris dilator muscle and the ciliary epithelium, which causes the iris root to be more articulated. A component of pupillary block is often present. The angle may be further compromised following dilation of the pupil as the peripheral iris bunches up and obstructs the trabecular meshwork. Plateau iris may be suspected if the central anterior chamber appears to be of normal depth and the iris plane appears to be rather flat for an eye with angle closure. This suspicion can be confirmed with gonioscopy or by the presence of the "double hump" sign on ultrasound biomicroscopy. The diagnosis of plateau iris can only be made by gonioscopy or another technique for imaging the angle. The condition will be missed if the examiner relies solely on the slit-lamp examination or the Van Herick method of angle examination.

The management of plateau iris includes either laser iridotomy to remove any component of pupillary block or lensectomy if cataract is present. Eyes with plateau iris remain predisposed to angle closure despite a patent iridotomy as a result of the peripheral iris

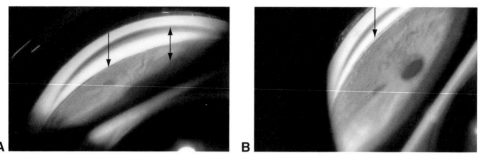

Figure 5-3 A, Plateau iris syndrome with a flat iris plane but shallow angle recess *(arrow).* Note that the midperipheral angle appears deeper *(double arrow)* than the narrow angles associated with pupillary block. **B,** Plateau iris syndrome, with a much deeper angle recess *(arrow)* following laser peripheral iridoplasty. *(Courtesy of M. Roy Wilson, MD.)*

anatomy. Thus, careful assessment of the angle following iridotomy or lensectomy is necessary to determine whether additional treatment to further deepen the angle is required. PAS have been reported to begin at the Schwalbe line and then to extend in a posterior direction over the trabecular meshwork, scleral spur, and angle recess. The reverse is seen in pupillary block–induced angle closure, in which PAS form in the posterior to anterior direction. These patients may be treated with long-term miotic therapy. However, argon laser peripheral iridoplasty may be more useful in individuals with this condition to flatten and thin the peripheral iris (Fig 5-3). Repeated gonioscopy at regular intervals is necessary because the threat of chronic angle closure may remain despite measures to deepen the angle recess.

Pavlin CJ, Foster FS. Plateau iris syndrome: changes in angle opening associated with dark, light, and pilocarpine administration. *Am J Ophthalmol.* 1999;128(3):288–291.

Secondary Angle Closure With Pupillary Block

Lens-Induced Angle Closure

Phacomorphic glaucoma
The mechanism of phacomorphic glaucoma is typically multifactorial. However, by definition, a significant component of the pathological angle narrowing is related to the acquired mass effect of the cataractous lens itself. As with primary angle closure, pupillary block often plays an important role in this condition. Phacomorphic narrowing of the angle generally occurs slowly with formation of the cataract. However, in some cases, the onset may be acute and rapid, precipitated by marked lens swelling (intumescence) as a result of cataract formation and the development of pupillary block in an eye that is otherwise not anatomically predisposed to closure (Figs 5-4, 5-5). Distinguishing between primary angle closure and phacomorphic angle closure is not always straightforward and may not be necessary since the treatment of both conditions is similar; but disparities between the 2 eyes in ACD, gonioscopy, and degree of cataract should suggest a phacomorphic process (Fig 5-6). (See also BCSC Section 11, *Lens and Cataract.*) A laser iridotomy

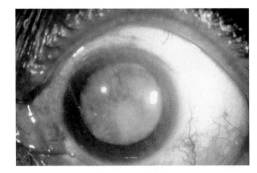

Figure 5-4 Phacomorphic glaucoma. Lens intumescence precipitates pupillary block and secondary angle closure in an eye not anatomically predisposed to angle closure. *(Courtesy of Steven T. Simmons, MD.)*

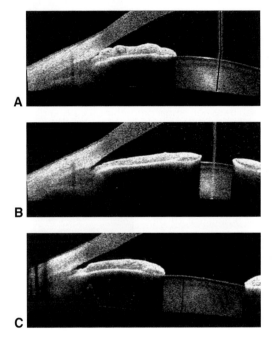

Figure 5-5 Phacomorphic glaucoma. **A,** In this example, the angle remains narrow despite a patent iridotomy. **B,** In bright light the angle is transiently made deeper by pupil constriction. **C,** In this case, a more long-term solution is accomplished by thinning the peripheral iris with argon laser iridoplasty. Lensectomy is also a viable treatment strategy. *(Courtesy of Yaniv Barkana, MD.)*

followed by cataract extraction in a quiet eye is the preferred treatment. In many cases, the iridotomy is unnecessary, as cataract surgery is the definitive treatment in eyes that have the potential for improved vision. Cholinergic agents have a minimal role in the treatment of this condition because they may further narrow the angle and worsen the vision in the presence of cataract. Further, the miotic pupil will make subsequent cataract surgery more difficult.

Ectopia lentis

Ectopia lentis is defined as displacement of the lens from its normal anatomical position (Fig 5-7). With forward displacement, pupillary block may occur, resulting in iris bombé, shallowing of the anterior chamber angle, and secondary angle closure. This may present

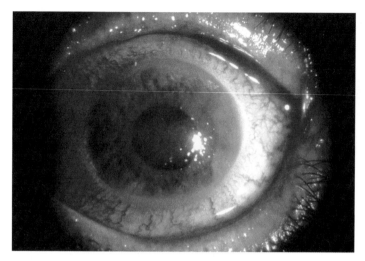

Figure 5-6 Phacomorphic glaucoma often presents clinically as acute angle-closure glaucoma. Disparities in the anterior chamber depths and degree of cataract between the 2 eyes can help the clinician distinguish between a phacomorphic process and primary angle-closure glaucoma. *(Courtesy of Steven T. Simmons, MD.)*

Figure 5-7 Ectopia lentis: dislocation of the lens into the anterior chamber through a dilated pupil. *(Courtesy of Ron Gross, MD.)*

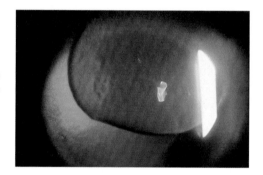

clinically as an acute event with pain, conjunctival hyperemia, and vision loss, or as a chronic ACG with PAS formation secondary to repeated attacks. Two laser iridotomies 180° apart is the treatment of choice to relieve the pupillary block and temporize until more definitive lensectomy, if indicated from a visual function standpoint. Lens extraction is usually indicated to restore vision and to reduce the risk of recurrence of pupillary block and development of chronic angle closure. See Table 5-2 for a list of conditions that can cause this entity.

Microspherophakia, a congenital disorder in which the lens has a spherical or globular shape, may cause ectopia lentis and subsequent pupillary block and ACG (Fig 5-8). Treatment with cycloplegia may tighten the zonule, flatten the lens, and pull it posteriorly, breaking the pupillary block. Miotics may make the condition worse by increasing the pupillary block and by rotating the ciliary body forward, loosening the zonule and allowing the lens to become more globular. Microspherophakia is often familial and may occur as an isolated condition or as part of either Weill-Marchesani or Marfan syndrome. Finally, the most common form of acquired zonular insufficiency and crystalline lens subluxation occurs in the exfoliation syndrome (Fig 5-9).

Table 5-2 Common Causes of Ectopia Lentis

Exfoliation syndrome
Trauma
Marfan syndrome
Homocystinuria
Microspherophakia
Weill-Marchesani syndrome

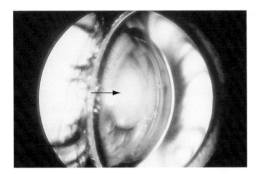

Figure 5-8 Ectopia lentis. In a case of microspherophakia, the lens *(arrow)* is trapped anteriorly by the pupil, resulting in iris bombé and a dramatic shallowing of the anterior chamber. *(Courtesy of G. L. Spaeth, MD.)*

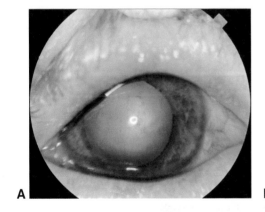

A

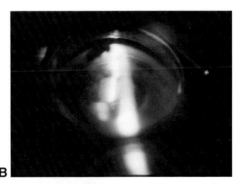

B

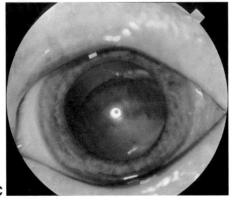

C

Figure 5-9 The exfoliation syndrome is a common cause of subluxation of the crystalline lens. **A,** Right eye of patient with complete dislocation of the lens. **B,** Gonioscopic view of the same eye reveals that the dislocated lens is in the inferior vitreous cavity. **C,** Left eye of same patient showing subluxation of the lens. *(Courtesy of Thomas W. Samuelson, MD.)*

Aphakic or pseudophakic angle-closure glaucoma

Pupillary block may occur in *aphakic* and *pseudophakic* eyes. An intact vitreous face can block the pupil and/or an iridectomy in aphakic or pseudophakic eyes or in a phakic eye with a dislocated lens. Generally, the anterior chamber shallows and the iris shows considerable bombé configuration. Treatment with mydriatic and cycloplegic agents may restore the aqueous flow through the pupil but may also make performing a laser iridotomy difficult initially. Topical β-adrenergic antagonists, α_2-adrenergic agonists, carbonic anhydrase inhibitors, and hyperosmotic agents can be effective in reducing IOP prior to the placement of an iridotomy. One or more laser iridotomies may be required.

A variant of this problem occurs with *anterior chamber intraocular lenses.* Pupillary block develops with apposition of the iris, vitreous face, and/or lens optic. The lens haptic or vitreous may obstruct the iridectomy or the pupil, and the peripheral iris bows forward around the anterior chamber IOL to occlude the chamber angle. The central chamber remains deep relative to the peripheral chamber in this instance, because the lens haptic and optic prevent the central portions of the iris and vitreous face from moving forward. Laser iridotomies, often multiple, are required to relieve the block.

Pupillary block may also occur following posterior capsulotomy when vitreous obstructs the pupil. A condition referred to as *capsular block* may also be seen, whereby retained viscoelastic or fluid in the capsular bag pushes a posterior chamber IOL anteriorly, which may narrow the angle.

Secondary Angle Closure Without Pupillary Block

A number of disorders can lead to secondary angle closure without pupillary block, and several are discussed in this section. This form of secondary angle closure may occur through 1 of 2 mechanisms:

- contraction of an inflammatory, hemorrhagic, or vascular membrane, band, or exudate in the angle, leading to PAS
- forward displacement of the lens–iris interface, often accompanied by swelling and anterior rotation of the ciliary body

Neovascular Glaucoma

This common, severe type of secondary ACG is caused by a variety of disorders characterized by retinal or ocular ischemia or ocular inflammation (Table 5-3). The most common causes are diabetic retinopathy, central retinal vein occlusion, and ocular ischemic syndrome. The disease is characterized by fine arborizing blood vessels on the surface of the iris, pupil margin, and trabecular meshwork, which are accompanied by a fibrous membrane. The contraction of the fibrovascular membrane results in the formation of PAS, leading to the development of secondary ACG. In some cases, a fibrous membrane may be evident without active angle neovascularization. Moreover, angle vessels may be present without vessels on the iris surface.

Neovascularization of the anterior segment usually presents in a classic pattern, which starts with fine vascular tufts at the pupillary margin (Fig 5-10). As these vessels grow,

Table 5-3 Disorders Predisposing to Neovascularization of the Iris and Angle

Systemic vascular disease Carotid occlusive disease* Carotid artery ligation Carotid cavernous fistula Giant cell arteritis Takayasu (pulseless) disease	**Other ocular disease** Chronic uveitis Chronic retinal detachment Endophthalmitis Stickler syndrome Retinoschisis
Ocular vascular disease Diabetic retinopathy* Central retinal vein occlusion* Central retinal artery occlusion Branch retinal vein occlusion Sickle cell retinopathy Coats disease Eales disease Retinopathy of prematurity Persistent fetal vasculature Syphilitic vasculitis Anterior segment ischemia	**Intraocular tumors** Uveal melanoma Metastatic carcinoma Retinoblastoma Reticulum cell sarcoma **Ocular therapy** Radiation therapy **Trauma**

*Most common causes.

they extend radially over the iris. The neovascularization crosses the ciliary body and scleral spur as fine single vessels that then branch as they reach and involve the trabecular meshwork (see Chapter 3, Fig 3-6). Often the trabecular meshwork takes on a reddish coloration. With contraction of the fibrovascular membrane, PAS develop and coalesce, gradually closing the angle (Fig 5-11). Because the fibrovascular membrane typically does not grow over healthy corneal endothelium, the PAS end at the Schwalbe line, distinguishing this condition from other secondary ACGs that result from an abnormal corneal endothelium, such as ICE syndrome, which is discussed in the following section (Figs 5-12, 5-13).

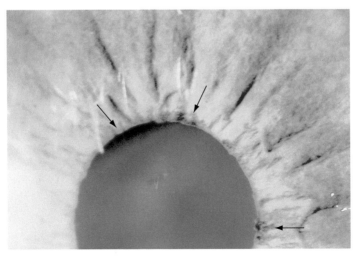

Figure 5-10 The initial presentation of iris neovascularization is usually small vascular tufts *(arrows)* at the pupillary margin. *(Courtesy of Steven T. Simmons, MD.)*

Figure 5-11 Iris neovascularization. With progressive angle involvement, PAS develop with contraction of the fibrovascular membrane, resulting in secondary neovascular glaucoma. *(Courtesy of Steven T. Simmons, MD.)*

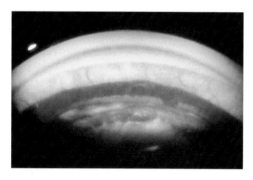

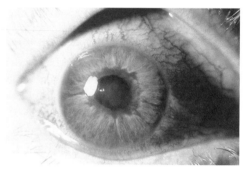

Figure 5-12 With end-stage neovascular glaucoma, total angle closure occurs, obscuring the iris neovascularization. The PAS end at the Schwalbe line because the fibrovascular membrane does not grow over healthy corneal endothelium. *(Courtesy of Steven T. Simmons, MD.)*

Figure 5-13 With growth, iris neovascularization extends from the pupillary margin radially toward the anterior chamber angle. *(Courtesy of Steven T. Simmons, MD.)*

Clinically, patients often present with an acute or subacute glaucoma associated with reduced vision, pain, conjunctival hyperemia, microcystic corneal edema, and high IOP. While performing gonioscopy in patients suspected of having neovascularization, the clinician may find it helpful to use a bright slit-lamp beam of light and high magnification in order to best visualize these fine vessels.

In rare instances, anterior segment neovascularization may occur without demonstrable retinal ischemia, as in Fuchs heterochromic iridocyclitis and other types of uveitis, exfoliation syndrome, or isolated iris melanomas. When an ocular cause cannot be found, carotid artery occlusive disease should be considered. In establishing a correct diagnosis, the clinician should distinguish dilated iris vessels associated with inflammation from newly formed abnormal blood vessels.

Because the prognosis for neovascular glaucoma is poor, prevention and early diagnosis are desirable. Gonioscopy is vitally important to the early diagnosis because angle neovascularization can occur without iris neovascularization. In central retinal vein occlusion (CRVO), approximately 10% of patients develop angle neovascularization alone. The most common cause of iris neovascularization is ischemic retinopathy, and panretinal photocoagulation should be performed whenever possible. The treatment of choice when the ocular media are clear is panretinal photocoagulation. When cloudy media prevent laser therapy, panretinal cryotherapy should be considered as an alternative to vitrectomy to clear the media with endophotocoagulation or subsequent panretinal photocoagulation. Frequently, marked involution of the neovascularization occurs. The resulting decrease in neovascularization after panretinal photocoagulation may reduce or normalize the IOP, depending on the degree of synechial closure that has occurred. Even in the presence of total synechial angle closure, panretinal photocoagulation may improve the success rate of subsequent glaucoma surgery by eliminating the angiogenic stimulus and may decrease the risk of hemorrhage at the time of surgery. More recently, anti-VEGF agents have been successfully employed to promote regression of the neovascular tissue prior to filtering surgery (Fig 5-14).

Medical management of neovascular glaucoma yields variable success but often is a temporizing measure until more definitive surgical or laser treatment is undertaken. Topical β-adrenergic antagonists, α_2-adrenergic agonists, carbonic anhydrase inhibitors, cycloplegics, and corticosteroids may be useful in reducing IOP and decreasing inflammation either as a long-term remedy or prior to filtering surgery. Filtering surgery has a better chance of success once the neovascularization has regressed after panretinal photocoagulation. The use of the antifibrotics 5-fluorouracil and mitomycin C has been shown to increase the success rate of and decrease the final IOP following trabeculectomy in patients with neovascular glaucoma. A variety of glaucoma drainage devices have also been successfully implanted to control the IOP in neovascular glaucoma and, in many cases, glaucoma drainage device implantation is the surgical procedure of choice. If these therapies fail, either endoscopic or transscleral cyclophotocoagulation, or less often, cyclocryotherapy, may help reduce the IOP.

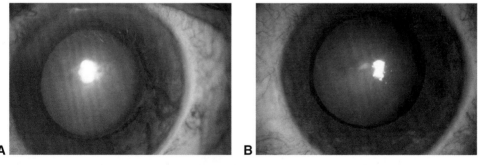

A   **B**

Figure 5-14   A, Slit-lamp photograph of florid iris neovascularization taken 15 minutes before injection of bevacizumab. **B,** Regression of iris neovascularization 4 days after treatment with bevacizumab. *(Courtesy of Nicholas P. Bell, MD.)*

Iliev ME, Domig D, Wolf-Schnurrbursch U, Wolf S, Sarra GM. Intravitreal bevacizumab (Avastin) in the treatment of neovascular glaucoma. *Am J Ophthalmol.* 2006;142(6): 1054–1056.

Jonas JB, Spandau UH, Schlichtenbrede F. Intravitreal bevacizumab for filtering surgery. *Ophthalmic Res.* 2007;39(2):121–122.

Sivak-Callcott JA, O'Day DM, Gass JD, Tsai JC. Evidence-based recommendations for the diagnosis and treatment of neovascular glaucoma. *Ophthalmology.* 2001;108(10): 1767–1776.

Iridocorneal Endothelial Syndrome

Iridocorneal endothelial (ICE) syndrome is a group of disorders characterized by abnormal corneal endothelium that causes variable degrees of iris atrophy, secondary ACG, and corneal edema. BCSC Section 8, *External Disease and Cornea,* discusses the corneal aspects of ICE syndrome. Three clinical variants have been described: Chandler syndrome, essential (progressive) iris atrophy, and Cogan-Reese syndrome (iris nevus).

The condition is clinically unilateral, presents between 20 and 50 years of age, and occurs more often in women. No consistent association has been found with another ocular or systemic disease, and familial cases are very rare. Patients typically present with elevated IOP, decreased vision due to corneal edema, secondary chronic ACG, or an abnormal iris appearance. In each of the 3 clinical variants, the abnormal corneal endothelium takes on a "beaten bronze" appearance, similar to corneal guttae seen in Fuchs corneal endothelial dystrophy. Microcystic corneal edema may be present without elevated IOP, especially in Chandler syndrome. The unaffected eye may have subclinical irregularities of the corneal endothelium without other manifestations of the disease.

High PAS are characteristic of ICE syndrome (Fig 5-15), and these often extend anterior to the Schwalbe line. Similar to neovascular glaucoma, the degree of angle closure does not always correlate to the elevation in IOP, because some angles may be functionally closed by the endothelial membrane without overt synechial formation.

Various degrees of iris atrophy and corneal changes distinguish the specific clinical entities. The essential iris atrophy variant of ICE syndrome is characterized by severe progressive iris atrophy resulting in heterochromia, corectopia, ectropion uveae, iris stromal and pigment epithelial atrophy, and hole formation (Fig 5-16). In Chandler syndrome, minimal iris atrophy and corectopia occur, and the corneal and angle findings predominate (Fig 5-17). Chandler syndrome is the most common of the clinical variants and

Figure 5-15 The classic high PAS seen in ICE syndrome. These PAS extend anterior to the Schwalbe line in this patient with essential iris atrophy. With angle closure, the secondary glaucoma occurs. *(Courtesy of Steven T. Simmons, MD.)*

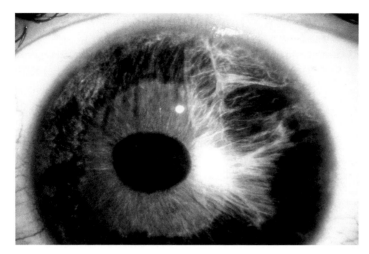

Figure 5-16 ICE syndrome. Corectopia and hole formation are typical findings in essential iris atrophy. *(Courtesy of Steven T. Simmons, MD.)*

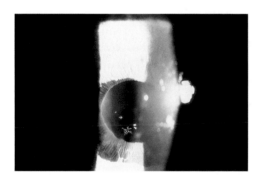

Figure 5-17 Ectropion uveae in a patient with Chandler syndrome. *(Courtesy of Steven T. Simmons, MD.)*

makes up approximately 50% of the cases of ICE syndrome. The iris atrophy also tends to be less severe in Cogan-Reese syndrome. This condition is distinguished by tan pedunculated nodules or diffuse pigmented lesions on the anterior iris surface.

Glaucoma occurs in approximately 50% of patients with ICE syndrome, and the glaucoma tends to be more severe in essential iris atrophy and Cogan-Reese syndrome. In this condition, the corneal endothelium migrates posterior to the Schwalbe line onto the trabecular meshwork. Electron microscopy has shown this endothelial layer to vary in thickness, with areas of single and multiple endothelial layers and surrounding collagenous and fibrillar tissue. Unlike with normal corneal endothelium, filopodial processes and cytoplasmic actin filaments are present, supporting the migratory nature of these cells. PAS are formed when this migratory endothelium and its surrounding collagenous, fibrillar tissue contract. A viral cause has been postulated for the mechanism of ICE syndrome after lymphocytes were seen on the corneal endothelium of affected patients.

The diagnosis of ICE syndrome must always be considered in young to middle-aged patients who present with unilateral, secondary ACG. It is particularly important to maintain a high index of suspicion as this condition may mimic primary OAG when the iris and corneal features are subtle. Specular microscopy can confirm the diagnosis by demonstrating an asymmetric loss of endothelial cells and atypical endothelial cell morphology in the involved eye.

Therapy is directed toward the corneal edema and secondary glaucoma. Hypertonic saline solutions and medications to reduce the IOP, when elevated, can be effective in controlling the corneal edema. The ACG can be treated medically with aqueous suppressants and prostaglandin analogues. Miotics are often ineffective. When medical therapy fails, filtering surgery (trabeculectomy or a glaucoma drainage device) can be effective. Late failures have been reported with trabeculectomy secondary to endothelialization of the fistula. The fistula can be reopened in some cases with the Nd:YAG laser. Laser trabeculoplasty has no useful role in treating glaucoma related to ICE syndrome.

Tumors

Tumors in the posterior segment of the eye or anterior uveal cysts may cause a unilateral secondary ACG. Primary choroidal melanomas, ocular metastases, and retinoblastoma are the most common tumors to cause secondary angle closure. The mechanism of the ACG is determined by the size, location, and pathology of the tumor. Choroidal and retinal tumors tend to shift the lens–iris interface forward as the tumors enlarge, causing secondary angle closure. Breakdown of the blood–aqueous barrier and inflammation from tissue necrosis can result in posterior and PAS formation, further exacerbating other underlying mechanisms of angle closure. Iris neovascularization can occur frequently with retinoblastomas, medulloepitheliomas, and choroidal melanomas, resulting in secondary angle closure and neovascular glaucoma.

Inflammation

Secondary ACG can result from ocular inflammation. Fibrin and increased aqueous proteins from the breakdown of the blood–aqueous barrier may predispose to the formation of posterior synechiae (Fig 5-18) and PAS. If left untreated, these posterior synechiae can result in a secluded pupil, iris bombé, and secondary angle closure (Fig 5-19).

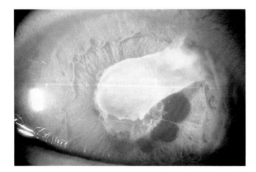

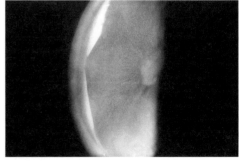

Figure 5-18 Inflammatory glaucoma. A fibrinous anterior chamber reaction and posterior synechiae formation are shown in a patient with ankylosing spondylitis. *(Courtesy of Steven T. Simmons, MD.)*

Figure 5-19 Inflammatory glaucoma. A secluded pupil is shown in a patient with long-standing uveitis with classic iris bombé and secondary angle closure. *(Courtesy of Steven T. Simmons, MD.)*

Inflammation may prompt PAS to form through peripheral iris edema, organization of inflammatory debris in the angle, and the bridging of the angle by large keratic precipitates (sarcoidosis). Unlike with PAC, in which the PAS occur preferentially in the superior angle, with inflammatory etiologies they occur most frequently in the inferior angle (Fig 5-20). These PAS tend to be nonuniform in shape and height, which further differentiates inflammatory disease from PAC (Fig 5-21). In rare instances, ischemia secondary to inflammation may cause rubeosis iridis and neovascular glaucoma.

Ocular inflammation can lead to the shallowing and closure of the anterior chamber angle by uveal effusion, resulting in anterior rotation of the ciliary body. Significant posterior uveitis causing massive exudative retinal detachment or choroidal effusions may lead to ACG through forward displacement of the lens–iris interface. Treatment is primarily directed at the underlying cause of the uveitis. Aqueous suppressants and corticosteroids are the primary agents for reducing elevated IOP and preventing synechial angle closure.

Interstitial keratitis may be associated with OAG or ACG. The angle closure may be caused by chronic inflammation and PAS formation or by multiple cysts of the iris pigment epithelium.

Samples JR. Management of glaucoma secondary to uveitis. *Focal Points: Clinical Modules for Ophthalmologists.* San Francisco: American Academy of Ophthalmology; 1995, module 5.

Aqueous Misdirection

Aqueous misdirection is also known as *malignant glaucoma, ciliary block glaucoma,* and *posterior aqueous diversion syndrome.* This rare but potentially devastating form of glaucoma usually presents following ocular surgery in patients with a history of angle closure or PAS. It may also occur spontaneously in eyes with an open angle following cataract surgery or various laser procedures. The disease presents with uniform flattening of both the central and peripheral anterior chamber, which is typically markedly asymmetrical to the fellow eye (Fig 5-22). This is in contrast to acute PACG, which presents with iris bombé and a shallow peripheral anterior chamber (Fig 5-23). Classically, the condition is

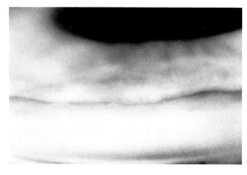

Figure 5-20 Inflammatory glaucoma. Keratic precipitates can be seen bridging the inferior anterior chamber angle in this patient with long-standing uveitis, resulting in the formation of PAS. *(Courtesy of Joseph Krug, MD.)*

Figure 5-21 Inflammatory glaucoma. PAS in uveitis occur preferentially in the inferior anterior chamber angle and are nonuniform in height and shape, as shown in this photograph. *(Courtesy of Joseph Krug, MD.)*

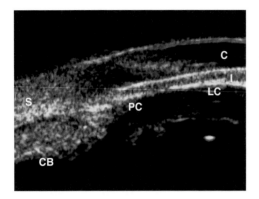

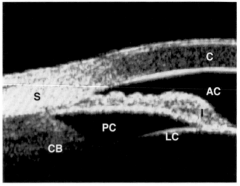

Figure 5-22 Aqueous misdirection seen by UBM. Expansion of the vitreous pushes the lens and ciliary body forward, causing a uniform shallowing of the anterior chamber. The central portion of the anterior lens capsule *(LC)* is nearly in contact with the cornea *(C)*. *PC* = posterior chamber; *CB* = ciliary body; *I* = iris; *S* = sclera. *(From Lundy DC. Ciliary block glaucoma. Focal Points: Clinical Modules for Ophthalmologists. San Francisco: American Academy of Ophthalmology; 1999, module 3. Courtesy of Jeffrey M. Liebmann, MD.)*

Figure 5-23 Acute angle closure seen by UBM. Pupillary block leads to forward bowing of the peripheral iris. The peripheral chamber is shallow, whereas the central chamber is relatively deeper by comparison. *C* = cornea; *AC* = anterior chamber; *PC* = posterior chamber; *LC* = lens capsule; *CB* = ciliary body; *I* = iris; *S* = sclera. *(From Lundy DC. Ciliary block glaucoma. Focal Points: Clinical Modules for Ophthalmologists. San Francisco: American Academy of Ophthalmology; 1999, module 3. Courtesy of Jeffrey M. Liebmann, MD.)*

thought to result from anterior rotation of the ciliary body and posterior misdirection of the aqueous, in association with a relative block to aqueous movement at the level of the lens equator, vitreous face, and ciliary processes. More recently, some have proposed that primary angle closure and malignant glaucoma may result from the simultaneous presence of several factors, including a small eye, a propensity for choroidal expansion, and reduced vitreous fluid conductivity.

Clinically, the anterior chamber is shallow or flat with anterior displacement of the lens, pseudophakos, or vitreous face. Optically clear "aqueous" zones may be seen in the vitreous, highlighting the underlying pathology. In the early postoperative setting, aqueous misdirection is often difficult to distinguish from choroidal effusion, pupillary block, or suprachoroidal hemorrhage. Often the level of IOP, time frame following surgery, patency of an iridectomy, or presence of a choroidal effusion or suprachoroidal hemorrhage helps the clinician make the appropriate diagnosis and initiate treatment. In some cases, unfortunately, the clinical picture is difficult to interpret and surgical intervention may be required to make the diagnosis.

Medical management includes the triad of intensive cycloplegic therapy; aggressive aqueous suppression with β-adrenergic antagonists, α_2-adrenergic agonists, and carbonic anhydrase inhibitors; and shrinking of the vitreous with hyperosmotic agents. Miotics should not be used and can make aqueous misdirection worse. In aphakic and pseudophakic eyes, the anterior vitreous can be disrupted with the Nd:YAG laser. Argon laser photocoagulation of the ciliary processes has reportedly been helpful in treating this condition; this procedure may alter the adjacent vitreous face. Approximately 50% of patients can be controlled with laser iridotomy and medical management, whereas the other half will require surgical intervention alone. The definitive surgical treatment is pars plana vitrectomy with anterior hyaloido-zonulectomy combined with an anterior chamber deepening procedure. BCSC Section 12, *Retina and Vitreous,* discusses vitrectomy in greater detail.

Lundy DC. Ciliary block glaucoma. *Focal Points: Clinical Modules for Ophthalmologists.* San Francisco: American Academy of Ophthalmology; 1999, module 3.

Quigley HA, Friedman DS, Congdon NG. Possible mechanisms of primary angle-closure and malignant glaucoma. *J Glaucoma.* 2003;12(2):167–180.

Nonrhegmatogenous Retinal Detachment and Uveal Effusions

A nonrhegmatogenous retinal detachment occurs as a result of subretinal fluid in which no retinal break is present. A suprachoroidal effusion or hemorrhage refers to blood or fluid in the potential space between the choroid and the sclera. Retinoblastoma, Coats disease, metastatic carcinoma, choroidal melanoma, suprachoroidal hemorrhage, choroidal effusion/detachment, infections (HIV), and subretinal neovascularization in age-related macular degeneration with extensive effusion or hemorrhage can cause nonrhegmatogenous retinal detachments or suprachoroidal mass effect that may result in secondary angle closure related to forward displacement of the lens–iris interface. See BCSC Section 12, *Retina and Vitreous,* for further discussion.

In a *rhegmatogenous retinal detachment,* the subretinal fluid can escape through the retinal tear and equalize the hydraulic pressure on both sides of the retina. In a nonrhegmatogenous retinal detachment, by contrast, the subretinal fluid accumulates and becomes a space-occupying lesion in the vitreous, which may progressively push the retina forward against the lens like a hydraulic press. The fluid or hemorrhage may accumulate rapidly, and as it pushes the retina forward to a retrolenticular position, in severe cases it can flatten the anterior chamber completely. The retina may be dramatically visible behind the lens on slit-lamp examination.

Epithelial and Fibrous Ingrowth

Epithelial and fibrous proliferation are rare surgical complications that can cause severe secondary glaucomas. Epithelial and fibrous ingrowth occur when epithelium and/or connective tissue invades the anterior chamber through a defect in a wound site. Fortunately, improved surgical and wound closure techniques have greatly reduced the incidence of these entities. Fibrous ingrowth is more prevalent than epithelial ingrowth. Risk factors for the development of these entities include prolonged inflammation, wound dehiscence, delayed wound closure, or a Descemet membrane tear. Epithelial ingrowth has also been reported following Descemet-stripping automated endothelial keratoplasty.

Epithelial ingrowth presents as a grayish, sheetlike growth on the trabecular meshwork, iris, ciliary body, and posterior surface of the cornea. It is often associated with vitreous incarceration, wound gape, ocular inflammation, hypotony secondary to choroidal effusions, and corneal edema (Figs 5-24, 5-25). The epithelial ingrowth consists of nonkeratinized stratified squamous epithelium with an avascular subepithelial connective tissue layer.

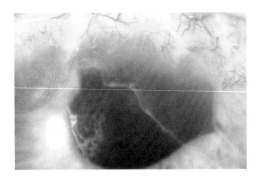

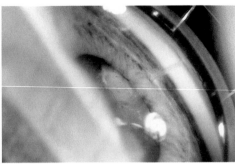

Figure 5-24 Epithelial ingrowth appears as a grayish, sheetlike growth on the endothelial surface of the cornea, usually originating from a surgical incision or traumatic wound. The epithelial ingrowth shown here originated from a cataract surgery incision. *(Courtesy of Steven T. Simmons, MD.)*

Figure 5-25 Epithelial ingrowth. The precipitating causes of epithelial ingrowth include vitreous incarceration in corneal and scleral wounds, as seen in this photograph, as well as wound gape, ocular inflammation, and hypotony secondary to choroidal effusions. *(Courtesy of Steven T. Simmons, MD.)*

The argon laser produces characteristic white burns on the epithelial membrane on the iris surface, which help to confirm the diagnosis of epithelial ingrowth and to determine the extent of involvement. If the diagnosis remains in question, a cytologic examination of an aqueous aspirate can be performed. Radical surgery is sometimes necessary to remove the intraocular epithelial membrane and the affected tissues and to repair the fistula, but the prognosis remains poor; thus the decision to intervene is made based on the extent of disease, the visual potential, the status of the fellow eye, and social-medical circumstances relevant to the affected individual.

Fibrovascular tissue may also proliferate into an eye from a penetrating wound. Unlike epithelial proliferation, fibrous ingrowth progresses slowly and is often self-limited. A common cause of corneal graft failure, fibrous ingrowth appears as a thick, gray-white, vascular retrocorneal membrane with an irregular border. The ingrowth often involves the angle, resulting in PAS and the destruction of the trabecular meshwork (Fig 5-26). The resultant secondary ACG is often difficult to control. Medication is the preferred treatment of the secondary glaucomas that present without a pupillary block mechanism, although surgical intervention may be required. See Chapters 7 and 8 for further discussion.

Figure 5-26 Fibrous ingrowth appears as a thick, grayish, vascular retrocorneal membrane that results in high PAS and destruction of the trabecular meshwork. *(Courtesy of Steven T. Simmons, MD.)*

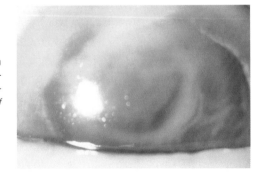

Trauma

Angle-closure glaucoma without pupillary block may develop following ocular trauma from the formation of PAS associated with angle recession or from contusion, hyphema, and inflammation. See Chapter 4 for discussion of trauma.

Retinal Surgery and Retinal Vascular Disease

Scleral buckling operations, especially encircling bands, can produce shallowing of the anterior chamber angle and frank ACG, often accompanied by choroidal effusion and anterior rotation of the ciliary body, causing a flattening of the peripheral iris with a relatively deep central anterior chamber. Usually, the anterior chamber deepens with the opening of the anterior chamber angle over days to weeks with medical therapy consisting of cycloplegics, anti-inflammatory agents, β-adrenergic antagonists, carbonic anhydrase inhibitors, and hyperosmotic agents. If medical management is unsuccessful, argon laser iridoplasty, drainage of suprachoroidal fluid, or adjustment of the scleral buckle may be required. Iridectomy is usually of little benefit in this condition. The scleral buckle can impede venous drainage by compressing a vortex vein, elevating episcleral venous pressure and IOP. Such cases may respond only to moving the scleral buckle or releasing tension on the band.

Following a pars plana vitrectomy, ACG may result from the injection of air, long-acting gases such as sulfur hexafluoride and perfluorocarbons (perfluoropropane and perfluoroethane), or silicone oil. These substances are less dense than water and rise to the top of the eye, and an iridectomy may be beneficial. The iridectomy should be located inferiorly to prevent obstruction of the iridectomy site by the oil or gas. Eyes that have undergone complicated vitreoretinal surgery and have developed elevated IOP require individualized treatment plans. Treatment options include the following: removal of the silicone oil; release of the encircling element; removal of expansile gases; or primary glaucoma surgery, such as trabeculectomy, implantation of glaucoma drainage devices, or cilioablation.

Following panretinal photocoagulation, IOP may become elevated by an angle-closure mechanism. The ciliary body is thickened and rotated anteriorly, and often an anterior annular choroidal detachment occurs. Generally, this secondary glaucoma is self-limited, and therapy is directed at temporary medical management with cycloplegic agents, topical corticosteroids, and aqueous suppressants.

Central retinal vein occlusion (CRVO) sometimes causes early shallowing of the chamber angle, presumably because of swelling of the choroid and ciliary body. In rare cases, the angle becomes sufficiently compromised to cause ACG. The chamber deepens and the glaucoma resolves over 1 to several weeks. Medical therapy for the elevated IOP, combined with administration of topical corticosteroids and cycloplegia, is usually preferred. However, if the contralateral eye of a patient with CRVO has a potentially occludable anterior chamber angle, the ophthalmologist must consider an underlying pupillary block mechanism and the possible need for bilateral iridectomy.

Nanophthalmos

A nanophthalmic eye is normal in shape but unusually small, with a shortened axial length (<20 mm), a small corneal diameter, and a relatively large lens for the volume of the eye.

Thickened sclera may impede drainage from the vortex veins. These eyes are markedly hyperopic and highly susceptible to ACG, which occurs at an earlier age than in primary angle closure. Intraocular surgery is frequently complicated by choroidal effusion and nonrhegmatogenous retinal detachment. Choroidal effusion may occur spontaneously, and it can induce ACG. Laser iridotomy, argon laser peripheral iridoplasty, and medical therapy are the safest ways to manage glaucoma in these patients. Surgery should be avoided if possible because of the high rate of surgical complications. When intraocular surgery is employed, prophylactic posterior sclerotomies may reduce the severity of intraoperative choroidal effusion. Additional treatment options include lensectomy for angles that remain compromised despite a patent iridotomy. In such cases, a limited core vitrectomy is sometimes needed to provide adequate ACD to accomplish safe lens removal.

Persistent Fetal Vasculature

The contracting retrolental tissue seen in persistent fetal vasculature (PFV; formerly known as *persistent hyperplastic primary vitreous*) and in retinopathy of prematurity can cause progressive shallowing of the anterior chamber angle with subsequent ACG. These conditions are discussed in more detail in BCSC Section 6, *Pediatric Ophthalmology and Strabismus,* and Section 12, *Retina and Vitreous.* In PFV, the onset of this complication usually occurs at 3–6 months of age during the cicatricial phase of the disease. However, the ACG may occur later in childhood.

PFV is usually unilateral and often associated with microphthalmos and elongated ciliary processes. The contracture of the hyperplastic primary vitreous and swelling of a cataractous lens may result in subsequent ACG.

Flat Anterior Chamber

A flat anterior chamber from any cause can result in the formation of PAS. Debate continues concerning how long a postoperative flat chamber should be treated conservatively before surgical intervention is undertaken. Hypotony in an eye with a postoperative flat chamber following cataract surgery or filtering surgery indicates a wound leak until proven otherwise. A Seidel test should be performed to locate the leak. Simple pressure patching or bandage contact lens application will often cause the leak to seal and the chamber to re-form. If the chamber does not re-form, the leak should be repaired surgically to prevent permanent synechial closure of the angle or other complications of hypotony.

Some ophthalmologists repair the wound leak and re-form a flat chamber following cataract surgery within 24 hours. Others prefer observation in conjunction with corticosteroid therapy for several days to prevent synechiae formation. Although iridocorneal contact is well tolerated, if the hyaloid face or an IOL is in contact with the cornea, the chamber should be re-formed without delay to minimize corneal endothelial damage. Early intervention should also be considered in the presence of corneal edema, excessive inflammation, or posterior synechiae formation.

Drug-Induced Secondary Angle-Closure Glaucoma

Topiramate, a sulfamate-substituted monosaccharide, is an oral medication prescribed in the treatment of epilepsy, depression, headaches, and pseudotumor cerebri. In some patients using this medication, a syndrome characterized by acute myopic shift and acute bilateral ACG can occur. Patients presenting with this syndrome experience bilateral, sudden loss of vision with acute myopia, bilateral ocular pain, and headache, usually within 1 month of initiating topiramate. In addition to myopia, ocular findings of this syndrome include a uniformly shallow anterior chamber with anterior iris and lens displacement, microcystic corneal edema, elevated IOP (40–70 mm Hg), a closed anterior chamber angle, and a ciliochoroidal effusion/detachment (Fig 5-27). The underlying mechanism of this syndrome is the ciliochoroidal effusion, which causes the relaxation of zonular fibers and the profound anterior displacement of the lens–iris complex, causing the secondary ACG and high myopia.

The bilateral nature of this form of angle closure should alert the clinician to the possibility of an idiosyncratic response to topiramate. Treatment of this syndrome involves early recognition of the causal systemic medication and immediate discontinuation of the topiramate. In addition to discontinuation of the medication, medical treatment for the elevated IOP is initiated, generally in the form of aqueous suppressants. Systemic agents such as acetazolamide may also be administered orally or intravenously. Aggressive cycloplegia may help deepen the anterior chamber and relieve the attack. The secondary ACG usually resolves within 24–48 hours with medical treatment, and the myopia resolves within 1–2 weeks of discontinuing the topiramate. Because pupillary block is not an underlying mechanism of this syndrome, a peripheral iridectomy is not indicated. Other sulfonamides, such as acetazolamide, have been reported to cause a similar clinical syndrome.

Epstein DL, Allingham RR, Schuman JS, eds. *Chandler and Grant's Glaucoma.* 4th ed. Baltimore: Williams & Wilkins; 1997.

Ritch R, Shields MB, Krupin T, eds. *The Glaucomas.* 2nd ed. St Louis: Mosby; 1996.

Shields MB. *Textbook of Glaucoma.* 4th ed. Philadelphia: Williams & Wilkins; 2000.

Stamper RL, Lieberman MF, Drake MV, eds. *Becker-Shaffer's Diagnosis and Therapy of the Glaucomas.* 7th ed. St Louis: Mosby; 1999.

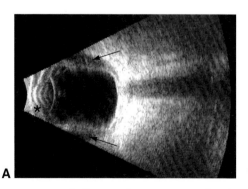
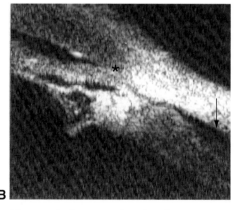

A   B

Figure 5-27 **A,** B-scan ultrasonogram of patient with very shallow anterior chamber *(asterisk)* and topiramate-induced angle-closure glaucoma. The choroidal effusion is clearly evident *(arrows)*. **B,** Ultrasonographic view of extremely shallow anterior chamber and closed angle *(asterisk)*. The posterior choroidal effusion is clearly visible *(arrow)*. *(Courtesy of Jonathan Eisengart, MD.)*

CHAPTER 6

Childhood Glaucoma

BCSC Section 6, *Pediatric Ophthalmology and Strabismus,* also discusses many of the topics covered in this chapter.

Childhood glaucomas are a heterogeneous group of disorders that result in elevated intraocular pressure (IOP) and subsequent damage to the optic nerve. Various presentations and etiologies characterize these rare glaucomas. Although the pediatric glaucomas share many characteristics with adult-onset glaucoma, there are numerous management issues unique to the pediatric population.

Classification

Multiple systems have been used to classify the childhood glaucomas, including those based on anatomical anomalies, age of onset, inheritance, and associated systemic disorders. *Primary* pediatric glaucomas are developmental glaucomas with congenital anomalies of the filtration angle (Table 6-1). Although there is some overlap in the classification of the pediatric glaucomas—for example, the glaucoma associated with Sturge-Weber syndrome has been classified as both a primary and a secondary glaucoma (Table 6-2)—primary pediatric glaucomas can be divided into the following:

- congenital glaucoma (congenital open-angle glaucoma)
- juvenile open-angle glaucoma
- glaucoma associated with systemic diseases
- glaucoma associated with other ocular anomalies

Children with primary congenital glaucoma (PCG) present with the classic features of this condition, including enlarged and/or cloudy corneas, Haab striae, and elevated IOP. PCG may present at birth or prior to 1 month of age (newborn PCG), within the first 2 years of life (infantile PCG), or after age 2 (late-diagnosed PCG). Juvenile open-angle glaucoma develops later in childhood or in early adulthood. Numerous systemic diseases can cause primary pediatric glaucoma, including chromosomal disorders, connective tissue disorders (ie, Marfan and Stickler syndromes), and the phakomatoses. In addition, primary pediatric glaucoma can be associated with defective development of the anterior segment, such as aniridia or Peters anomaly.

Secondary glaucomas in childhood arise from multiple etiologies, including trauma, intraocular neoplasms, inflammation, lens-induced disorders, surgical interventions, angle closure, infection, neovascularization, corticosteroid use, or elevated episcleral venous pressure (see Table 6-2).

Table 6-1 Classification Scheme for Primary Childhood Glaucomas

I. Congenital glaucomas
  A. Newborn glaucoma
  B. Infantile glaucoma
  C. Late-diagnosed glaucoma
II. Juvenile (open-angle) glaucoma
III. Associated with ocular abnormalities (anterior segment developmental abnormality)
  A. Axenfeld-Rieger syndrome
  B. Aniridia
  C. Congenital iris ectropion syndrome
  D. Iridotrabecular dysgenesis (iris hypoplasia)
  E. Peters anomaly
  F. Congenital microcornea with myopia
  G. Sclerocornea
  H. Congenital hereditary endothelial dystrophy
  I. Posterior polymorphous dystrophy
  J. Megalocornea
IV. Associated with systemic abnormalities
  A. Chromosomal disorders
    1. Trisomy 13 (Patau syndrome)
    2. Trisomy 15
    3. Trisomy 18 (Edward syndrome)
    4. Trisomy 21 (Down syndrome)
    5. Turner syndrome (XO)
  B. Connective tissue abnormalities
    1. Marfan syndrome
    2. Stickler syndrome
    3. Others (see Table 6-2)
  C. Phakomatoses
    1. Sturge-Weber syndrome (isolated vs with CNS involvement)
    2. Neurofibromatosis 1
    3. Nevus of Ota (ocular melanosis)
    4. von Hippel–Lindau syndrome
  D. Other
    1. Axenfeld-Rieger syndrome
    2. Hepatocerebrorenal syndrome (Zellweger syndrome)
    3. Kniest dysplasia
    4. Hallermann-Streiff syndrome
    5. Michel syndrome
    6. Nail-patella syndrome
    7. Oculodentodigital dysplasia
    8. Prader-Willi syndrome
    9. Rubinstein-Taybi syndrome
    10. Waardenburg syndrome
    11. Walker-Warburg syndrome
    12. Cutis marmorata telangiectasia congenita

Adapted from Yanovitch TL, Freedman SF. Pediatric glaucoma. *Focal Points: Clinical Modules for Ophthalmologists.* San Francisco: American Academy of Ophthalmology; 2012, module 3.

Table 6-2 Classification Scheme for Secondary Childhood Glaucomas

I. Secondary to trauma
   A. Acute glaucoma
   B. Late-onset glaucoma with angle recession
   C. Arteriovenous fistula
II. Secondary to intraocular neoplasm
   A. Retinoblastoma
   B. Juvenile xanthogranuloma
   C. Leukemia
   D. Melanoma
   E. Melanocytoma
   F. Iris rhabdomyosarcoma
   G. Aggressive nevi of the iris
III. Secondary to uveitis
   A. Open-angle glaucoma
   B. Angle-blockage glaucoma
      1. Synechial angle closure
      2. Iris bombé with pupillary block
      3. Trabecular endothelialization
IV. Lens-induced
   A. Subluxation or dislocation and pupillary block
      1. Marfan syndrome
      2. Homocystinuria
      3. Weill-Marchesani syndrome
      4. Ectopia lentis
      5. Hyperlysinemia
   B. Spherophakia with pupillary block
   C. Phacolytic glaucoma
V. After surgery for congenital cataract
   A. Lens tissue trabecular obstruction
   B. Pupillary block (angle closure)
   C. Chronic open-angle glaucoma associated with angle abnormalities
VI. Steroid-induced
VII. Secondary to rubeosis
   A. Retinoblastoma
   B. Coats disease
   C. Familial exudative vitreoretinopathy
   D. Medulloepithelioma
   E. Chronic retinal detachment
VIII. Secondary angle-closure glaucomas
   A. Retinopathy of prematurity
   B. Persistent fetal vasculature
   C. Microphthalmos
   D. Nanophthalmos
   E. Iris stromal cysts
   F. Ciliary body cysts
   G. Congenital pupillary iris–lens membrane
   H. Retinoblastoma
   I. Cystinosis
   J. Central retinal vein occlusion
   K. Topiramate-induced

(Continued)

Table 6-2 *(continued)*

  IX. Malignant glaucoma
   X. Glaucoma associated with increased episcleral venous pressure
       A. Sturge-Weber syndrome (isolated vs with CNS involvement)
       B. Cavernous or dural venous fistula
       C. Orbital disease
  XI. Secondary to maternal rubella
 XII. Secondary to intraocular infection
       A. Acute recurrent toxoplasmosis
       B. Acute herpetic iritis

Adapted from Yanovitch TL, Freedman SF. Pediatric glaucoma. *Focal Points: Clinical Modules for Ophthalmologists.* San Francisco: American Academy of Ophthalmology; 2012, module 3.

Genetics

Most cases of PCG occur sporadically, and 10%–40% of cases have a familial pattern of inheritance, usually an autosomal recessive pattern with incomplete or variable penetrance. Linkage studies have identified 3 genetic loci of PCG—GLC3A, GLC3B, and GLC3C—but it is likely that additional loci exist (see Chapter 1, Table 1-4). Two main genes for PCG have been identified:

- *CYP1B1* (the drug-metabolizing enzyme cytochrome P450, family 1, subfamily B, polypeptide 1) within the GLC3A locus
- *LTBP2* (latent transforming growth factor beta-binding protein 2) within the GLC3C locus

Most cases of juvenile open-angle glaucoma have an autosomal dominant inheritance pattern, although sporadic cases occasionally occur. Juvenile open-angle glaucoma has been linked to mutations in the *TIGR* (trabecular meshwork inducible glucocorticoid response)/*MYOC* (myocillin) gene located at the GLC1A locus.

Primary pediatric glaucoma is associated with many ocular abnormalities, including aniridia (mentioned previously), Axenfeld-Rieger syndrome, and Peters anomaly. Aniridia results from mutations in the paired box 6 gene *(PAX6)*. Two-thirds of cases of aniridia are autosomal dominant and one-third are sporadic. Axenfeld-Rieger syndrome has an autosomal dominant pattern of inheritance and presents with a variety of phenotypes. Mutations in the *PITX2* (paired-like homeodomain transcription factor 2) gene, located at 4q25, and in the *FOXC1* (forkhead box C1) gene, located at 6p25, have been linked to this syndrome; the variable interaction between these 2 genes may underlie the diverse phenotypic expression in Axenfeld-Rieger syndrome. Peters anomaly has been associated with mutations in *PITX2, FOXC1, CYP1B1,* and *PAX6.*

Genetic testing should be considered for parents of pediatric glaucoma patients and for adults whose glaucoma had its onset in childhood or early adulthood.

Akarsu AN, Turacli ME, Aktan SG, et al. A second locus (GLC3B) for primary congenital glaucoma (Buphthalmos) maps to the 1p36 region. *Hum Mol Genet.* 1996;5(8):1199–1203.

Sarfarazi M, Stoilov I, Schenkman JB. Genetics and biochemistry of primary congenital glaucoma. *Ophthalmol Clin North Am.* 2003;16(4):543–554.

Yeung HH, Walton DS. Clinical classification of childhood glaucomas. *Arch Ophthalmol.* 2010;128(6):680–684.

Primary Congenital Glaucoma

Primary congenital glaucoma in infancy presents with the classic triad of epiphora, photophobia, and blepharospasm. Until age 3, elevated IOP causes the cornea to stretch, which leads to increased corneal diameter and enlargement of the globe (buphthalmos). The corneal stretching produces *Haab striae,* or breaks in Descemet membrane, and leads to the development of corneal edema and corneal opacification (Fig 6-1). As the cornea swells, the child may become irritable and photophobic. After age 3, the cornea does not continue to enlarge, but persistently elevated IOP may result in scleral stretching and progressive myopia.

PCG accounts for the majority of primary pediatric glaucomas. Most cases are bilateral (70%) and are diagnosed within the first year of life (>75%). PCG occurs more frequently in males (65%) than females. The incidence varies with ethnicity, ranging from 1 in 1250 live births in Slovakian Roms to 1 in 18,500 live births in Great Britain. Consanguinity greatly increases the risk. Without a family history of PCG, an affected parent has a 2% chance of having a child with PCG.

Newborn PCG occurs in approximately 25% of cases and confers a worse prognosis than does infantile PCG. More than half the patients with newborn PCG progress to legal blindness. The prognosis is also worse for patients whose glaucoma is diagnosed after 1 year of age and for those with corneal diameters larger than 14 mm at diagnosis. The prognosis is best for patients whose glaucoma is diagnosed between the ages of 3 and 12 months, with the vast majority responding to angle surgery.

PCG is characterized by increased outflow resistance through the trabecular meshwork. Barkan hypothesized that a membrane covering the anterior chamber angle reduced outflow facility. Although this membrane has not been identified, there appears to be a developmental anomaly of the neural crest–derived tissue of the anterior chamber angle,

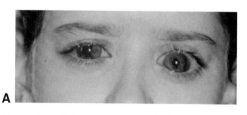
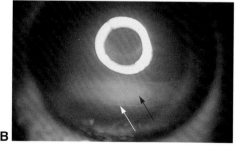

Figure 6-1 Primary congenital glaucoma. **A,** Buphthalmos in child with history of congenital glaucoma. Pupils are altered after multiple surgical procedures. **B,** Haab striae may lead to corneal edema. *White arrow* points to edge of Haab striae, and *red arrow* points to center of Haab striae with corneal edema and opacification. *(Part A courtesy of Jody Piltz-Seymour, MD; part B courtesy of Sharon Freedman, MD.)*

with dysgenesis and compression of the trabecular meshwork and an anterior insertion of the iris root (Fig 6-2).

The differential diagnosis of PCG is extensive and is presented in Table 6-3. PCG should be considered in the differential diagnosis of any child who presents with tearing.

Since PCG is a relatively rare disease, primary care doctors and general ophthalmologists may never have seen a case. Milder cases have fewer signs and symptoms and may be misdiagnosed as nasolacrimal duct obstruction; this misdiagnosis results in delayed diagnosis and irreversible damage (see Table 6-3). Physicians must be vigilant about

Figure 6-2 Typical view through a Koeppe lens of the anterior chamber angle in an infant with congenital glaucoma. *(Courtesy of Sharon Freedman, MD.)*

Table 6-3 Differential Diagnosis for Symptoms and Signs of Primary Congenital Glaucoma

Conditions associated with epiphora
Nasolacrimal duct obstruction
Corneal epithelial defect or abrasion
Conjunctivitis
Keratitis
Ocular inflammation (uveitis, trauma)

Conditions associated with corneal enlargement or apparent enlargement
X-linked megalocornea
Exophthalmos
Shallow orbits (eg, craniofacial dysostoses)
Axial myopia

Conditions associated with corneal clouding
Birth trauma with breaks in Descemet membrane
Keratitis: maternal rubella, herpes, phlyctenules
Corneal dystrophies: Congenital hereditary endothelial dystrophies, posterior polymorphous dystrophy
Corneal malformations: dermoid tumors, sclerocornea, choristomas, Peters anomaly
Keratomalacia
Metabolic disorders with associated corneal abnormalities: mucopolysaccharidoses, sphingolipidoses, cystinoses
Skin disorders affecting the cornea: congenital ichthyosis, congenital dyskeratosis

Conditions associated with optic nerve abnormalities
Optic nerve pit
Optic nerve coloboma
Optic nerve hypoplasia
Optic nerve malformation
Optic nerve atrophy
Physiologic cupping, particularly in a large optic nerve

adequately assessing and referring infants who present with the classic triad of epiphora, photophobia, and blepharospasm. Left untreated, almost all cases of PCG will progress to blindness.

Treatment of PCG typically requires surgical intervention, which is discussed later in this chapter (see the section Surgical Management). Medical therapy has limited long-term value but may be used to temporize or reduce corneal edema to improve visualization during surgery.

Walton DS, Katavounidou G. Newborn primary congenital glaucoma: 2005 update. *J Pediatr Ophthalmol Strabismus.* 2005;42(6):333–341.

Juvenile Open-Angle Glaucoma

Juvenile open-angle glaucoma (JOAG) is a form of primary open-angle glaucoma that presents with elevated IOP between the ages of 4 and 35. Since most cases of JOAG are inherited as an autosomal dominant trait, many families may be aware of their risk of developing this condition, leading to earlier screening and detection. Although the IOP is elevated, it does not usually cause corneal enlargement or Haab striae; rather, progressive myopia may continue to develop until 10 years of age. The angles appear normal. Medical therapy is usually unsuccessful, and most patients require trabeculectomy or implantation of a glaucoma drainage device. Angle procedures may be helpful in select cases.

Developmental Glaucomas of Childhood With Associated Ocular or Systemic Anomalies

The childhood glaucomas may be associated with various ocular and systemic abnormalities, as summarized in Tables 6-1 and 6-2. Following are discussions of the more common of these conditions.

Axenfeld-Rieger Syndrome

Axenfeld-Rieger (A-R) syndrome is a spectrum of disorders characterized by bilateral anomalous development of the neural crest–derived anterior segment structures. Affected structures include the anterior chamber angle, the iris, and the trabecular meshwork. Autosomal dominant inheritance occurs in most cases, but A-R syndrome can also occur sporadically. Approximately 50% of cases are associated with glaucoma that usually develops in middle or late childhood.

Although this syndrome was initially separated into Axenfeld anomaly (posterior embryotoxon with multiple adherent peripheral iris strands), Rieger anomaly (Axenfeld anomaly plus iris hypoplasia and corectopia), and Rieger syndrome (Rieger anomaly plus developmental defects of the teeth or facial bones, including maxillary hypoplasia, redundant periumbilical skin, pituitary abnormalities, or hypospadias), these disorders are now considered variations of the same clinical entity and are combined under the name *Axenfeld-Rieger syndrome.*

The typical corneal abnormality is a posterior embryotoxon (a prominent and anteriorly displaced Schwalbe line), with the remainder of the cornea being normal. Iridocorneal adhesions to the Schwalbe line range from threadlike to broad bands of iris tissue. The iris itself may range from normal to markedly atrophic with corectopia, hole formation, and ectropion uveae. The disorder is bilateral, with no sex predilection. A-R syndrome can be distinguished from other conditions that involve abnormalities of the iris, cornea, and anterior chamber, as outlined in Table 6-4.

Peters Anomaly

Peters anomaly is a developmental condition presenting with an annular corneal opacity (leukoma) in the central visual axis. The leukoma corresponds to a defect in the corneal endothelium and underlying Descemet membrane and posterior stroma. Typically, there are adhesions between iris strands, and these strands extend from the collarette to the corneal opacity. The lens may be in its normal position, with or without a cataract, or the lens may be adherent to the posterior layers of the cornea. Patients with corneolenticular adhesions have a higher likelihood of ocular abnormalities, such as microcornea and angle anomalies, and of systemic abnormalities, including those of the heart, genitourinary tract, musculoskeletal system, ear, palate, and spine.

Peters anomaly is usually sporadic, although autosomal dominant and autosomal recessive forms have been reported. The majority of cases are bilateral, and angle abnormalities cause glaucoma in approximately 50% of affected patients.

The glaucoma associated with Peters anomaly is very difficult to treat because of the iridocorneal dysgenesis. Angle surgery is performed if possible; alternative treatments include medications, trabeculectomy, glaucoma drainage devices, and cyclodestructive procedures.

Table 6-4 Differential Diagnosis for Axenfeld-Rieger Syndrome

Condition	Differentiating Features
Iridocorneal endothelial syndrome	Unilateral Middle-age onset Corneal endothelial abnormalities Progressive changes
Isolated posterior embryotoxon	Lack of glaucoma-associated or iris changes
Aniridia	Iris hypoplasia Associated corneal and macular changes
Iridoschisis	Splitting of iris layers with atrophy of anterior layer
Peters anomaly	Corneal leukoma
Ectopia lentis et pupillae	Lens subluxation, pupillary displacement, axial myopia, retinal detachment, enlarged corneal diameters, cataract, prominent iris processes in the anterior chamber angle
Oculodentodigital dysplasia	Microphthalmia, microcornea, iris abnormalities, cataracts, glaucoma

Adapted from Morrison JC, Pollack IP. *Glaucoma: Science and Practice.* New York: Thieme Medical Publishers; 2003:188.

Aniridia

Aniridia is a bilateral congenital disorder characterized by iris hypoplasia. Most patients with aniridia have only a rudimentary stump of iris; however, the iris appearance may vary greatly, with some patients having nearly complete but thin irides. Aniridia is often associated with other ocular anomalies, including small corneas, cataracts that may be present at birth or develop later in life, and optic nerve and foveal hypoplasia with resulting pendular nystagmus and reduced vision.

Approximately 50%–75% of patients with aniridia develop glaucoma. Though occasionally associated with congenital glaucoma, glaucoma in aniridia usually develops after the rudimentary iris stump rotates anteriorly to progressively cover the trabecular meshwork, resulting in synechial angle closure. This is a gradual process, and glaucoma may not occur until the second decade of life or later. Primary maldevelopment of the drainage angle may also result in elevated IOP at a younger age.

Patients with aniridia may have limbal stem cell abnormalities that eventually result in a corneal pannus, which begins in the peripheral cornea and slowly extends centrally. There may be a role for limbal stem cell transplants in these patients.

Most cases of aniridia are familial and are transmitted with an autosomal dominant inheritance pattern; however, about one-third of cases are isolated sporadic mutations. Approximately 20% of sporadic cases are associated with a large chromosomal deletion that includes the Wilms tumor 1 gene *(WT1),* a tumor suppressor gene, which results in an increased risk of Wilms tumor; relatively few cases of Wilms tumor are seen in the familial form.

There are 2 less common forms of aniridia that are associated with systemic abnormalities. WAGR (Wilms tumor, aniridia, genitourinary anomalies, and mental retardation) syndrome is an autosomal dominant form seen in 13% of patients with aniridia. *Gillespie syndrome,* an autosomal recessive form of aniridia, is associated with cerebellar ataxia and intellectual disability and occurs in 2% of those with aniridia.

Prophylactic goniosurgery in infants with a strong family history of aniridic glaucoma may be beneficial. Young children with progressive angle narrowing may also benefit from goniosurgery if the angle is not fully closed. Once the angle is closed, trabeculectomy, glaucoma drainage devices, and cyclophotocoagulation may be required for long-term control. Thus, it is important to closely follow the angle anatomy with serial gonioscopy.

Sturge-Weber Syndrome

Sturge-Weber syndrome (also known as *encephalotrigeminal angiomatosis*) is a phakomatosis with ipsilateral facial cutaneous hemangioma (nevus flammeus or port-wine stain), ipsilateral cavernous hemangioma of the choroid, and ipsilateral leptomeningeal angioma. The condition is usually unilateral but can present bilaterally in rare instances. There is no race or sex predilection, and no inheritance pattern has been established. Glaucoma occurs in 30%–70% of children with this syndrome and is more common when the nevus flammeus involves the eyelids. When seen in infants with this syndrome, the glaucoma is thought to be due to congenital anterior chamber anomalies (similar to congenital glaucoma). Elevated episcleral venous pressure may be involved in glaucoma that develops after the first decade of life. Involvement of the central nervous system may cause seizures, focal neurological defects, or intellectual disability. Trabeculectomy should be performed with caution in patients with Sturge-Weber syndrome because their risk of choroidal effusion and choroidal hemorrhage is substantially increased.

Neurofibromatosis

Neurofibromatosis (NF) is the most common phakomatosis. Two forms of NF are recognized. Neurofibromatosis 1 (NF1), also known as *von Recklinghausen disease* or *peripheral neurofibromatosis,* is the most common type, with a prevalence of 1 in 3000–5000 persons. NF1 is localized to band 11 of the long arm of chromosome 17 and is inherited in an autosomal dominant fashion in approximately 50% of cases, with the other cases being sporadic. Ectropion uveae is a common ocular finding whose presence in a neonate should prompt a workup for NF. Other ocular findings include Lisch nodules, optic nerve gliomas, eyelid neurofibromas, and glaucoma. Systemic findings include cutaneous café-au-lait spots, cutaneous neurofibromas, and axillary or inguinal freckling.

Neurofibromatosis 2, or *central neurofibromatosis,* is defined by the presence of bilateral acoustic neuromas and is not associated with glaucoma.

Secondary Glaucomas

Many of the causes of secondary glaucoma in infants and children are similar to those in adults (see Table 6-2). Trauma, inflammation, steroid use, and topiramate-induced angle closure are frequent causes of secondary glaucoma in all age groups. Lens-associated disorders causing angle-closure glaucoma include Marfan syndrome, homocystinuria, Weill-Marchesani syndrome, and microspherophakia. Posterior segment disorders such as persistent fetal vasculature (PFV); retinopathy of prematurity (ROP); and familial exudative vitreoretinopathy (FEVR); as well as tumors of the retina, iris, or ciliary body can also result in glaucoma. Retinoblastoma, juvenile xanthogranuloma, and medulloepithelioma are some of the intraocular tumors known to lead to secondary glaucoma in infants and children. Rubella and congenital cataract are important conditions that are also associated with secondary pediatric glaucoma.

Aphakic Glaucoma

Of children who undergo surgery for congenital cataract, 15%–50% or more develop glaucoma. Although most aphakic glaucoma develops within 3 years of cataract surgery, the patient is at risk of developing glaucoma for his or her entire life and therefore requires lifelong follow-up. Risk factors for the development of aphakic glaucoma include cataract surgery in the first year of life, postoperative complications, and small corneal diameter. While the underlying mechanism is unclear, it appears that congenital anomalies, surgically induced inflammation, and altered intraocular anatomy postoperatively may play a role. Removal of all residual cortex during cataract surgery may reduce the occurrence of pediatric aphakic glaucoma.

Aponte EP, Diehl N, Mohney BG. Incidence and clinical characteristics of childhood glaucoma: a population-based study. *Arch Ophthalmol.* 2010;128(4):478–482.

Beck AD. Diagnosis and management of pediatric glaucoma. *Ophthalmol Clin North Am.* 2001;14(3):501–512.

Chen TC, Bhatia LS, Halpern EF, Walton DS. Risk factors for the development of aphakic glaucoma after congenital cataract surgery. *J Pediatr Ophthalmol Strabismus.* 2006;43(5): 274–280.

Papadopoulos M, Cable N, Rahi J, Khaw PT; BIG Eye Study Investigators. The British Infantile and Childhood Glaucoma (BIG) Eye Study. *Invest Ophthalmol Vis Sci.* 2007; 48(9):4100–4106.

Tai TY, Mills MD, Beck AD, et al. Central corneal thickness and corneal diameter in patients with childhood glaucoma. *J Glaucoma.* 2006;15(6):524–528.

Yanovitch TL, Freedman SF. Pediatric glaucoma. *Focal Points: Clinical Modules for Ophthalmologists.* San Francisco: American Academy of Ophthalmology; 2012, module 3.

Evaluating the Pediatric Glaucoma Patient

Evaluating the pediatric glaucoma patient is very different from evaluating the adult patient with glaucoma. Ophthalmologists should be prepared with an orderly system for evaluating infants and young children in both the office and the operating room when required. All equipment needed for the examination should be readily available. For examinations under anesthesia (EUAs), the ophthalmologist should have a prepared checklist and dedicated storage that houses all supplies needed for the examination (Table 6-5). Efficiency in performing measurements and recording data in the operating room can minimize the time that the patient is under anesthesia.

History

The ophthalmologist should ask questions that will elicit information about the patient's signs and symptoms. When evaluating an infant, the ophthalmologist should ask the caregiver whether the baby is fussy or irritable, whether the child is not feeding well or is

Table 6-5 Supplies for Examining Children Under Anesthesia

Examination form/checklist
Topical medications
  Anesthetics
  Mydriatics (use only if not proceeding with angle surgery)
  Coupling or balanced salt solution for gonioscopy
  Glycerol
  Pilocarpine and apraclonidine if proceeding with angle surgery
Tonometer: Tono-Pen, Perkins, or pneumotonometer
Calipers
Koeppe or other angle lens
Direct ophthalmoscope
Portable slit lamp
A-scan ultrasonic test system
B-scan ultrasonic test system
Retinoscope
Indirect ophthalmoscope and lens
Pachymeter
Portable fundus camera

losing weight, and whether the baby cries when taken outside, into the sunshine. The caregiver's observations regarding corneal clouding should be sought, specifically as to whether the clouding is intermittent or constant.

For evaluation of school-aged children, the history should include any failed vision screenings, any change in academic performance, and complaints about trouble seeing the blackboard. It is helpful to know which extracurricular activities the child is involved in. A complete history should include the names of previous physicians who have been consulted; all prior ocular and systemic medical and surgical treatments; family history of congenital glaucoma and other ocular and systemic disorders; medication use (with particular attention to all forms of steroids); and allergies.

Visual Acuity

Testing of visual acuity in infants and young children is discussed in BCSC Section 6, *Pediatric Ophthalmology and Strabismus*. Refraction should be performed and may identify myopia from axial enlargement, and/or astigmatism from corneal irregularity. Decreased vision may result from end-stage glaucomatous optic nerve damage, amblyopia, corneal scarring, or other associated ocular disorders (retinal detachment, macular edema, cataract, lens dislocation).

External Examination

The ophthalmologist should look for buphthalmos and other signs and symptoms of PCG, including epiphora and blepharospasm (see Fig 6-1). The examination should be directed at features of primary and secondary glaucomas other than PCG, including chromosomal abnormalities, phakomatoses, connective tissue disorders, and Axenfeld-Rieger syndrome.

Anterior Segment Examination

As discussed previously, corneal enlargement and opacification are important signs of the onset of glaucoma in patients younger than 3 years. Corneal diameter should be measured with calipers or a ruler. The normal corneal diameter is approximately 10–10.5 mm in full-term newborns, increasing to 11–12 mm by age 1. Eyes with congenital glaucoma may have a corneal diameter greater than 12 mm in the first year of life. Corneal edema may be due to elevated IOP or Haab striae and may range from mild haze to dense opacification of the corneal stroma (see Fig 6-1). Retroillumination after pupillary dilation may help visualize Haab striae. Evaluation for other anterior segment anomalies, such as aniridia, iridocorneal adhesions, and corectopia, may provide insight into the underlying diagnosis.

Tonometry

Accurate tonometry is vital in the assessment of the childhood glaucomas. IOP may be falsely elevated in the uncooperative or struggling child. Often, the clinician can successfully measure the IOP of an infant younger than 6 months without general anesthesia or sedation by performing the measurement while the infant is feeding or immediately thereafter. For this group of patients, the Tono-Pen (Reichert Ophthalmic Instruments, Depew, NY) or pneumotonometer works best for in-office tonometry. The Perkins tonometer can also be helpful for children who are too young to cooperate for Goldmann tonometry at the slit lamp. The rebound tonometer is a newer instrument that does not require topical anesthesia and that may play a future role in office and home IOP measurements in the pediatric patient. Initial reports indicate that measurements in patients with congenital glaucoma were higher with rebound tonometry than with the Perkins tonometer.

Anesthesia is usually required for accurate IOP assessment of older infants (>6 months) and young children. However, most general anesthetic agents and sedatives can profoundly lower IOP. Exceptions include chloral hydrate, which does not affect IOP, and ketamine, which may raise IOP. In addition, in preparation for general anesthesia, infants may become dehydrated, which can also reduce IOP. Increased IOP during general anesthesia may result from endotracheal intubation, upward drift of the eyes, or possible induced laryngospasm. It is best to coordinate with the anesthesiologist before the child is brought to the operating room and arrange to take the IOP measurement immediately after induction of general anesthesia (preferably before intubation), which should ensure that the anesthesia has not yet maximally lowered the IOP.

The normal IOP in newborns is in the low teens, increasing to adult levels of 10–20 mm Hg by middle childhood. Glaucoma should be suspected if IOPs are elevated or asymmetric in a cooperative or anesthetized child.

Martinez-de-la-Casa JM, Garcia-Feijoo J, Saenz-Frances F, et al. Comparison of rebound tonometer and Goldmann handheld applanation tonometer in congenital glaucoma. *J Glaucoma.* 2009;18(1):49–52.

Central Corneal Thickness

The role of pachymetry in the diagnosis and management of pediatric glaucoma is unclear. The average central corneal thickness (CCT) is 540–560 μm in children without glaucoma. CCT is lower than average in eyes with congenital glaucoma and in children with Down syndrome; CCT is higher than average in eyes with aphakic glaucoma and aniridia. The effect of CCT on the accuracy of IOP measurements in these groups is unclear, and nomograms cannot accurately be used to "correct" IOP measurements for differences in CCT measurements.

Gonioscopy

Gonioscopy provides important information about the mechanism of the pediatric glaucoma as well as evidence of prior surgeries. An EUA is usually required for gonioscopic examination of younger children. A Koeppe lens allows direct visualization of the angle structures. In older children, indirect gonioscopy can be performed with a 4-mirror goniolens at the slit lamp.

The normal anterior chamber angle of an infant differs from the normal adult angle in several ways. The trabecular meshwork is less pigmented, the Schwalbe line less prominent, and the junction between the scleral spur and ciliary body band less distinct in normal infant angles than in normal adult angles. In PCG, the anterior chamber is deep, with a high anterior iris insertion. The angle recess is absent, and the iris root appears as a scalloped line of glistening tissue. This tissue has been referred to as the *Barkan membrane,* although it is not a true membrane but probably represents thickened and compacted trabecular meshwork (see Fig 6-2).

In JOAG, the angle usually appears normal. In aniridia, gonioscopy reveals a rudimentary iris root with progressive narrowing and synechial closure.

Optic Nerve and Fundus Evaluation

Visualization and documentation of the optic nerve are crucial to the evaluation and management of childhood glaucomas. Indirect ophthalmoscopy is usually inadequate for accurate assessment of the optic nerve. Direct ophthalmoscopy can be performed in the office or operating room. In patients with small pupils, viewing can be enhanced by performing direct ophthalmoscopy through a Koeppe lens without a dimple. In older children, slit-lamp biomicroscopy can be performed. Photographs provide the best documentation and help in the evaluation of changes over time.

The typical newborn without glaucoma has a small physiologic cup (cup–disc ratio [CDR] of <0.3) with a pink rim. In PCG, there is stretching of the optic canal and backward bowing of the lamina cribrosa, causing generalized cup enlargement. Enlarged or increasing CDR or CDR asymmetry greater than 0.2 between the 2 eyes is suggestive of glaucomatous cupping. Cupping may be reversible if the IOP is lowered; however, lowering IOP cannot reverse any existing atrophy of the optic nerve axons.

Axial Length

Serial measurements of axial length using A-scan ultrasonography can document progressive globe enlargement in patients with PCG. Axial length may stabilize or decrease with control of IOP, and this stabilization or decrease is a critical marker of successful surgical control of IOP.

Other Testing

B-scan ultrasonography should be performed whenever media opacities, particularly corneal edema, preclude fundus evaluation. Scanning laser ophthalmoscopy and optical coherence tomography can provide useful longitudinal data in older children with clear media; however, no normative data are available in children.

Treatment Overview

Surgical Management

Medications have limited long-term value in the treatment of most cases of PCG, and surgery is the preferred, definitive therapy. Goniotomy and trabeculotomy *ab externo* are the procedures of choice for the treatment of PCG. Either procedure is appropriate if the cornea is clear; trabeculotomy should be performed if the cornea is cloudy. In patients with clear corneas, angle surgery with either goniotomy or trabeculotomy yields a 70%–80% success rate. Angle surgery may also be used to treat other forms of childhood glaucoma, including glaucoma associated with aniridia, Axenfeld-Rieger syndrome, or Sturge-Weber syndrome. Trabeculectomy and glaucoma drainage device implantation should be reserved for those cases of congenital glaucoma in which goniotomy or trabeculotomy has failed or for treatment of other forms of childhood glaucoma. Cyclophotocoagulation is necessary in some intractable cases, but because of the risk of phthisis, it should be avoided if possible.

Glaucoma surgery in children poses unique difficulties. For example, in PCG, the anatomical landmarks are distorted in the buphthalmic eye, and the thin sclera presents additional difficulties during trabeculotomy and trabeculectomy. The surgeon undertaking surgery in pediatric glaucoma patients should have experience with these particular intraoperative issues and should be able to provide the necessary environment for evaluating these patients postoperatively. Since additional surgery is often required, the surgeon should develop a long-term plan in order to keep surgical options available for future use and to minimize the risk of visual compromise.

The decision to proceed with angle surgery is often made during an EUA; ideally, if glaucoma is diagnosed, angle surgery should be performed during the same anesthesia session in order to minimize the number of general anesthesia sessions the child will require. If angle surgery is anticipated, it is best not to dilate the eye during the EUA. This protects the lens during the surgical procedure.

In goniotomy, the angle is visualized with a surgical gonioscopic contact lens, a needle knife is passed across the anterior chamber, and a superficial incision is made in the uveal trabecular meshwork (Fig 6-3). A clear cornea is required in order to visualize the chamber angle.

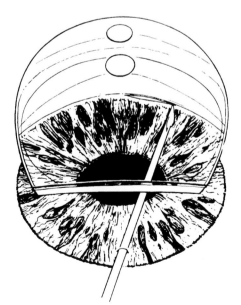

Figure 6-3 Goniotomy incision as seen through a surgical contact lens.

In trabeculotomy, the Schlemm canal is cannulated from an *ab externo* approach, and the trabecular meshwork is opened by breaking through the Schlemn canal into the anterior chamber. The procedure begins with creation of a conjunctival flap, beneath which a partial-thickness scleral flap is created, similar to trabeculectomy. Beneath the partial-thickness scleral flap, the surgeon identifies the Schlemm canal either by creating a radial incision into the sclera or by dissecting a deep scleral flap and noting the canal at the edges of this flap. Alternatively, the surgeon can identify the canal edges after unroofing the Schlemm canal with a single deep scleral flap. A fine wirelike instrument (trabeculotome) is inserted into the Schlemn canal and then rotated into the anterior chamber, tearing the trabecular meshwork (Fig 6-4). Alternatively, a 6-0 nonabsorbable polypropylene suture (Prolene) can be fed through the Schlemm canal for 360° and pulled tautly into the anterior chamber. When using either the trabeculotome or suture, the surgeon must take care to avoid creating a false passage or entering the subretinal or suprachoroidal spaces.

A recent innovation in trabeculotomy is the use of a fiber-optic microcatheter to cannulate the Schlemm canal until the cannula passes 360°. The ends of the catheter can then be grasped and pulled in opposite directions to perform a 360° trabeculotomy.

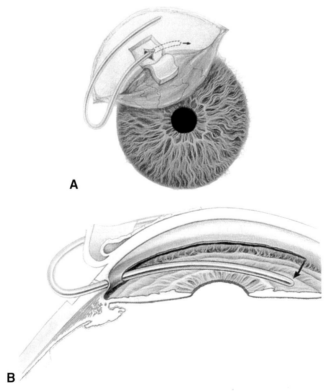

A

B

Figure 6-4 Trabeculotomy. **A,** Probe is gently passed along the Schlemm canal with little resistance for 6–10 mm. **B,** By rotating the probe internally *(arrow),* the surgeon ruptures the trabeculum, and the probe appears in the anterior chamber with minimal bleeding. *(Reproduced and modified with permission from Kolker AE, Hetherington J, eds.* Becker-Shaffer's Diagnosis and Therapy of the Glaucomas. *5th ed. St Louis: Mosby; 1983.)*

Many surgeons fill the anterior chamber with viscoelastic at the start of goniotomy and trabeculotomy in order to prevent collapse of the chamber and to tamponade bleeding intraoperatively. Thorough removal of the viscoelastic at the end of the procedure is necessary to prevent a postoperative spike in IOP.

Although the success rates of the 2 angle surgeries are similar, each procedure has its advantages and disadvantages. When the cornea is clear, goniotomy has the following advantages over trabeculotomy: there is no postoperative conjunctival scarring, the presence of which can limit future filtering surgery; the procedure is much faster, and there is less trauma to the anterior segment tissues. Trabeculotomy offers the following advantages: the approach to trabeculotomy is more familiar to surgeons experienced in adult glaucoma procedures; trabeculotomy can be performed in an opacified cornea; and it can be converted to a trabeculectomy if the Schlemm canal cannot be cannulated.

Complications associated with these procedures include hyphema, infection, lens damage, and uveitis. Descemet membrane may be stripped during trabeculotomy. General anesthesia may cause serious complications in children; to minimize the risks associated with general anesthesia, bilateral procedures are performed in some children.

Angle surgery is successful in 70%–80% of infants with PCG who present between 3 months and 1 year of age, although a second procedure may be required. A second angle procedure should be performed if the first surgery is not successful. Trabeculectomy or implantation of a glaucoma drainage device should be considered when 2 or more angle surgeries are not successful in lowering the IOP; when adjunctive medical therapy is inadequate; or in children who have forms of glaucoma other than PCG, although angle surgery is often successful in aphakic glaucoma and in new onset of glaucoma in aniridia.

If angle surgery is not successful, the next procedure should be trabeculectomy or implantation of a glaucoma drainage device. The surgeon must consider several factors when deciding between these 2 options. Trabeculectomy has a low success rate in children younger than 2 years and in aphakic eyes. Bleb scarring and failure are very prevalent without the use of antifibrotics, but there are serious risks of bleb leaks and bleb infections when these agents are used. Until the child is old enough to understand good hygiene, mitomycin C (MMC)–augmented trabeculectomy should be performed with caution in the pediatric patient to avoid the risk of blebitis and endophthalmitis.

Glaucoma drainage devices are useful for lowering IOP, and they avoid the risk of bleb-related infections. Success rates vary with different drainage devices, diagnoses, and patient age. Complications include anterior migration of the drainage device with resultant corneal damage, tube blockage, cataract, motility disturbances, bleb encapsulation with elevated IOP, and pupil distortion. The IOPs are usually higher after implantation of these devices than after trabeculectomy, and most of these children will need to continue using topical glaucoma medications. The various styles and sizes of glaucoma drainage devices can help individualize the surgery to the patient's situation.

Cyclodestruction is reserved for cases refractory to other surgical and medical treatments. Cyclodestructive procedures lower IOP by destroying regions of the ciliary body to decrease aqueous production. Cyclodestructive techniques include cyclocryotherapy, transscleral cyclophotocoagulation (CPC) with the Nd:YAG or diode laser, and endoscopic cyclophotocoagulation (ECP). When these techniques are used in pediatric patients, general anesthesia is required. One disadvantage of cyclodestructive techniques is that it can be difficult to titrate the results. Another disadvantage is that the potential complications—which include hypotony, uveitis, phthisis, and blindness—are serious. The rate of complications is lower with cyclodestructive laser procedures than with cryotherapy. The most common cyclodestructive modalities currently used are transscleral CPC with the diode laser and ECP. CPC is a noninvasive procedure performed transsclerally, whereas ECP is an intraocular procedure in which the laser energy is applied under direct visualization, thereby causing less damage to adjacent tissues. ECP is particularly useful in eyes with distorted anterior segment anatomy and in eyes with prior unsuccessful CPC or cryotherapy. CPC and ECP can be very useful for providing additional IOP lowering after glaucoma drainage device surgery.

Medical Management

Although surgical management is the mainstay of PCG care, medications are frequently required in the treatment of PCG and other childhood glaucomas. Medications can be used to lower IOP before surgery in order to reduce corneal edema and improve visualization during surgery. They may also be used after surgical procedures in order to provide additional IOP lowering. Medical therapy may be useful for forms of childhood glaucoma other than PCG, including JOAG, inflammatory, and aphakic glaucoma and other secondary glaucomas. The safety and efficacy of most FDA-approved glaucoma medications have not been studied in controlled clinical trials specifically in children, although extensive clinical experience guides most clinicians. A full discussion of glaucoma medications can be found in Chapter 7.

β-Adrenergic antagonists

β-Adrenergic antagonists, or β-blockers, decrease aqueous production in the ciliary body and are useful for controlling IOP in children. Topical β-adrenergic antagonists are considered first-line therapy for glaucoma in children. These agents must be used with caution, however, as they have considerable systemic absorption and can cause bronchospasm, bradycardia, and hypotension in susceptible children. β-Blockers should therefore be avoided in children with asthma or significant cardiac disease. To decrease the risk of bronchospasm, the clinician may consider administering the cardioselective β-blocker betaxolol. The risk of adverse effects can also be diminished by occluding the nasolacrimal drainage system for 3 minutes after administration of the medication and by prescribing timolol 0.25% or levobunolol 0.25% instead of the more commonly used 0.5%, particularly in younger children. The clinician should teach parents how to occlude the nasolacrimal drainage system. Patients with lighter irides may respond as well to timolol 0.25% or levobunolol 0.25% as they do to 0.5%.

Carbonic anhydrase inhibitors

Carbonic anhydrase inhibitors (CAIs) decrease IOP by reducing aqueous production. Topical therapy with dorzolamide or brinzolamide has a minimal risk of systemic side effects and is an excellent second-line therapy after the topical β-adrenergic antagonists. There is some concern about the use of topical dorzolamide or brinzolamide in eyes with compromised corneas or after corneal transplantation, although these contraindications are not absolute. Systemic CAIs (acetazolamide and methazolamide) provide slightly more IOP lowering than do the topical preparations, but they have numerous systemic side effects. The pediatric dosage of acetazolamide is 10–20 mg/kg/day. CAIs should not be used in patients with known serious sulfa allergies. Adverse effects include anorexia, diarrhea, weight loss, tingling of the perioral areas and fingers, hypokalemia, and metabolic acidosis; children using diuretics are particularly at risk of experiencing these effects. Because of the risk of these adverse effects and of rare but life-threatening reactions such as Stevens-Johnson syndrome and aplastic anemia, systemic CAIs are reserved for patients at high risk of vision loss due to glaucoma.

α-Adrenergic agonists

α-Adrenergic agonists lower IOP by both diminishing aqueous production and increasing uveoscleral outflow. The $α_2$-adrenergic agonist brimonidine crosses the blood–brain barrier and therefore has significant effects on the central nervous system. Infants and young children are particularly susceptible to brimonidine's adverse effects, including apnea, hypotension, bradycardia, hypotonia, hypothermia, and somnolence. $α_2$-Adrenergic agonists are contraindicated in children younger than 3 years. There is some debate about the age at which children can safely use brimonidine. In general, this agent should be used with caution in children between the ages of 3 and 10. The lowest dose should be used and punctal occlusion employed to minimize systemic absorption.

The α-agonist apraclonidine is better tolerated systemically in children, but the risk of follicular conjunctivitis increases with long-term use. Apraclonidine acts as a vasoconstrictor and can be used to minimize bleeding during intraocular surgery.

Prostaglandin analogues

Prostaglandin analogues lower IOP by increasing uveoscleral outflow. They have minimal systemic side effects in children and have been shown to effectively lower IOP in JOAG. They can exacerbate uveitis in postoperative glaucoma patients and should be avoided with uncontrolled uveitis. Their once-daily dosing is helpful for minimizing the stress involved in administering eyedrops to children. Adverse effects include conjunctival hyperemia, hypertrichiasis, periocular pigmentation (reversible), and darkening of irides (permanent) except in blue-eyed patients.

Cholinergic agonists

Cholinergic agonists (miotics) lower IOP by increasing aqueous outflow through the trabecular meshwork. With the newer medications that are available, these agents are rarely used on a long-term basis, but they have a role intraoperatively by inducing miosis, which facilitates angle surgery.

Prognosis and Follow-Up

The long-term prognosis for pediatric glaucoma patients has greatly improved with the development of effective surgical techniques. This is particularly true for PCG patients who are asymptomatic at birth and who present with onset of symptoms between 3 and 12 months of age; IOP can be controlled with angle surgery in approximately 80% of these children. When symptoms are present at birth or when the disease is diagnosed after 12 months of age, the outlook for surgical control of IOP is more guarded.

Pediatric patients whose IOP is controlled by surgery may still experience morbidities related to the previous IOP elevation. These can cause serious lifelong visual compromise and include amblyopia, corneal scarring, strabismus, anisometropia, cataract, lens subluxation, susceptibility to trauma (as occurs in an eye with a thinned sclera), and recurrent glaucoma in the affected or unaffected eye. Clinicians should address these conditions and be prepared to coordinate care with other specialists as needed.

Amblyopia is a common cause of visual compromise, particularly in patients with unilateral glaucoma, corneal opacification, and/or anisometropia. The clinician should aggressively treat amblyopia, addressing conditions contributing to its development, such as refractive error, strabismus, cataract, and corneal clouding. Elevated IOP can lead to buphthalmos in patients with PCG and to progressive myopia and anisometropia in patients with juvenile glaucoma. Haab striae and corneal scarring may cause astigmatism. Refractive errors should be corrected with spectacles, and use of protective eyewear should be encouraged.

Strabismus may result from glaucoma drainage devices or amblyopia. When performing surgery to correct strabismus, the surgeon should try to minimize conjunctival scarring in anticipation of future glaucoma surgeries and should be cognizant of the sites of prior trabeculectomies and glaucoma drainage device implants.

All cases of childhood glaucoma require lifelong follow-up to monitor IOP and to observe for any complications of prior surgeries and any secondary vision-threatening issues. As relapses of glaucoma may occur even years later, care should be coordinated between glaucoma specialists and pediatric specialists. Educating parents about the need for lifelong care of the child with glaucoma and involving these children in their own care enhance the long-term management of this challenging disease.

Barkan O. Goniotomy for the relief of congenital glaucoma. *Br J Ophthalmol.* 1948;32(9): 701–728.

Beck AD, Lynch MG. 360-degree trabeculotomy for primary congenital glaucoma. *Arch Ophthalmol.* 1995;113(9):1200–1202.

Bothun ED, Guo Y, Christiansen SP, et al. Outcome of angle surgery in children with aphakic glaucoma. *J AAPOS.* 2010;14(3):235–239. Epub 2010 Mar 11.

Coppens G, Stalmans I, Zeyen T, Casteels I. The safety and efficacy of glaucoma medications in the pediatric population. *J Pediatr Ophthalmol Strabismus.* 2009;46(1):12–18.

Moore W, Nischal KK. Pharmacologic management of glaucoma in childhood. *Paediatr Drugs.* 2007;9(2):71–79.

Neely DE, Plager DA. Endocyclophotocoagulation for management of difficult pediatric glaucomas. *J AAPOS.* 2001;5(4):221–229.

O'Malley Schotthoefer E, Yanovitch TL, Freedman SF. Aqueous drainage device surgery in refractory pediatric glaucomas: I. Long-term outcomes. *J AAPOS.* 2008;12(1):33–39.

O'Malley Schotthoefer E, Yanovitch TL, Freedman SF. Aqueous drainage device surgery in refractory pediatric glaucoma: II. Ocular motility consequences. *J AAPOS.* 2008;12(1): 40–45.

Sarkisian SR Jr. An illuminated microcatheter for 360-degree trabeculectomy in congenital glaucoma: a retrospective case series. *J AAPOS.* 2010;14(5):412–416.

Wright TM, Freedman SF. Exposure to topical apraclonidine in children with glaucoma. *J Glaucoma.* 2009;18(5):395–398.

CHAPTER 7

Medical Management of Glaucoma

In the management of patients with glaucoma, the ophthalmologist must decide whom, when, and how to treat. This chapter deals largely with the last of these decisions and specifically relates to the medical management of primary open-angle glaucoma (POAG). The major clinical trials on open-angle glaucoma have provided an evidence base for the use of medical treatment to lower intraocular pressure (IOP) in glaucoma. These trials are summarized in Chapter 4.

Risk calculators such as the Scoring Tool for Assessing Risk (STAR) and one based on data pooled from the Ocular Hypertension Treatment Study and the European Glaucoma Prevention Study, STAR II, have been used clinically in assessing the risk of glaucoma development in an individual patient with untreated ocular hypertension. The information obtained from these tools can help guide the clinician in deciding which ocular hypertensive patients to treat. These risk calculators are now available for mobile use through smartphone applications.

In patients with established glaucoma, 3 principal factors guide the decision of whether to treat and how aggressively to treat: the life expectancy of the patient, the stage of disease at the time of presentation, and the rate of disease progression. In addition, other factors are taken into consideration, such as the degree of IOP elevation, the presence or absence of optic disc hemorrhages, and the family history.

The stage of disease is important, as a patient who is converting from ocular hypertension to mild glaucoma has a lower risk of significant vision loss compared with a patient who has advanced glaucoma (eg, visual field loss threatening central fixation) at the time of presentation, irrespective of the rate of progression. Likewise, a young patient presenting with glaucoma has a higher risk of vision loss in the long term, because of his or her longer life expectancy, compared with an older patient presenting with the same stage of disease and the same IOP level. Also, a patient demonstrated to have a faster rate of visual field progression has a higher risk of vision loss than one with a slow rate of visual field progression (see Chapter 3 for discussion of visual fields).

The goal of currently available glaucoma therapy is to preserve visual function by lowering IOP to a level that is likely to prevent further optic nerve damage. The treatment regimen chosen should achieve this goal with the lowest risk, fewest adverse effects, and the least amount of disruption to the patient's life, taking into account the cost of treatment. Although the goal of treatment is to prevent vision loss, current treatments are aimed at lowering IOP and, in the short term, the efficacy of treatment is gauged according to the IOP level. The concept of *target pressure* was introduced because some patients require lower IOP levels than do others to stabilize their glaucoma. In general, the patients who require lower target pressures are those with more advanced optic neuropathy, although patients who develop optic nerve damage in the presence of IOP levels that are never elevated also require low target levels.

Despite the significance of the concept of target pressure, it is important not to set a rigid target pressure for the individual patient, as there is no evidence base for doing so. Ideally, the target pressure level should be a broad range (eg, <21 mm Hg, <18 mm Hg, or <15 mm Hg) with an upper IOP limit that is unlikely to lead to further optic nerve damage in a given patient. The range should be individualized for the patient, based on the following: IOP level at which damage is thought to have occurred, severity of the damage, life expectancy of the patient, and associated risk factors.

The more advanced the disease on initial presentation, the lower the target pressure required for preventing further progression in the average patient. Once the optic nerve is damaged, it can incur additional damage more easily. If severe vision loss is already present, then further damage is likely to have a disproportionately greater impact on the patient. An initial IOP reduction of 20% from baseline is a suggested minimum. However, there is no guarantee that reduction of IOP to the target pressure range will prevent disease progression. If further progression does occur, the target pressure range may require revision.

Once the target pressure range has been determined, the clinician must decide how to achieve this goal, medically or surgically. Regardless of which is chosen, the anticipated benefits of any therapeutic regimen should justify the risks, and regimens associated with substantial adverse effects should be reserved for patients with a high probability of progressive vision loss. For example, it may be illogical to expose a patient to the adverse effects of multiple topical medications or oral carbonic anhydrase inhibitors (CAIs) unless significant damage to the visual field and optic nerve has occurred or the IOP is very high.

The interrelationship between medical and surgical therapy is complex, with the choice of treatment varying according to the type of glaucoma. Further, it is not always clear which modality is better. The treatment of angle-closure glaucoma with pupillary block and of primary congenital glaucoma is primarily surgical, either laser or incisional, with medical therapy playing a secondary role. Initial treatment of POAG has commonly been medical, with surgery undertaken only if medical treatment fails or is not well tolerated. The treatment of secondary glaucoma is similar to that of primary glaucoma, with some exceptions, and the underlying cause of the glaucoma should be addressed if possible. However, the Glaucoma Laser Trial (GLT) found that, as initial glaucoma therapy, argon laser trabeculoplasty was at least as effective as medications. The Collaborative Initial Glaucoma Treatment Study (CIGTS) reported that medical therapy was essentially equally as effective as surgical therapy in preventing POAG progression. In fact, with medical therapy, the rate of progression at 5 years was substantially less than had been anticipated. This has been attributed to the definition of *progression* that was used in the study and to the aggressive IOP lowering obtained in both groups. Surgical therapy is discussed in detail in Chapter 8.

When a patient starts a medication, some clinicians favor using a unilateral treatment trial in order to assess the medication's efficacy. The continued efficacy of a therapeutic regimen should be reevaluated periodically. To assess a patient's existing regimen, a reverse therapeutic trial can be performed, which entails stopping a medication in 1 eye, and then comparing the effect in the treated eye with that in the untreated eye.

The AGIS Investigators. The Advanced Glaucoma Intervention Study (AGIS): 4. Comparison of treatment outcomes within race: seven-year results. *Ophthalmology.* 1998;105(7):1146–1164.

The AGIS Investigators. The Advanced Glaucoma Intervention Study (AGIS): 7. The relationship between control of intraocular pressure and visual field deterioration. *Am J Ophthalmol.* 2000;130(4):429–440.

Kass MA, Heuer DK, Higginbotham EJ, et al. The Ocular Hypertension Treatment Study: a randomized trial determines that topical ocular hypotensive medication delays or prevents the onset of primary open-angle glaucoma. *Arch Ophthalmol.* 2002;120(6):701–713.

Leske MC, Heijl A, Hussein M, et al. Factors for glaucoma progression and the effect of treatment: the Early Manifest Glaucoma Trial. *Arch Ophthalmol.* 2003;121(1):48–56.

Lichter PR, Musch DC, Gillespie BW, et al. Interim clinical outcomes in the Collaborative Initial Glaucoma Treatment Study comparing initial treatment randomized to medications or surgery. *Ophthalmology.* 2001;108(11):1943–1953.

Medeiros FA, Weinreb RN, Sample PA, et al. Validation of a predictive model to estimate the risk of conversion from ocular hypertension to glaucoma. *Arch Ophthalmol.* 2005;123(10):1351–1360.

Ocular Hypertension Treatment Study Group; European Glaucoma Prevention Study Group; Gordon MO, et al. Validated prediction model for the development of primary open-angle glaucoma in individuals with ocular hypertension. *Ophthalmology.* 2007;114(1):10–19.

Medical Agents

Ocular hypotensive agents are divided into several groups based on chemical structure and pharmacologic action. The groups of agents in common clinical use include

- prostaglandin analogues
- β-adrenergic antagonists (nonselective and selective)
- adrenergic agonists
- carbonic anhydrase inhibitors (oral and topical)
- parasympathomimetic (miotic) agents, including cholinergic and anticholinesterase agents
- combination medications
- hyperosmotic agents

The actions and adverse effects of the various glaucoma medications, along with other information, are listed in Table 7-1. See also BCSC Section 2, *Fundamentals and Principles of Ophthalmology,* for additional discussion of the mechanisms of action of these medications.

Netland PA, ed. *Glaucoma Medical Therapy: Principles and Management.* 2nd ed. Ophthalmology Monograph 13. New York: Oxford University Press; 2007.

Table 7-1 Glaucoma Medications

Class/Compound	Concentration	Dosing	Method of Action	IOP Decrease	Side Effects Ocular	Side Effects Systemic	Comments, Including Time to Peak Effect and Washout
Prostaglandin analogues							
Latanoprost	.005%	Once daily (nighttime)	Not known, but presumably by increasing uveoscleral outflow	25%–32%	Increased pigmentation of iris and lashes, hypertrichosis, trichiasis, distichiasis, hair growth around the eyes, blurred vision, keratitis, anterior uveitis, conjunctival hyperemia, exacerbation of herpes keratitis, CME	Flulike symptoms, joint/muscle pain, headache	±IOP-lowering effect with miotic Peak: 10–14 hours Washout: 4–6 weeks Maximum IOP-lowering effect may take up to 6 weeks to occur
Travoprost	.004%	Once daily (nighttime)	Same as above	25%–32%	Same as above	Same as above	Same as above
Bimatoprost	0.03, 0.01%	Once daily (nighttime)	Increase uveoscleral and trabecular outflow	27%–33%	Same as above	Same as above	Same as above
Tafluprost	0.0015%	Once daily (nighttime)	Increases uveoscleral outflow	Equivalent to latanoprost	Same as above	Same as above	Peak: unknown Washout: unknown
β-Adrenergic antagonists (β-blockers)							
Nonselective							
Timolol maleate	0.25% and 0.50% solution or gel Also 0.1% gel	Solutions: 1–2 times daily Gels: once daily	Decrease aqueous production	20%–30%	Blurring, irritation, corneal anesthesia, punctate keratitis, allergy; possible aggravation of myasthenia gravis	Bradycardia, heart block, bronchospasm, lowered blood pressure, decreased libido, CNS depression, mood swings, reduced exercise tolerance	May be less effective if patient taking systemic β-blockers; short-term escape, long-term drift; diabetic patients may experience reduced glucose tolerance and masking of hypoglycemic signs/symptoms Peak: 2–3 hours Washout: 1 month
Timolol hemihydrate	0.5%	As above	Same as above	20%–30%	Same as above	Same as above	Less expensive Peak: 2–6 hours
Levobunolol	0.25, 0.5%	As above	Same as above	20%–30%	Same as above	Same as above	Report of iritis
Metipranolol	0.3%	2 times daily	Same as above	20%–30%	Same as above	Same as above	Peak: 2 hours
Carteolol hydrochloride	1.0%	1–2 times daily				Intrinsic sympathomimetic	May have less effect on nocturnal pulse, blood pressure Peak: 4 hours Washout: 1 month

Class/Compound	Concentration	Dosing	Method of Action	IOP Decrease	Ocular	Systemic	Comments, Including Time to Peak Effect and Washout
Selective Betaxolol	0.25%	2 times daily	Same as above	15%–20%	Same as above	Fewer pulmonary complications	Peak: 2–3 hours Washout: 1 month
α₂-Adrenergic agonists							
Selective Apraclonidine hydrochloride	0.5, 1.0%	2–3 times daily	Decrease aqueous production, decrease episcleral venous pressure	20%–30%	Irritation, ischemia, allergy, eyelid retraction, conjunctival blanching, follicular conjunctivitis, puritis, dermatitis, ocular ache, photopsia, miosis	Hypotension, vasovagal attack, dry mouth and nose, fatigue	Useful in pre- or postlaser or cataract surgery Tachyphylaxis may limit long-term use. Peak: <1–2 hours Washout: 7–14 days
Brimonidine tartrate 0.2%	0.2%	2–3 times daily	Decreases aqueous production, increases uveoscleral outflow	20%–30%	Blurring, foreign-body sensation, eyelid edema, dryness, less ocular sensitivity/allergy than with apraclonidine	Headache, fatigue, hypotension, insomnia, depression, syncope, dizziness, anxiety, dry mouth	Primary adrenergic agent in current use; highly selective for α₂-receptor Brimonidine should not be used in infants and young children. Peak: 2 hours Washout: 7–14 days
Brimonidine tartrate in Purite 0.1%	0.1%	2–3 times daily	Same as above	Same as above	Same as above, except less allergy than with brimonidine 0.2%	Same as above, except less fatigue and depression than with brimonidine 0.2%	Same as above
Carbonic anhydrase inhibitors							
Oral Acetazolamide	250 mg 500 mg	2–4 times daily 2 times daily	Decrease aqueous production	15%–20%	None	Poor tolerance of carbonated beverages, acidosis, depression, malaise, hirsutism, flatulence, paresthesias, numbness, lethargy, blood dyscrasias, diarrhea, weight loss, renal stones, loss of libido, impotence, bone marrow depression, hypokalemia, cramps, anorexia, altered taste, increased serum urate, enuresis	May cause allergic reaction in persons with sulfa allergy Use with caution in patients susceptible to ketoacidosis or hepatic insufficiency

(Continued)

Table 7-1 *(continued)*

Class/Compound	Concentration	Dosing	Method of Action	IOP Decrease	Ocular	Systemic	Comments, Including Time to Peak Effect and Washout
					Side Effects		
Acetazolamide (parenteral)	500 mg 5–10 mg/kg	Usually every 6–8 hrs	Same as above	Same as above	Same as above	Same as above	Same as above
Methazolamide	25, 50, 100 mg	2–3 times daily	Same as above	Same as above	Same as above	Same as above	Same as above
Topical							
Dorzolamide	2%	2–3 times daily	Same as above	15%–20%	Induced myopia, blurred vision, stinging, keratitis, conjunctivitis, dermatitis	Less likely to induce systemic effects of CAI, but may occur; bitter taste	Peak: 2–3 hours Washout: 48 hours
Brinzolamide	1%	2–3 times daily	Same as above	Same as above	Same as above, except less stinging when compared to dorzolamide	Same as above	Same as above
Parasympathomimetic agents (miotics)							
Cholinergic agonists (direct acting)							
Pilocarpine HCl	0.5, 1.0, 2.0, 3.0, 4.0, 6.0%	2–4 times daily	Increase trabecular outflow	15%–25%	Posterior synechiae, keratitis, miosis, brow ache, cataract growth, angle-closure potential, myopia, retinal tear/detachment, dermatitis, change in retinal sensitivity, color vision changes, epiphora	Increased salivation, increased secretion (gastric), abdominal cramps	Exacerbation of cataract effect; more effective in lighter irides Peak: 1½–2 hours Washout: 48 hours
Pilocarpine gel	4.0%	Once daily (nighttime)	Increases trabecular outflow	15%–25%	Same as above	Same as above	Same as above Peak: 2–3 hours Washout: 48 hours
Anticholinesterase agent (indirect acting)							
Echothiophate iodide (Phospholine Iodide)	0.125%	1–2 times daily	Same as above	15%–25%	Intense miosis, iris pigment cyst, myopia, cataract, retinal detachment, angle closure, punctal stenosis, pseudopemphigoid, epiphora	Same as pilocarpine; more gastrointestinal difficulties	Increased inflammation with ocular surgery; may be helpful in aphakia, anesthesia risks (prolonged recovery); useful in eyelid-lash lice, cataract surgery postoperatively

					Side Effects		
Class/Compound	Concentration	Dosing	Method of Action	IOP Decrease	Ocular	Systemic	Comments, Including Time to Peak Effect and Washout
Fixed combinations							
Timolol/ Brinzolamide	0.5%/1%	2 times daily	Reduces aqueous secretion	25%–30%	Same as those of nonselective β-adrenergic antagonist, topical CAI	Same as those of nonselective β-adrenergic antagonist, topical CAI	
Timolol/Dorzolamide	0.5%/2%	2 times daily	Decreases aqueous production	25%–30%	Same as those of nonselective β-blocker, topical CAI	Same as those of nonselective β-blocker, topical CAI	Peak: 2–3 hours Washout: 1 month
Timolol/Latanoprost	0.5%/0.005%	Once daily (nighttime)	Same as nonselective β-blocker and latanoprost	Greater than monotherapy with each individually	Same as those of nonselective β-blocker and latanoprost	Same as those of nonselective β-blocker and latanoprost	Not currently available in US
Timolol/Travoprost	0.5%/0.004%	Once daily (nighttime)	Same as nonselective β-blocker and travoprost	Same as above	Same as those of nonselective β-blocker and travoprost	Same as nonselective β-blocker and travoprost	Not currently available in US
Timolol/Bimatoprost	0.5%/0.03%	Once daily (nighttime)	Same as nonselective β-blocker and bimatoprost	Same as above	Same as those of nonselective β-blocker and bimatoprost	Same as nonselective β-blocker and bimatoprost	Not currently available in US
Timolol/Brimonidine tartrate	0.5%/0.2%	2 times daily	Same as nonselective β-blocker and α-agonist	Same as above	Same as those of nonselective β-blocker and α-agonist	Same as those of nonselective β-blocker and α-agonist	
Hyperosmotic agents							
Mannitol (parenteral)	20%	0.5–2.0 g/kg body weight	Creates osmotic gradient; dehydrates vitreous		IOP rebound, increased aqueous flare	Urinary retention, headache, congestive heart failure, expansion of blood volume, diabetic complications, nausea, vomiting, diarrhea, electrolyte disturbance, renal failure, mental confusion, backache, myocardial infarction	Contraindicated in patients in renal failure or on dialysis; caution in heart failure; useful in acute increased IOP
Glycerol (oral)	50%	1–1.5 g/kg	Same as above		Similar to above	Similar to above; can cause problems in diabetic patients	Similar to above; may precipitate diabetic ketoacidosis

Prostaglandin Analogues

Currently, 4 prostaglandin analogues are approved for clinical use: latanoprost, travoprost, bimatoprost, and tafluprost.

Prostaglandin analogues act via pressure-dependent and pressure-independent mechanisms. The exact mechanism by which these drugs increase outflow is not known; however, it has been shown that latanoprost usage is associated with increased spaces between the muscle fascicles within the ciliary body, presumably increasing uveoscleral outflow.

Latanoprost and travoprost are prodrugs that penetrate the cornea and become biologically active after being hydrolyzed by corneal esterase. Both latanoprost and travoprost reduce IOP by 25%–32%. Bimatoprost lowers IOP by 27%–33%; fewer data are available for tafluprost, which appears to be similar in efficacy to latanoprost. All 4 of these drugs are used once daily, usually at night, and are less effective when used twice daily. Because some patients may respond better to one agent in this class than to another, switching drugs after a trial of 4–6 weeks may prove helpful.

An ocular side effect unique to this class of drugs is darkening of the iris and periocular skin as a result of an increased number of melanosomes within the melanocytes. Increased iris pigmentation is permanent, and the frequency of this effect depends on eye color at baseline. Most published data relate to latanoprost and suggest a risk of increased iris pigmentation of up to 33% after 5 years. In particular, up to 79% of persons with green-brown irides and up to 85% of persons with hazel (yellow-brown) irides may be affected, compared to 8% of persons with blue irides. There are no data to suggest that this color change confers any other risk to the patient. Other side effects reported in association with the use of a topical prostaglandin analogue include conjunctival hyperemia, hypertrichosis (Fig 7-1), trichiasis, distichiasis, hyperpigmentation of the eyelid skin, and hair growth around the eyes. These effects appear to be reversible with drug discontinuation. Exacerbation of underlying herpes keratitis and cystoid macular edema, especially in aphakic or uveitic eyes, has been reported. Uveitis appears to occur as an idiosyncratic reaction in approximately 1% of patients. Studies to date have demonstrated that the incidence of these side effects varies among these 4 agents. Hyperemia is more common with bimatoprost and travoprost. Because bimatoprost, latanoprost, and travoprost reach peak effect 10–14 hours after administration, bedtime application is recommended to maximize efficacy and decrease patient symptoms related to vascular dilation.

Alm A, Schoenfelder J, McDermott J. A 5-year, multicenter, open-label, safety study of adjunctive latanoprost therapy for glaucoma. *Arch Ophthalmol.* 2004;122(7):957–965.

Camras CB, Alm A, Watson P, Stjernschantz J. Latanoprost, a prostaglandin analog, for glaucoma therapy: efficacy and safety after 1 year of treatment in 198 patients. Latanoprost Study Group. *Ophthalmology.* 1996;103(11):1916–1924.

Higginbotham EJ, Schuman JS, Goldberg I, et al. One-year, randomized study comparing bimatoprost and timolol in glaucoma and ocular hypertension. *Arch Ophthalmol.* 2002;120(10):1286–1293.

Netland PA, Landry T, Sullivan EK, et al. Travoprost compared with latanoprost and timolol in patients with open-angle glaucoma or ocular hypertension. *Am J Ophthalmol.* 2001;132(4):472–484.

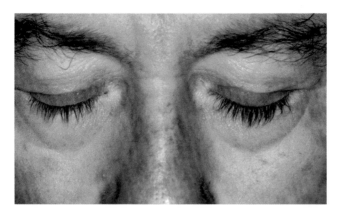

Figure 7-1 Hypertrichosis following latanoprost use (left eye). *(Courtesy of F. Jane Durcan, MD.)*

β-Adrenergic Antagonists

Topical β-adrenergic antagonists lower IOP by inhibiting cyclic adenosine monophosphate (cAMP) production in ciliary epithelium, thereby reducing aqueous humor secretion 20%–50% (2.5 μL/min to 1.9 μL/min), with a corresponding IOP reduction of 20%–30%. The effect of β-adrenergic antagonists, or β-blockers, on aqueous production occurs within 1 hour of instillation and can be present for up to 4 weeks after discontinuation. Evidence suggests that β-blockers decrease aqueous production during the day but have much less effect during sleep. As systemic absorption occurs, an IOP-lowering effect in the untreated contralateral eye can also be observed. Most β-blockers are approved for twice-daily therapy. In many cases, it is possible to use the nonselective agents once daily. Generally, dosing first thing in the morning is preferred in order to effectively blunt an early-morning pressure rise while minimizing the risk of systemic hypotension during sleep, a time when the effect of β-blockers is minimal. Many nonselective β-blockers are available in more than 1 concentration. In many patients, timolol 0.25% is as effective as timolol 0.5% in lowering IOP.

β-Blockers are additive in combination with miotics, adrenergic agonists, CAIs (both topical and systemic), and prostaglandin analogues. Combinations of β-blockers and nonselective adrenergic agonists are only slightly additive, whereas more effect can be expected when β-blockers are combined with an α_2-adrenergic agonist. When timolol is added to latanoprost, an additional IOP reduction of between 13% and 37% has been reported. Fixed combinations of a prostaglandin analogue and timolol, which are given once daily, are currently available in a number of countries, though not in the United States. However, these fixed combinations are slightly less effective than their individual components given separately.

Approximately 10%–20% of the patients treated with topical β-blockers fail to respond with significantly lower IOP. Patients already taking a systemic β-blocker may experience little additional IOP lowering from adding a topical β-blocker. Extended use of β-blockers may reduce their effectiveness, because the response of β-adrenergic receptors is affected by constant exposure to an agonist (long-term drift, tachyphylaxis). Similarly, receptor saturation (drug-induced up-regulation of β-adrenergic receptors) may occur within a few weeks, with loss of effectiveness (short-term escape).

Six topical β-adrenergic antagonists are approved for use for the treatment of glaucoma in the United States: betaxolol, carteolol, levobunolol, metipranolol, timolol maleate, and timolol hemihydrate. All except betaxolol are nonselective β_1 and β_2 antagonists. The activity of β_1 is largely cardiac and that of β_2, largely pulmonary. Because betaxolol is a selective β_1 antagonist, it is safer than the nonselective β-blockers for use in patients with pulmonary, central nervous system (CNS), or other systemic conditions. However, β-blocker–related adverse effects can still occur. In addition, betaxolol is less effective than the nonselective β-adrenergic antagonists.

The ocular and systemic adverse effects of β-adrenergic antagonists are listed in Table 7-1. They include bronchospasm, bradycardia, increased heart block, lowered blood pressure, reduced exercise tolerance, and CNS depression. Patients with diabetes may experience reduced glucose tolerance and masking of hypoglycemic signs and symptoms. Abrupt withdrawal of ocular β-blockers can exacerbate symptoms of hyperthyroidism. Although betaxolol is somewhat less effective than the other β-adrenergic antagonists in lowering IOP, it may be a safer alternative for some patients.

Before a β-blocker is prescribed, it is important to ask whether the patient has had asthma, as β-blockers may induce severe bronchospasm in susceptible patients. The pulse should be measured and β-blockers withheld if the pulse rate is slow or if more than first-degree heart block is present. Myasthenia gravis may also be aggravated by these drugs. The use of a gel vehicle decreases the plasma concentration of β-blockers compared to the equivalent solution.

Other adverse effects of β-blockers include lethargy, mood changes, depression, altered mentation, light-headedness, syncope, visual disturbance, corneal anesthesia, punctate keratitis, allergy, impotence, reduced libido, and alteration of serum lipids. In children, β-blockers should be used with caution, because of the relatively high systemic levels achieved. Although topical β-blockers have been shown to decrease high-density lipoprotein and increase cholesterol levels, there is no evidence that this influences cardiovascular risk. However, this effect on the plasma lipid profile should be considered, particularly in those patients taking medications that affect plasma lipids. Carteolol may have less effect on serum lipid levels than timolol.

Higginbotham EJ, Diestelhorst M, Pfeiffer N, Rouland JF, Alm A. The efficacy and safety of unfixed and fixed combinations of latanoprost and other antiglaucoma medications. *Surv Ophthalmol.* 2002;47(Suppl 1):S133–S140.

Novack GD. Ophthalmic beta blockers since timolol. *Surv Ophthalmol.* 1987;31(5):307–327.

Van Buskirk EM. Adverse reactions from timolol administration. *Ophthalmology.* 1980;87(5): 447–450.

Adrenergic Agonists

The nonselective adrenergic agonists epinephrine (adrenaline) and dipivefrin (a prodrug of epinephrine) increase conventional trabecular and uveoscleral outflow. Both have largely been superseded by other classes of drugs and are no longer used in the management of

POAG in most countries. Nonselective adrenergic agonists are generally not used concomitantly with β-blockers because of lack of additional efficacy.

α_2-Adrenergic agonists

These have replaced the use of nonselective adrenergic agents in clinical practice in the treatment of POAG. The ocular effects of α_1-adrenergic agonists include vasoconstriction, pupillary dilation, and eyelid retraction, whereas the ocular effects of α_2-adrenergic agonists are primarily IOP reduction and possibly neuroprotection. Apraclonidine and brimonidine are relatively selective α_2-agonists that have been developed for glaucoma therapy. Brimonidine is more selective for the α_2-receptor than is apraclonidine.

Apraclonidine hydrochloride (para-aminoclonidine) is an α_2-adrenergic agonist and clonidine derivative that prevents the release of norepinephrine at nerve terminals. It decreases aqueous production as well as episcleral venous pressure and improves trabecular outflow. However, its true ocular hypotensive mechanism is not fully understood. When administered preoperatively and postoperatively, apraclonidine is effective in diminishing the acute rise in IOP that follows argon laser iridotomy, argon laser trabeculoplasty, Nd:YAG laser capsulotomy, and cataract extraction. This agent may be effective for short-term lowering of IOP, but the development of topical sensitivity and tachyphylaxis in patients often limits long-term use.

Tachyphylaxis occurs less often with brimonidine than with apraclonidine. The incidence of ocular allergic reaction (eg, follicular conjunctivitis and contact blepharodermatitis; Fig 7-2) is also lower with brimonidine: up to 40% for apraclonidine, less than 15% for brimonidine tartrate 0.2% preserved with benzalkonium chloride, and less than 10% for brimonidine tartrate 0.1% preserved with Purite. Despite the relatively low incidence of true allergy with brimonidine, the incidence of long-term intolerance due to local adverse effects is high (>20%). Adverse effects usually take the form of local blepharoconjunctivitis and, in more severe cases, ectropion and granulomatous anterior uveitis, both of which are often misdiagnosed. Brimonidine 0.1% preserved with Purite has been shown to be as efficacious as brimonidine 0.2% preserved with benzalkonium chloride and to have a lower incidence of all side effects. It contains a lower concentration of brimonidine tartrate at a neutral pH. Cross-sensitivity to brimonidine in patients with known hypersensitivity to apraclonidine is minimal. Systemic adverse effects include dry

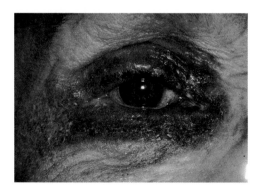

Figure 7-2 Contact blepharodermatitis following α-adrenergic agonist use. *(Courtesy of F. Jane Durcan, MD.)*

mouth and lethargy. Brimonidine should not be used in infants and young children because of the risk of respiratory arrest, as well as somnolence, hypotension, seizures, and serious derangements of neurotransmitters in the CNS, presumably due to increased CNS penetration of the drug. Brimonidine lowers IOP by decreasing aqueous production and increasing uveoscleral outflow. As with β-blockers, a peripheral mechanism may account for part of the IOP reduction with brimonidine 0.2%, as a 1-week, single-eye treatment trial caused a statistically significant reduction of 1.2 mm Hg in the fellow eye.

Brimonidine's peak IOP reduction is approximately 26% (2 hours postdose). At peak, it is comparable to a nonselective β-blocker and superior to the selective β-blocker betaxolol, although at trough (12 hours postdose), the reduction is only 14%–15%, or less than the reduction achieved with nonselective β-blockers. Though approved for therapy 3 times daily, brimonidine is commonly used twice daily, particularly when used as an adjunctive agent.

Caution is recommended when either apraclonidine or brimonidine is used in patients on a monoamine oxidase inhibitor (MAOI) or tricyclic antidepressant therapy. Apraclonidine has a much greater affinity for α_1-receptors than does brimonidine and is therefore more likely to produce vasoconstriction in the eye.

Robin AL. Argon laser trabeculoplasty medical therapy to prevent the intraocular pressure rise associated with argon laser trabeculoplasty. *Ophthalmic Surg.* 1991;22(1):31–37.

Schuman JS, Horwitz B, Choplin NT, David R, Albracht D, Chen K. A 1-year study of brimonidine twice daily in glaucoma and ocular hypertension: a controlled, randomized, multicenter clinical trial. *Arch Ophthalmol.* 1997;115(7):847–852.

Carbonic Anhydrase Inhibitors

Carbonic anhydrase inhibitors (CAIs) decrease aqueous humor formation by direct antagonist activity on ciliary epithelial carbonic anhydrase and perhaps, to a lesser extent only with systemic administration, by production of a generalized acidosis. The enzyme carbonic anhydrase is present in many other tissues, including corneal endothelium, iris, retinal pigment epithelium, red blood cells, brain, and kidney. More than 90% of the ciliary epithelial enzyme activity must be abolished to decrease aqueous production and lower IOP.

Topical CAI agents are available for long-term treatment of elevated IOP. Dorzolamide and brinzolamide are sulfonamide derivatives that reduce aqueous formation by direct inhibition of carbonic anhydrase in the ciliary body. They have fewer systemic side effects than the oral agents. Dorzolamide and brinzolamide are currently available for use 3 times daily, although the reduction in IOP is only slightly greater when compared to the IOP reduction with twice-daily therapy. For patients taking an oral CAI, there is no advantage to adding a topical CAI.

Common adverse effects of topical CAIs include bitter taste, blurred vision, and punctate keratopathy. Dorzolamide may cause transient burning because of its lower pH, whereas brinzolamide is a suspension, resulting in white deposits in the tear film. Eyes with compromised endothelial cell function may also be at risk of corneal decompensation.

The systemic agents can be given orally, intramuscularly, and intravenously. They are most useful in acute situations (eg, acute angle-closure glaucoma). Oral CAIs begin to act within 1 hour of administration, with maximal effect within 2–4 hours. Sustained-release acetazolamide can reach peak effect within 3–6 hours of administration. Because of the adverse effects of systemic CAIs, however, long-term therapy with these agents should be reserved for patients whose glaucoma is not controlled with topical therapy and who have refused surgery or in whom surgery would be inappropriate.

Systemic acetazolamide and methazolamide are the oral CAI agents most commonly used; another agent in this group is dichlorphenamide. Methazolamide has a longer duration of action and is less bound to serum protein than is acetazolamide; however, it is less effective than acetazolamide. Methazolamide and sustained-release acetazolamide are the best tolerated of the systemic CAIs. Methazolamide is metabolized by the liver, thereby decreasing some of the risk of systemic adverse effects. Acetazolamide is not metabolized and is excreted in urine.

Adverse effects of systemic CAI therapy are usually dose-related. Many patients develop paresthesias of the fingers or toes and complain of lassitude, loss of energy, and anorexia. Weight loss is common. Abdominal discomfort, diarrhea, loss of libido, impotence, and an unpleasant taste in the mouth, as well as severe mental depression, may also occur. There is an increased risk of the formation of calcium oxalate and calcium phosphate renal stones. Because methazolamide has greater hepatic metabolism and causes less acidosis, it may be less likely than acetazolamide to cause renal lithiasis.

CAIs are chemically derived from sulfa drugs; therefore, their use may cause an allergic reaction in individuals with a sulfa allergy. The level of cross-reactivity is low, however. Aplastic anemia is a rare but potentially fatal idiosyncratic reaction to CAIs. Thrombocytopenia and agranulocytosis can also occur. Although routine complete blood counts have been suggested, they are not predictive of this idiosyncratic reaction and are not routinely recommended. Hypokalemia is a potentially serious complication that is especially likely to occur when an oral CAI is used concurrently with another drug that causes potassium loss (eg, a thiazide diuretic). Serum potassium should be monitored regularly in such patients.

Oral CAIs are potent medications with significant adverse effects. Therefore, the lowest dose that reduces the IOP to an acceptable range should be used. Methazolamide is often effective in doses as low as 25–50 mg given 2 to 3 times daily. Sustained-release formulations may have fewer side effects. A typical dosing regimen for acetazolamide is 250 mg 4 times daily; for sustained release, 250–500 mg twice daily.

Fraunfelder FT, Fraunfelder FW, eds. *Drug-Induced Ocular Side Effects*. Boston: Butterworth-Heinemann; 2001.

Strahlman E, Tipping R, Vogel R. A double-masked, randomized 1-year study comparing dorzolamide (Trusopt), timolol, and betaxolol. International Dorzolamide Study Group. *Arch Ophthalmol*. 1995;113(8):1009–1016.

Parasympathomimetic Agents

Parasympathomimetic agents, or *miotics*, have been used in the treatment of glaucoma for more than 100 years. Traditionally, they were divided into 2 groups, direct-acting and indirect-acting anticholinesterase agents. However, indirect-acting agents fell out of use because of ocular and systemic adverse effects, and they are no longer available for glaucoma therapy, including echothiophate iodide, the agent typically used in the past.

Direct-acting agents affect the motor end plates in the same way as acetylcholine, which is transmitted at postganglionic parasympathetic junctions, as well as at other autonomic, somatic, and central synapses. Indirect-acting agents inhibit the enzyme acetylcholinesterase, thereby prolonging and enhancing the action of naturally secreted acetylcholine. *Pilocarpine* is the only direct-acting agent still used in the treatment of glaucoma.

Parasympathomimetics reduce IOP by causing contraction of the longitudinal ciliary muscle, which pulls the scleral spur to tighten the trabecular meshwork, increasing the outflow of aqueous humor. Pilocarpine can reduce IOP by 15%–25%. The currently accepted indications for miotic therapy include long-term treatment of elevated IOP in patients whose drainage angles are persistently occludable despite laser iridotomy, and prophylaxis for angle-closure glaucoma prior to iridectomy.

Miotic agents have been associated with numerous ocular side effects. Induced myopia resulting from ciliary muscle contraction is a side effect common to all cholinergic agents. Brow ache may accompany the ciliary spasm, and the miosis interferes with vision in dim light and in patients with lens opacities. Miotic agents have also been associated with retinal detachment; thus, a peripheral retinal evaluation is suggested before the initiation of therapy. Miotics may be cataractogenic, particularly the indirect-acting agents. In children, they may also induce formation of iris pigment epithelial cysts. In pediatric and adult patients, these agents may cause epiphora by both direct lacrimal stimulation and punctal stenosis. These agents may also cause ocular surface changes resulting in drug-induced pseudopemphigoid.

Other potential ocular side effects include increased bleeding during surgery and increased inflammation and severe fibrinous iridocyclitis postoperatively. Because miotics can break down the blood–aqueous barrier, they should be avoided if possible in patients with uveitic glaucoma. Use of miotics occasionally induces a paradoxical angle closure, particularly in eyes with phacomorphic narrow angles, because contraction of the ciliary muscle leads to forward movement of the lens–iris interface and an increase in the anteroposterior diameter of the lens, which may cause or exacerbate pupillary block in an eye with a large lens.

Systemic adverse effects, seen mainly with indirect-acting medications, include diarrhea, abdominal cramps, increased salivation, bronchospasm, and even enuresis. Depolarizing muscle relaxants such as succinylcholine cannot be used for up to 6 weeks after stopping indirect-acting agents.

Although miotic agents effectively lower IOP, they are poorly tolerated and have been associated with poor compliance because of the 2–4-times-daily regimen required. This class of agents is now rarely used in the treatment of POAG.

Pilocarpine absorbed to a polymer gel (pilocarpine gel) is administered once daily at bedtime. Although nocturnal dosing reduces problems from induced myopia and miosis, the gel is marketed at 4% concentration, which is still relatively poorly tolerated, especially in younger patients. On the other hand, pilocarpine is among the most affordable of agents, and miotics are much better tolerated in aphakic than in phakic eyes.

Hoskins HD Jr, Kass MA. Cholinergic drugs. In: Hoskins HD Jr, Kass MA, eds. *Becker-Shaffer's Diagnosis and Therapy of the Glaucomas.* 6th ed. St Louis: Mosby; 1989:420–434.

Combined Medications

Medications that are combined in a single bottle have the potential benefit of improved convenience and compliance, as well as reduced cost. Fixed combinations consisting of timolol and another agent—a CAI (dorzolamide, brinzolamide), an α_2-adrenergic agonist (brimonidine), or a prostaglandin analogue (latanoprost, travoprost, bimatoprost)—are available in many countries (see Table 7-1). In general, the efficacy of fixed combinations of timolol and a topical CAI is similar to that of these components given separately. However, the main outcome of twice-daily dosing may be to increase the risk of systemic β-blocker side effects, because nearly the full effect of a β-blocker can be achieved with once-daily dosing. The ocular side effects are the same as for both drugs individually. In general, except in emergent situations, fixed combinations such as those with topical CAIs should not be used until the clinician has established that timolol alone does not sufficiently lower the IOP.

Strohmaier K, Snyder E, DuBiner H, Adamsons I. Dorzolamide-Timolol Study Group. The efficacy and safety of the dorzolamide-timolol combination versus the concomitant administration of its components. *Ophthalmology.* 1998;105(10):1936–1944.

Hyperosmotic Agents

Hyperosmotic agents are used to control acute episodes of elevated IOP. Common hyperosmotic agents include oral glycerol and intravenous mannitol.

When given systemically, hyperosmotic agents lower the IOP by increasing the blood osmolality, which creates an osmotic gradient between the blood and the vitreous humor, drawing water from the vitreous cavity and reducing the IOP. Because of the increased gradient, the larger the dose administered and the more rapid the administration, the greater the subsequent IOP reduction. A substance distributed only in extracellular water, such as mannitol, is more effective than a drug distributed in total body water (eg, urea). When the blood–aqueous barrier is disrupted, the osmotic agent enters the eye faster than when the barrier is intact, thus reducing the effectiveness of the drug and its duration of action.

Hyperosmotic agents are rarely administered for longer than a few hours because their effects are transient as a result of the rapid reequilibration of the osmotic gradient. They become less effective over time, and a rebound elevation in IOP may occur if the agent penetrates the eye and reverses the osmotic gradient.

Adverse effects of these drugs include headache, mental confusion, backache, acute congestive heart failure, and myocardial infarction. The rapid increase in extracellular volume and cardiac preload caused by hyperosmotic agents may precipitate or aggravate congestive heart failure. Intravenous administration is more likely than oral administration to cause this problem. In addition, subdural and subarachnoid hemorrhages have been reported after treatment with hyperosmotic agents. Glycerol can precipitate hyperglycemia or even ketoacidosis in patients with diabetes, because it is metabolized into sugar and ketone bodies. Hyperosmotics, as well as oral CAIs, are contraindicated in patients in renal failure or on dialysis.

General Approach to Medical Treatment

Open-Angle Glaucoma

The ophthalmologist should tailor therapy for open-angle glaucoma to the individual needs of the patient. As noted previously, a target IOP range is established as a goal. However, the effectiveness of therapy can be established only by careful repeated scrutiny of the patient's optic nerve and visual field status.

Characteristics of the medical agents available for the treatment of glaucoma are summarized in Table 7-1. When making management decisions, the ophthalmologist should keep drug efficacy and patient compliance in mind. Treatment is usually initiated with a single topical medication, unless the starting IOP is extremely high, in which case 2 or more medications may be indicated. The selection of the agent for initial medical therapy should be individualized based on the efficacy, safety, and tolerability of the drug and the patient's status and needs. A brief discussion with the patient regarding treatment options can be effective for determining the optimal choice. Prostaglandin analogues, β-blockers, α$_2$-agonists, and topical CAIs are all reasonable choices for first-line therapy. The once-daily prostaglandin analogues are the most effective agents to lower IOP, and they have the best systemic safety profile. Thus, they are commonly the first class of medications used in most patients. Although β-blockers are the best tolerated locally, they have significant systemic side effects. Because of the variability of IOP, it may be helpful (unless the IOP is extremely high) to test the medication in 1 eye until the effectiveness of therapy has been established. At that point, both eyes can be treated.

If 1 drug is not adequate to reduce IOP to the desired range, the initial agent may be discontinued and another tried. If no single agent controls the pressure, a combination of topical agents should be used. Again, individualizing the choice of agent is helpful for selection of the second-line medication. These choices include miotic therapy for nonphakic patients and, in rare instances, systemic CAIs for short periods when the clinical situation warrants the risk of adverse effects associated with their use. Clearly, when the patient requires 3 or more medications, compliance becomes more difficult and the potential for local ocular and systemic side effects increases.

Patients may not be able to tolerate multiple topical agents because of preservative toxicity. Benzalkonium chloride (BAK) is the agent most commonly used as a preservative and is present in most currently available topical ophthalmic eyedrops. If a reaction is suspected, an alternative can be used, including preservative-free timolol maleate (unit dose), brimonidine 0.1% preserved with Purite, timolol in gel-forming solution preserved with benzododecinium bromide, preservative-free tafluprost, preservative-free dorzolamide, preservative-free timolol/dorzolamide fixed combination, and BAK-free travoprost, which is preserved in the bottle with an ionic buffered system. If the level of glaucoma damage permits, it may be beneficial, for rehabilitation of the ocular surface, to stop all topical medications and to have the patient use unpreserved artificial tears frequently. The temporary use of oral CAIs may be useful to lower IOP during this period, if clinically warranted.

Patients rarely associate systemic side effects with topical drugs and, consequently, seldom volunteer symptoms. The ophthalmologist must inquire about these symptoms. Communication with the primary care physician is important not only to provide information about the potential side effects of glaucoma medication but also to discuss the possible effects of other currently prescribed systemic medications on the glaucomatous process. Modification of systemic β-blocker therapy for hypertension, for example, may affect glaucoma control. Physicians should be aware that patient compliance may decline as the complexity and expense of the medical regimen increase.

Patients with open-angle glaucoma require careful monitoring. IOP, though important, is only one of several factors to monitor. Optic nerve photographs or drawings and visual fields must be compared periodically to ensure that the disease is stable (see Chapter 3). The condition of the patient and the severity of the disease determine how often each of these parameters must be checked. If the cupping or visual field damage shows evidence of progression despite apparent control of acceptable IOP, the ophthalmologist should consider other diseases (see the discussion of normal-tension glaucoma in Chapter 4). Other possible explanations include an IOP level that is too high for the particular patient's optic nerve, IOP that may be spiking at times when the patient is not in the physician's office, low central corneal thickness, sleep apnea, concomitant angle closure, and poor patient compliance.

Angle-Closure Glaucoma

The aim of medical treatment of acute angle closure is usually to lower the IOP in preparation for laser iridotomy. Rapid IOP reduction is required in order to prevent further damage to the optic nerve, to clear the cornea of edema, to reduce intraocular inflammation, to allow pupillary constriction, and to prevent formation of posterior and peripheral anterior synechiae (see Chapter 5). Medical therapy for chronic angle closure is the same as that for POAG, although miotics play a greater role. However, the use of miotics may induce a paradoxical increase in IOP if the angle is closed and the trabecular meshwork is nonfunctional.

Administration of Ocular Medications

Patients should be shown how to instill eyedrops properly and should be given instructions on nasolacrimal occlusion. Nasolacrimal occlusion can be used to reduce the systemic absorption of topical ocular medications and to prolong their ocular contact time. Teaching the patient to close the eyes for 1–3 minutes after instillation of the eyedrop will also promote corneal penetration and reduce systemic absorption of the drug. These procedures are especially important with the use of β-blockers. In addition, they ensure that there is a sufficient amount of time between the instillation of different medications. Eyedrops to be administered at the same time should be separated by at least 5 minutes to prevent washout of the first drug by the second. Patients should be taught how to space their medications, and instructional charts should be given. It may be useful to coordinate the administration of medication with a part of the daily routine, such as meals. A dosing aid device may also be considered, especially for patients who live alone or who are unable to successfully instill eyedrops.

Use of Glaucoma Medications During Pregnancy or by Nursing Mothers

Unfortunately, there is little definitive information concerning the use of glaucoma medications in pregnant women or nursing mothers. In 1979, the US Food and Drug Administration (FDA) introduced a classification system to indicate the potential teratogenicity of approved medications. Drugs are rated A, B, C, D, or X, with the X category being the most teratogenic. For example, brimonidine has a Pregnancy Category B rating, and all other glaucoma agents have a Pregnancy Category C rating. The rating *Pregnancy Category B* indicates that animal studies of the drug have revealed no harm to the fetus, but no adequate and well-controlled studies have been done in pregnant women; or, animal studies of this drug have shown an adverse effect, but adequate and well-controlled studies in pregnant woman have failed to demonstrate a risk to the fetus. The *Pregnancy Category C* rating indicates that no animal studies have been conducted and that it is not known whether the drug can cause harm when given to a pregnant woman. The drug should be used during pregnancy only if clearly indicated. This category also includes drugs that have shown an adverse effect in animal studies, but there are no adequate and well-controlled studies of these drugs in pregnant women.

Timolol, despite its Pregnancy Category C rating, tends to be used during pregnancy, because of its long track record. However, β-adrenergic antagonists, which are concentrated fivefold in breast milk, should be avoided in nursing mothers because of their potential adverse effects on infants. Brimonidine has been reported to cause respiratory arrest in infants and young children and should not be used in these patients. The CAIs have been shown to be teratogenic in rodents. Although human information is lacking, oral CAIs should not be used by women in their childbearing years or by those who are pregnant. Because prostaglandins increase uterine contractility and may induce labor, they should not be used during pregnancy. In general, it is prudent to minimize the use of medications in pregnant women whenever possible, and the clinician may want to consider laser trabeculoplasty or surgical intervention in cases where vision loss is a concern.

Brauner SC, Chen TC, Hutchinson BT, Chang MA, Pasquale LR, Grosskreutz CL. The course of glaucoma during pregnancy: a retrospective case series. *Arch Ophthalmol.* 2006;124(8):1089–1094.

Sheth BP. Drugs and pregnancy. *Focal Points: Clinical Modules for Ophthalmologists.* San Francisco: American Academy of Ophthalmology; 2007, module 7.

Use of Glaucoma Medications in Elderly Patients

There are specific considerations with regard to the use of glaucoma medications in elderly patients. First, elderly patients generally have greater difficulty instilling their medications than do younger patients; consequently, compliance may be affected. This may be due to tremor, poor coordination, or a comorbidity such as arthritis. Compliance will also be affected in an elderly patient with reduced mental capacity or poor memory and a complicated drug regimen, especially since this individual is most likely already taking multiple systemic medications for other ailments. Second, elderly persons have a greater susceptibility to the systemic adverse effects of glaucoma medications, as for example, α_2-agonists, the systemic side effects of which are often symptomatic in these patients. This is especially important to remember with the use of β-adrenergic antagonists. It has been shown that a significant proportion of asymptomatic elderly patients suffer a significant, but reversible, reduction in pulmonary function.

> Diggory P, Cassels-Brown A, Vail A, Abbey LM, Hillman JS. Avoiding unsuspected respiratory side-effects of topical timolol with cardioselective or sympathomimetic agents. *Lancet.* 1995;345(8965):1604–1606.

Generic Medications

Many of the β-blockers and, increasingly, other classes of glaucoma medications are available as generic agents. Although the generic agents may be less expensive, in most cases little data are available to prove or disprove equivalent efficacy and safety between brand-name and generic medications.

Compliance

Glaucoma medications are effective only if patients use them. Patient education is usually the first step in improving compliance. Understanding the disease and the nature and benefits of treatment enhances compliance. Education should also include a discussion of treatment alternatives. When patients are aware of the possible side effects of a medication, compliance is also enhanced.

In addition, it is vital to teach patients how to properly instill medications. The ophthalmologist should confirm that the patient or someone else will be successful in instilling eyedrops. Compliance is further enhanced by a drug regimen that is designed to be as simple as possible. The fewest number of medications, instilled with the least frequency, is optimal. When the patient requires multiple drugs and doses, it may be helpful to coordinate administration with daily events. The ophthalmologist must make sure that the patient understands the regimen. A written schedule is very helpful.

CHAPTER 8

Surgical Therapy for Glaucoma

Surgical treatment for glaucoma is usually undertaken when medical therapy is not appropriate, not tolerated, not effective, or not properly utilized by a particular patient, and the glaucoma remains uncontrolled with either documented progressive damage or a high risk of further damage. Surgery is usually the primary approach for both congenital glaucoma and angle-closure glaucoma with pupillary block. In patients with primary open-angle glaucoma (POAG), surgery has traditionally been considered when medical therapy has failed. Caution is especially important because of the potential adverse effects of surgery, including bleb-associated complications, cataracts, and infection. Early studies of trabeculectomy as initial therapy for glaucoma, which were performed before the introduction of some contemporary antiglaucoma medications, suggested that trabeculectomy might offer some advantages—better control of IOP, reduction in the number of patient visits to the physician, and possibly better preservation of the visual field, for example. The results of the Collaborative Initial Glaucoma Treatment Study (CIGTS; see Chapter 4) confirmed that initial surgical therapy achieves better IOP control than does initial medical therapy. However, this finding did not translate to better visual field stabilization in the average subject, because those subjects who received initial surgical treatment had a higher risk of cataract in the long term. In both groups, there was a low incidence of visual field progression. On the other hand, the 9-year follow-up data revealed a considerable subset (approximately 20%) that did show substantial visual field progression. Initial surgery led to less visual field progression than did initial medical therapy in subjects with advanced visual field loss at baseline, whereas subjects with diabetes had more visual field loss over time if treated initially with surgery. Based on the results of this study and on current practice, most clinicians defer incisional surgery for POAG until after initial treatment with medical or laser therapy. Surgical treatment may be accelerated in patients with advanced visual field loss at presentation.

When surgery is indicated, the clinical setting must guide the selection of the appropriate procedure. Each of the many possible procedures is appropriate in specific conditions and clinical situations.

Lichter PR, Musch DC, Gillespie BW, et al. Interim clinical outcomes in the Collaborative Initial Glaucoma Treatment Study comparing initial treatment randomized to medications or surgery. *Ophthalmology.* 2001;108(11):1943–1953.

Migdal C, Gregory W, Hitchings R. Long-term functional outcome after early surgery compared with laser and medicine in open-angle glaucoma. *Ophthalmology.* 1994;101(10):1651–1657.

Musch DC, Gillespie BW, Lichter PR, Niziol LM, Janz NK; CIGTS Study Investigators. Visual field progression in the Collaborative Initial Glaucoma Treatment Study: the impact of treatment and other baseline factors. *Ophthalmology.* 2009;116(2):200–207.

Musch DC, Gillespie BW, Niziol LM, et al. Cataract extraction in the Collaborative Initial Glaucoma Treatment Study: incidence, risk factors, and the effect of cataract progression and extraction on clinical and quality-of-life outcomes. *Arch Ophthalmol.* 2006;124(12):1694–1700.

Surgery for Open-Angle Glaucoma

Laser Trabeculoplasty

Laser trabeculoplasty (LTP) is a technique whereby laser energy is applied to the trabecular meshwork in discrete spots, usually covering 180° to 360° per treatment. Various modalities of LTP exist, including argon laser trabeculoplasty (ALT), diode laser trabeculoplasty, and selective laser trabeculoplasty (SLT).

Mechanism

Several possible mechanisms of action were initially proposed for the increased outflow facility following successful LTP. The treated area of trabecular meshwork may shrink, causing stretching of adjacent areas. However, most investigators believe that chemical mediators, specifically interleukin-1β and tumor necrosis factor-α, are released from trabecular meshwork cells, increasing outflow facility through induction of specific matrix metalloproteinases. SLT results in selective absorption of energy by trabecular pigmented cells, sparing adjacent cells and tissues from thermal damage. The number of monocytes/macrophages in the trabecular meshwork increases substantially after SLT, and this increase may play a role in lowering IOP.

Indications

Historically, LTP was indicated when a glaucoma patient who was on maximum-tolerated medical therapy and whose angle was open on gonioscopy required lower IOP. Currently, many clinicians initiate some form of medical therapy before advancing to LTP, but LTP may be considered as an initial step in the management of glaucoma. In addition, patients who cannot tolerate or comply with initial medical therapy may be candidates for LTP.

The Glaucoma Laser Trial (GLT) was a multicenter randomized clinical trial to assess the efficacy and safety of ALT as an alternative to treatment with topical medication in patients with newly diagnosed, previously untreated POAG. Within the first 2 years of follow-up, ALT as initial therapy appeared to be as effective as medication. However, more than half of the eyes treated initially with laser required the addition of 1 or more medications to control IOP over the course of the study. Further, the medication protocols used in the study no longer resemble the medical regimens commonly employed for the treatment of POAG.

LTP effectively reduces IOP in patients with POAG, pigmentary glaucoma, exfoliation syndrome, and steroid-induced glaucoma. Aphakic and pseudophakic eyes may respond less favorably than phakic eyes. IOP control does not seem to be diminished by subsequent cataract extraction. When effective, LTP is expected to lower IOP 20%–25%. LTP is not effective for treating certain types of secondary glaucoma, such as uveitic glaucoma.

Glaucoma Laser Trial Research Group. The Glaucoma Laser Trial (GLT) and glaucoma laser trial follow-up study: 7. Results. *Am J Ophthalmol.* 1995;120(6):718–731.

Glaucoma Laser Trial Research Group. The Glaucoma Laser Trial (GLT): 2. Results of argon laser trabeculoplasty versus topical medicines. *Ophthalmology.* 1990;97(11):1403–1413.

Contraindications

There are few contraindications for LTP for the treatment of POAG when the angle is accessible. LTP is not advised in patients with inflammatory glaucoma, iridocorneal endothelial (ICE) syndrome, neovascular glaucoma, synechial angle closure, or developmental glaucoma. LTP can be tried in angle recession, but the underlying tissue alterations may cause it to be ineffective. Another relative contraindication for LTP is the lack of effect in the fellow eye. If the eye has advanced damage and high IOP, LTP is unlikely to achieve the target pressure.

Preoperative evaluation

As with all ocular surgery, the preoperative evaluation for LTP should include a detailed medical and ocular history and a comprehensive eye examination. Particular attention must be paid to visual field examination, gonioscopy, and optic nerve evaluation; the angle must be open on gonioscopy. The degree of pigmentation in the angle will determine the power setting: the more pigmented the trabecular meshwork, the less energy required for both argon and selective lasers to achieve the necessary effect.

Technique

In the argon laser procedure, a 50-μm laser beam of 0.1-second duration is focused through a goniolens at the junction of the anterior nonpigmented and the posterior pigmented edge of the trabecular meshwork (Fig 8-1). Application to the posterior trabecular meshwork tends to result in inflammation, pigment dispersion, prolonged IOP elevation, and peripheral anterior synechiae (PAS) formation. The power setting (300–1000 mW) should be titrated to achieve the desired endpoint: blanching of the trabecular meshwork or production of a tiny bubble. If a large bubble appears, the power is reduced and titrated to achieve the proper effect. As LTP was originally described, laser energy was applied to the entire circumference (360°) of the trabecular meshwork. But evidence suggests that many patients achieve a satisfactory reduction in IOP and have a lower risk of short-term pressure elevation when only half of the circumference is treated, with approximately 40–50 applications over 180° of the meshwork.

The procedure with the diode laser is similar: a 75-μm laser beam is focused through a goniolens with a power setting of 600–1000 mW and duration of 0.1 second.

Selective laser trabeculoplasty

Selective laser trabeculoplasty is an FDA-approved procedure in which the laser targets intracellular melanin. A frequency-doubled (532-nm) Q-switched Nd:YAG laser with a 400-μm spot size is used to deliver 0.4–1.0 mJ of energy for 0.3 ns. Results of clinical studies suggest that the procedure is safe and effective, with IOP-lowering effects similar to

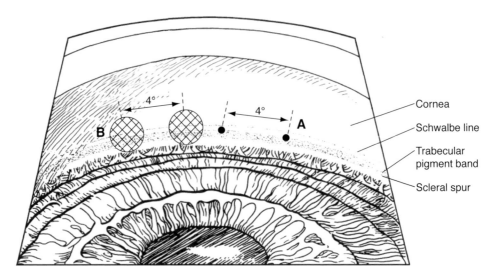

Figure 8-1 Position of argon laser trabeculoplasty *(A)* and selective laser trabeculoplasty *(B)* treatment in the trabecular meshwork. *(Modified with permission from Solish AM, Kass MA. Laser trabeculoplasty. In: Waltman SR, Keates RH, Hoyt CS, eds.* Surgery of the Eye. *New York: Churchill Livingstone; 1988:1.)*

those achieved with ALT. Histologic studies have shown that treatment with SLT causes less coagulative damage and fewer structural changes of the trabecular meshwork compared to treatment with ALT.

Damji KF, Bovell AM, Hodge WG, et al. Selective laser trabeculoplasty versus argon laser trabeculoplasty: results from a 1-year randomized clinical trial. *Br J Ophthalmol.* 2006;90(12):1490–1494.

Kramer TR, Noecker RJ. Comparison of the morphologic changes after selective laser trabeculoplasty and argon laser trabeculoplasty in human eye bank eyes. *Ophthalmology.* 2001;108(4):773–779.

Latina MA, Sibayan SA, Shin DH, Noecker RJ, Marcellino G. Q-switched 532-nm Nd:YAG laser trabeculoplasty (selective laser trabeculoplasty): a multicenter, pilot, clinical study. *Ophthalmology.* 1998;105(11):2082–2090.

McIlraith I, Strasfeld M, Colev G, Hutnik CM. Selective laser trabeculoplasty as initial and adjunctive treatment for open-angle glaucoma. *J Glaucoma.* 2006;15(2):124–130.

Weinreb RN, Ruderman J, Juster R, Wilensky JT. Influence of the number of laser burns administered on the early results of argon laser trabeculoplasty. *Am J Ophthalmol.* 1983;95(3):287–292.

Complications

The most common complication of LTP is a transient rise in IOP, which occurs in approximately 20% of patients. IOP has been reported to reach 50–60 mm Hg, and this transient rise may cause additional damage to the optic nerve. This rise is less common when only 180° of the angle is treated per session.

IOP elevations are of particular concern in patients with advanced cupping. Rises in IOP are usually evident within the first 1–4 hours of treatment, and all patients should be monitored closely for this complication. The adjunctive use of topical apraclonidine or brimonidine has been shown to blunt postoperative pressure elevation. Other medications shown to blunt these IOP spikes include β-blockers, pilocarpine, and carbonic anhydrase inhibitors (CAIs). Hyperosmotic agents and oral CAIs may be helpful in eyes with IOP spikes not responsive to topical medications.

Low-grade iritis may follow LTP. Some surgeons routinely administer topical anti-inflammatory drugs for 4–7 days after LTP; others use them only if inflammation develops. Other complications of LTP include hyphema, the formation of PAS, and the rare persistent elevation of IOP requiring filtering surgery.

Results and long-term follow-up

From 4 to 6 weeks should be allowed before the full effect of the first treatment is evaluated and a decision about additional treatment is made. Approximately 80% of patients with medically uncontrolled open-angle glaucoma (OAG) experience a drop in IOP for a minimum of 6–12 months following LTP. Longer-term data have shown that 50% of patients with an initial response maintain a significantly lower IOP level for 3–5 years after treatment. The success rate at 10 years is approximately 30%. The highest success rates are seen in older patients with POAG and in pseudoexfoliative glaucoma. Eyes with pigmentary glaucoma may show a good initial decrease in IOP, but with continued pigment shedding, this decrease may not be sustained.

Elevation of IOP may recur in some patients after months or even years of control. Additional laser treatment may be helpful in some patients, especially if the entire angle has not been treated previously. Re-treatment of an angle that has been fully treated (approximately 80–100 spots over 360°) has a lower success rate and a higher complication rate than does primary treatment.

Chung PY, Schuman JS, Netland PA, Lloyd-Muhammad RA, Jacobs DS. Five-year results of a randomized, prospective, clinical trial of diode vs argon laser trabeculoplasty for open-angle glaucoma. *Am J Ophthalmol.* 1998;126(2):185–190.

Mitrev PV, Schuman JS. Lasers in glaucoma management. *Focal Points: Clinical Modules for Ophthalmologists.* San Francisco: American Academy of Ophthalmology; 2001, module 9.

Ritch R, Shields MB, Krupin T, eds. *The Glaucomas.* 2nd ed. St Louis: Mosby; 1996.

Wise JB, Witter SL. Argon laser therapy for open-angle glaucoma: a pilot study. *Arch Ophthalmol.* 1979;97(2):319–322.

Incisional Surgery for Open-Angle Glaucomas

Incisional surgery is indicated in OAG when nonsurgical therapies cannot maintain the IOP at a level considered low enough to prevent further pressure-related damage to the optic nerve or visual field loss. The glaucoma may be uncontrolled for various reasons:

- Maximum-tolerated medical therapy fails to adequately reduce IOP.
- Glaucomatous optic neuropathy or visual field loss is progressing despite apparent "adequate" reduction of IOP with medical therapy.
- The patient cannot comply with the necessary medical regimen.

Although incisional procedures to lower IOP are traditionally referred to as *filters,* it would be more correct physiologically and anatomically to refer to them as *fistulizing procedures.* In this discussion, the popular term *filter* is used because it remains in widespread use. The goal of filtering surgery is to create a new pathway (fistula) that allows aqueous humor to flow out of the anterior chamber through the surgical opening in the sclera and into the subconjunctival and sub-Tenon spaces. The filtering procedure most commonly used is the guarded trabeculectomy. Full-thickness procedures have largely fallen into disuse because of both the high complication rate and the introduction of antifibrotic agents.

Indications

Incisional surgery is indicated in a patient with OAG when optic nerve function is decreasing or is likely to decrease and the patient is already on maximum-tolerated medical therapy and is unlikely to achieve a sufficient reduction in IOP with laser treatment. In advanced disease, many clinicians consider filtering surgery earlier.

This statement raises several important considerations. The presence of glaucoma with a high probability of progressive optic nerve damage is a clear indication for incisional surgery. With the potential complications of glaucoma surgery, however, it is not reasonable to perform incisional surgery in an eye with ocular hypertension and a low risk of developing optic neuropathy. In less clear-cut situations—for example, when 1 eye has sustained significant optic nerve damage and the IOP is high in the fellow eye despite maximum-tolerated medical therapy—some surgeons would recommend surgery prior to unequivocal detection of damage.

Medical therapy can be confirmed as the maximum-tolerated therapy when it is advanced beyond the tolerated level and patient intolerance is documented. This approach is clearly unnecessary and frustrating for both physician and patient. An alternative concept is *core therapy,* in which treatment consists of those medications likely to work well in combination. If a patient does not have a satisfactory IOP response, the physician may make a few alterations, but it is likely that further medical intervention will simply delay indicated surgery. Although a large number of drugs are available for use in this setting, IOP response diminishes each time a drug is added. Also, determining the maximum tolerated level does not require the use of every class of IOP-lowering medication.

Failure of medical therapy may be the result of poor patient compliance with therapy, in itself a relative indication for surgery. Some patients may use their medications only shortly before an office visit. Thus, there may be progression despite apparently acceptable IOP. It is difficult to elicit an accurate history in this situation. When the ophthalmologist suspects poor patient compliance, it may be appropriate to move to surgery sooner, because further changes in medical therapy are unlikely to improve IOP control.

Although the hallmark of glaucoma is progressive optic nerve damage, it is actually relatively uncommon to make a surgical decision based on the detection of progressive change in the appearance of the optic nerve or retinal nerve fiber layer. The main clinical indications for surgery are progression of visual field damage and uncontrolled IOP, even though multiple visual field examinations may be required in order to determine with certainty that a damaged visual field has become more damaged. In many cases, the decision to proceed with surgery is made even in the absence of documented progression and is based on a clinical judgment that the IOP is too high for the stage of the disease. Thus, an IOP of 25 mm Hg is not an indication for surgery in an eye with ocular hypertension, but this IOP level might be an indication for IOP-lowering surgery in the setting of advanced glaucomatous optic neuropathy. It is not always necessary to perform LTP before proceeding to trabeculectomy.

Weinreb RN, Mills RP, eds. *Glaucoma Surgery: Principles and Techniques.* 2nd ed. Ophthalmology Monograph 4. San Francisco: American Academy of Ophthalmology; 1998:20.

Contraindications

Relative contraindications for glaucoma filtering surgery can be ocular or systemic. A blind eye (no light perception) is usually not considered for incisional surgery. Ciliary body ablation is a better alternative for lowering IOP in such eyes, if pressure reduction is necessary for pain control; but even this procedure is not without risk. The risk of sympathetic ophthalmia should always be kept in mind when any procedure on a blind eye or an eye with poor visual potential is considered. Conditions that predispose to trabeculectomy failure, such as active anterior segment neovascularization (rubeosis iridis) or active iritis, are relative contraindications. The underlying problem should be addressed first, if possible; or a surgical alternative such as implantation of a glaucoma drainage device should be considered. It may be extremely difficult to perform a successful trabeculectomy in an eye that has sustained extensive conjunctival injury (eg, after retinal detachment surgery or chemical trauma) or that has an extremely thin sclera from prior surgery or necrotizing scleritis, and in such cases the likelihood of success is also reduced because of an increased risk of scarring.

The success rate of filtering surgery is decreased in younger or aphakic/pseudophakic patients. However, with the advent of phacoemulsificaton for cataract extraction and the use of antifibrotic agents during trabeculectomy, glaucoma filtering surgery can significantly improve IOP in pseudophakic patients. A lower success rate is also found in patients with certain types of secondary glaucomas and in those who previously had unsuccessful filtering procedures. In addition, black patients have a higher failure rate with filtering surgery.

Fontana H, Nouri-Mahdavi K, Caprioli J. Trabeculectomy with mitomycin C in pseudophakic patients with open-angle glaucoma: outcomes and risk factors for failure. *Am J Ophthalmol.* 2006;141(4):652–659.

Shingleton BJ, Alfano C, O'Donoghue MW, Rivera J. Efficacy of glaucoma filtration surgery in pseudophakic patients with or without conjunctival scarring. *J Cataract Refract Surg.* 2004;30(12):2504–2509.

Preoperative evaluation

When considering a surgical procedure, the ophthalmologist must take into account factors such as the patient's general health and presumed life expectancy and the status of the fellow eye. The patient must be medically stable enough to endure an invasive ocular procedure under local anesthesia. The preoperative evaluation should determine and document factors that may affect surgical planning, as well as those that determine the structural and functional status of the eye.

Control of preoperative inflammation with corticosteroids helps reduce postoperative iritis and scarring of the filtering bleb. Discontinuation of anticholinesterase agents (in the rare instances when they are used), with temporary use of alternative medications, at least 3–6 weeks before surgery helps reduce bleeding and iridocyclitis. Systemic CAIs should be discontinued postoperatively and topical CAIs used in the fellow eye, if needed. Blepharitis should be controlled preoperatively.

Before surgery, the IOP should be reduced as closely as possible to normal levels so that the risk of expulsive choroidal hemorrhage is minimized. Antiplatelet and anticoagulant medications should be discontinued if possible, in consultation with the patient's primary care physician. Systemic hypertension should be controlled.

Patients should be informed of the purpose of and expectations for surgery: to arrest or delay progressive vision loss caused by their glaucoma. Patients should understand that glaucoma surgery alone rarely improves vision and that they may still need to use glaucoma medications postoperatively; that surgery may fail completely; that they could lose vision as a result of surgery; and that glaucoma may progress despite successful surgery.

It is important to note that a patient with very advanced visual field loss or field loss that is impinging on fixation is at risk, in rare instances, of loss of central acuity following a surgical procedure. The most common cause of vision loss after trabeculectomy is cataract development. Hypotony maculopathy and cystoid macular edema may also cause vision loss. Loss of central vision in the absence of other explanations ("wipeout") may occur, but only in rare instances. Advanced age, preoperative visual field with macular splitting, and early postoperative hypotony are risk factors for wipeout. Early, undetected, postoperative elevation of IOP may also be associated with wipeout. Bleb infections and endophthalmitis may occur long after filtering surgery and may also cause vision loss.

> Costa VP, Smith M, Spaeth GL, Gandham S, Markovitz B. Loss of visual acuity after trabeculectomy. *Ophthalmology.* 1993;100(5):599–612.
> Greenfield DS. Dysfunctional glaucoma filtration blebs. *Focal Points: Clinical Modules for Ophthalmologists.* San Francisco: American Academy of Ophthalmology; 2002, module 4.

Trabeculectomy technique

Knowledge of both the internal and external anatomy of the limbal area is essential for successful incisional surgery. Trabeculectomy is a guarded partial-thickness filtering procedure in which a block of peripheral corneoscleral tissue is removed beneath a scleral flap. The scleral flap provides resistance and limits the outflow of aqueous, thereby reducing the complications associated with early hypotony, such as flat anterior chamber, cataract, serous choroidal effusion and hemorrhagic choroidal detachment, hypotony maculopathy, and optic nerve edema.

The use of antifibrotic agents (discussed in more detail later) such as mitomycin C and 5-fluorouracil, along with releasable sutures or laser suture lysis, enhances the longevity of guarded procedures, results in lower IOPs, and avoids some of the complications associated with full-thickness procedures, such as hypotony, flat anterior chamber, and choroidal hemorrhage.

A successful trabeculectomy involves reduction of IOP and avoidance or management of complications. Unlike with cataract surgery, the success of trabeculectomy often depends on appropriate and timely postoperative intervention to influence the functioning of the filter. Complete healing of the conjunctival incision, without scarring of the scleral flap to the scleral bed, and the absence of excessive subconjunctival scarring are the goals of this procedure.

A trabeculectomy can be broken down into several basic steps:

- *Exposure:* A corneal or limbal traction suture can rotate the globe down, providing excellent exposure of the superior sulcus and limbus, which can be very helpful for a limbus-based conjunctival flap (Fig 8-2). A superior rectus bridle suture has the same effect but is more likely to cause postoperative ptosis and subconjunctival hemorrhage. The speculum should be adjusted to keep pressure off the globe.
- *Conjunctival incision:* Traditionally, the trabeculectomy has been positioned at 12 o'clock or in either superior quadrant, depending on surgeon preference. There is evidence that with the use of antiproliferative agents, the trabeculectomy bleb should be positioned at 12 o'clock to reduce the risk of bleb exposure and dysesthesia. A fornix-based or limbus-based conjunctival flap can be used (Figs 8-3, 8-4). Each technique has advantages and disadvantages. The fornix-based flap is easier to fashion but requires very careful suturing to achieve a watertight closure at the end of the procedure. The advantage of a fornix-based conjunctival flap is the development of a subconjunctival scar anterior to the scleral flap, which encourages posterior aqueous flow and formation of a more posterior drainage bleb. The limbus-based conjunctival flap is technically more challenging, but it permits a secure closure well away from the limbus. The incision should be positioned 8–10 mm posterior to the limbus, and care should be taken to avoid the tendon of the superior rectus muscle. The advantage of a limbus-based flap is that it has a reduced risk of postoperative incision leakage; a potential disadvantage is the possible creation of a subconjunctival scar posterior to the scleral flap, impeding posterior flow of aqueous and encouraging more localized bleb formation closer to the limbus.

    The clinical situation will influence the placement of the conjunctival incision. For instance, in a deep-set eye with tight orbit, it may be anatomically difficult to create a limbus-based conjunctival flap. Conversely, if a patient is traveling long

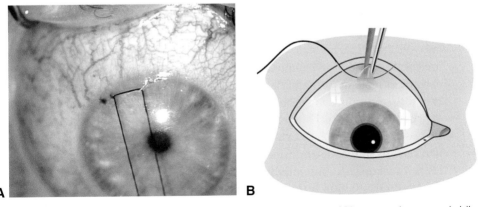

A **B**

Figure 8-2 Exposure for trabeculectomy: a corneal traction suture **(A)** or superior rectus bridle suture **(B)** is inserted. *(Part A courtesy of Keith Barton; part B courtesy of Alan Lacey. Both parts reproduced with permission of Moorfields Eye Hospital.)*

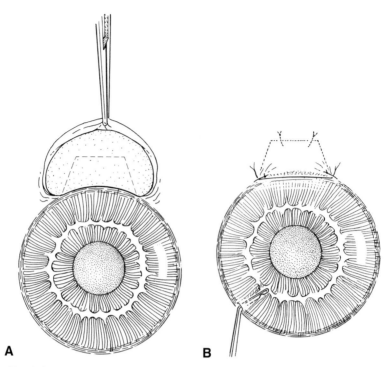

Figure 8-3 Fornix-based conjunctival flap. **A,** Drawing shows initial incision through conjunctiva and the insertion of the Tenon capsule. The arc length of the initial incision is approximately 6–7 mm. The tissue adjacent to the incision is undermined with blunt scissors before the scleral flap is prepared. **B,** The incision is closed either at both ends with interrupted sutures or purse-string sutures or with a running mattress suture. *(Modified with permission from Weinreb RN, Mills RP, eds.* Glaucoma Surgery: Principles and Techniques. *2nd ed. Ophthalmology Monograph 4. San Francisco: American Academy of Ophthalmology; 1998:43.)*

distances for postoperative care, the surgeon might elect to create a limbus-based conjunctival flap, as doing so would reduce both the risk of postoperative incision leakage and the number of postoperative visits that would be required to treat it.

- *Scleral flap:* The exact size and shape of the scleral flap do not seem to be critical. Rather, it is the relationship of the flap to the underlying sclerostomy (discussed later) that provides resistance to outflow. Although flap design will vary by surgeon preference, a common technique involves creating a 3- to 4-mm triangular, trapezoidal, or rectangular flap (Fig 8-5). If a fornix-based conjunctival flap is used, it is best to avoid dissecting the flap anteriorly into clear cornea, since anterior flap dissection facilitates early wound leakage.

- *Paracentesis* (Fig 8-6): To enable the surgeon to control the anterior chamber, a paracentesis should be performed next. This allows instillation of balanced salt solution or viscoelastic and intraoperative testing of the patency of the filtration site. Balanced salt solution is instilled through the paracentesis, and sutures are added to the scleral flap until flow is minimal. If a postoperative flat chamber occurs, the paracentesis is already in place and can be used to re-form the chamber. Using the existing paracentesis is much safer than trying to create a paracentesis in an eye with a flat chamber.

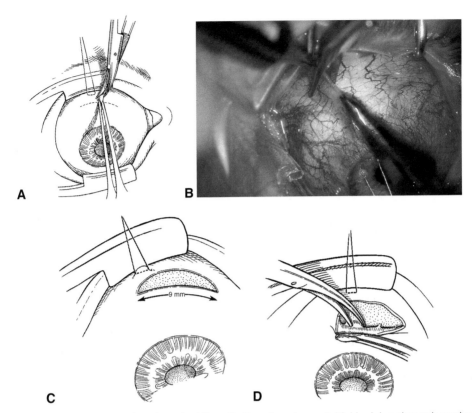

Figure 8-4 Limbus-based conjunctival flap. **A,** Drawing shows initial incision through conjunctiva and Tenon capsule. **B,** Clinical photograph corresponding to A shows the initial incision for creation of a limbus-based conjunctival flap. **C,** Completion of conjunctiva–Tenon incision 8–10 mm posterior to limbus. **D,** Anterior dissection of conjunctiva–Tenon flap with excision of Tenon episcleral fibrous adhesions. *(Parts A, C, and D modified with permission from Weinreb RN, Mills RP, eds. Glaucoma Surgery: Principles and Techniques. 2nd ed. Ophthalmology Monograph 4. San Francisco: American Academy of Ophthalmology; 1998:29–31. Part B courtesy of Robert D. Fechtner, MD.)*

- *Sclerostomy/keratectomy:* In a strict sense, the term *trabeculectomy* is inaccurate, because the procedure usually involves a peripheral posterior keratectomy rather than removal of trabecular meshwork. There is no advantage to extending the block posteriorly into sclera, and the risk of bleeding from the iris root and ciliary body is greater. The sclerostomy/keratectomy is commonly created with the use of a punch, although a block may also be cut with a fine blade (Fig 8-7). Aqueous drainage is generally not restricted by the size of the sclerostomy/keratectomy. A very small hole can drain more aqueous than is required to control IOP. However, the sclerostomy/keratectomy must be large enough to avoid occlusion by iris, but small enough so that it is overlapped on all sides by scleral flap. Insertion of a shunt (eg, EX-PRESS, Alcon, Ft Worth, TX) may be used to standardize the size of the sclerostomy/keratectomy. More overlap, a thicker flap, and tighter sutures are generally associated with less flow; the converse is also true.
- *Iridectomy:* An iridectomy is performed to reduce the risk of iris occluding the sclerostomy, especially in phakic and narrow-angle eyes, and to prevent pupillary block

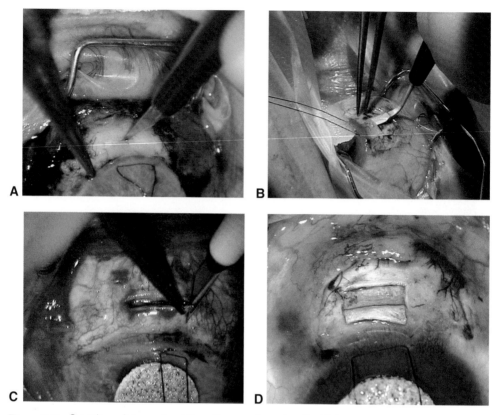

Figure 8-5 Creation of the scleral flap. Preparation of split-thickness scleral flap 4 mm wide and 2–2.5 mm from front to back. **A,** Posterior margin is dissected with a fine blade. **B,** A crescent knife is used to dissect a partial-thickness scleral tunnel. **C,** The sides of the tunnel are opened to create a flap. **D,** The final appearance. *(Courtesy of Keith Barton. Reproduced with permission of Moorfields Eye Hospital.)*

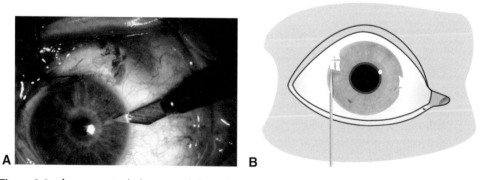

Figure 8-6 A paracentesis is created through clear cornea. This may be radial **(A)** or oblique **(B).** *(Part A courtesy of Keith Barton; part B courtesy of Alan Lacey. Both parts reproduced with permission of Moorfields Eye Hospital.)*

(see Fig 8-7D). An iridectomy may not always be necessary in pseudophakic eyes with deep anterior chambers. Care should be taken to avoid amputation of the ciliary processes or disruption of the zonular fibers or hyaloid face.

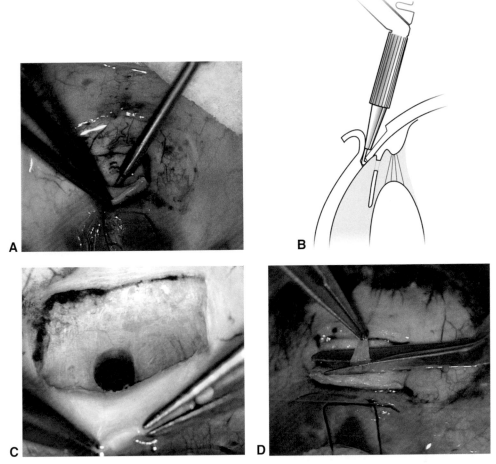

Figure 8-7 The surgeon can create a sclerostomy by **(A)** inserting a punch under the scleral flap; **(B)** snaring the posterior lip of the anterior chamber entry site; and **(C)** removing a punch (0.75–1 mm) of peripheral posterior cornea. A peripheral iridectomy is then made (shown here in an albino eye) with the use of iridectomy scissors **(D)**. *(Clinical photographs courtesy of Keith Barton; drawing courtesy of Alan Lacey. All parts reproduced with permission of Moorfields Eye Hospital.)*

- *Closure of scleral flap:* With the advent of laser suture lysis and releasable sutures (discussed later under "Flap management"), many surgeons close the flap more tightly, thereby minimizing postoperative shallowing of the anterior chamber. After a few days or weeks, these techniques may be used to release and promote flow. It is important to test the integrity of the scleral flap before closing the conjunctiva. When mitomycin C is used, suture tension and suture numbers should be adjusted until optimal spontaneous flow can be seen. To ensure that the trabeculectomy will still function after suture adjustment, the surgeon can test the flow. It should be possible to induce flow with gentle depression of the posterior scleral lip (Fig 8-8).
- *Closure of conjunctiva:* Many techniques have been developed for conjunctival closure (Fig 8-9). It is imperative that the closure be watertight at the completion of the procedure. For a fornix-based flap, conjunctiva is secured at the limbus. Several techniques have been developed for this closure, including interrupted sutures at

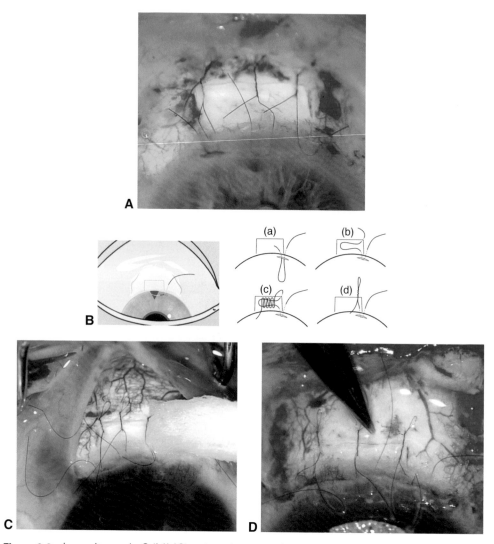

Figure 8-8 In a mitomycin C (MMC) trabeculectomy, the scleral flap is closed relatively tightly so that spontaneous drainage is minimal. Closure may be performed with the use of releasable sutures **(A, B)** that can be removed later at the slit lamp in order to increase flow, or with interrupted sutures that may be removed by laser later. **B** shows the order in which each movement is made. In both cases, the surgeon should check the flow at the end of scleral closure using a sponge **(C)** or fluorescein **(D)**. *(Clinical photographs courtesy of Keith Barton; drawing courtesy of Alan Lacey. All parts reproduced with permission of Moorfields Eye Hospital.)*

each end of the incision; a running mattress suture; and purse-string closures at each end of the incision, with or without mattress sutures in between. For a limbus-based flap, conjunctiva and Tenon capsule are closed separately or in a single layer with a running suture.

Jones E, Clarke J, Khaw PT. Recent advances in trabeculectomy technique. *Curr Opin Ophthalmol.* 2005;16(2):107–113.

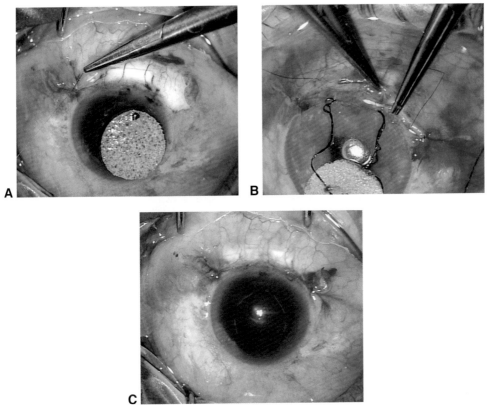

Figure 8-9 Conjunctival closure. Careful conjunctival closure is essential to prevent aqueous leakage, especially when a fornix-based conjunctival flap is used. Closing each extremity of the incision tightly with a purse-string suture **(A)** stretches the limbal edge of the conjunctiva, facilitating tight closure at the limbus. One or more conjunctival mattress sutures **(B)** prevent conjunctival recession. **C** shows an inflated bleb. *(Courtesy of Keith Barton. Reproduced with permission of Moorfields Eye Hospital.)*

Wise JB. Mitomycin-compatible suture technique for fornix-based conjunctival flaps in glaucoma filtration surgery. *Arch Ophthalmol.* 1993;111(7):992–997.

Antifibrotic agents

The application of antifibrotic agents such as 5-fluorouracil (5-FU) and mitomycin C (MMC) results in lower IOP following trabeculectomy. However, the rate of serious postoperative complications may increase, and these agents must not be used indiscriminately. Because their use is associated with an increased risk of hypotony maculopathy, antifibrotic agents should be used with caution in primary trabeculectomies on young patients with myopia.

The pyrimidine analog 5-FU inhibits fibroblast proliferation and has proven useful in reducing scarring after filtering surgery. The agent undergoes intracellular conversion to the active deoxynucleotide 5-fluoro-2′-deoxyuridine 5′-monophosphate (FdUMP), which interferes with DNA synthesis through its action on thymidylate synthetase.

Although 5-FU was originally advocated for use in high-risk groups such as patients with aphakic or pseudophakic eyes, neovascular glaucoma, or a history of failed operations, it is now used on a routine basis by many surgeons. This agent may be used intraoperatively (50 mg/mL on a surgical sponge) in a fashion similar to that described next for MMC. Regimens for postoperative administration vary according to the observed healing response. Individual doses of 5–10 mg in 0.1–0.5 cc can be injected. The total dose can be titrated to the observed healing response and corneal toxicity. Complications such as corneal epithelial defects commonly occur and require discontinuation of 5-FU injections. The site of the 5-FU injection can be varied: either 180° away from the trabeculectomy site or in the upper fornix adjacent to the bleb. As this agent is highly alkaline, the surgeon should avoid injecting 5-FU close to the scleral flap to reduce the risk of intraocular exposure.

Derived from *Streptomyces caespitosus,* MMC is a naturally occurring compound with antibiotic and antineoplastic activities. It acts as an alkylating agent after enzyme activation, resulting in DNA crosslinking. MMC is a potent antifibrotic agent that is most commonly administered intraoperatively in the following manner: a surgical sponge soaked in MMC is placed within the subconjunctival space so that it is in contact with sclera at the planned trabeculectomy site. Concentrations in current usage are typically between 0.1 and 0.5 mg/mL with a duration of application from 0.5 to 5 minutes. Most surgeons use the higher concentrations for shorter durations and vice versa. Few data are available to compare regimens, and most surgeons increase concentration or duration based on risk factors for trabeculectomy failure. The technique of MMC application has evolved to cover a larger area with increased posterior exposure in an attempt to develop a more diffuse, low-lying bleb (Fig 8-10) instead of a localized, elevated bleb (Fig 8-11), which is inherently at greater risk of infection. Because MMC is toxic and highly mutagenic, intracameral exposure must be avoided.

Flap management

Techniques allowing tighter initial closure of the scleral flap help prevent early postoperative hypotony. Two of these techniques are the use of releasable flap sutures and the placement of additional sutures that can be cut postoperatively to facilitate outflow following trabeculectomy. In laser suture lysis (LSL), the conjunctiva is compressed with either a Zeiss goniolens or a lens designed for suture lysis (such as a Hoskins, Ritch, Mandelkorn, or Blumenthal lens), and the argon green laser (set at 300–600 mW at a duration of 0.02–0.1 second with a spot size of 50–100 μm) or red laser can usually lyse the selected nylon suture with one application. It is important to avoid creating a full-thickness conjunctival burn. Shorter duration of laser energy and avoidance of pigment or blood are helpful for preventing such a burn. Most surgeons wait at least 48 hours before performing LSL. Filtration is best enhanced if lysis or suture release is completed within 2 to 4 weeks of the surgery or before the occurrence of flap fibrosis. This period may be lengthened to several months when antifibrotic agents have been used.

Postoperative considerations in filtering surgery

The success of glaucoma surgery depends on careful postoperative management. Topical corticosteroids are typically administered intensively (at least 4 times daily) initially and tapered as the clinical course dictates. Topical antibiotics or cycloplegic agents may also

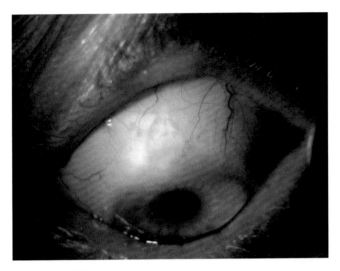

Figure 8-10 Diffuse conjunctival bleb. *(Courtesy of F. Jane Durcan, MD.)*

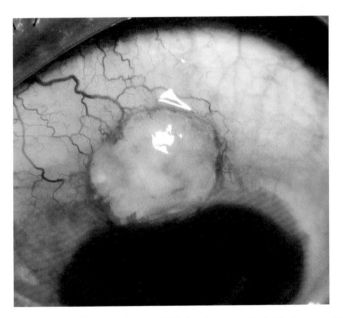

Figure 8-11 Localized conjunctival bleb. *(Courtesy of Jody Piltz-Seymour, MD.)*

be used. Topical corticosteroids should be tapered according to the degree of conjunctival hyperemia, which may continue for 2 months or more, rather than in response to the visible anterior chamber reaction, which usually resolves more quickly. Long-term use of prophylactic antibiotics is generally not recommended. Trabeculectomies require intensive early postoperative care, and frequent office visits are necessary in the first postoperative month. During this period, it is common for bleb massage to be performed, 5-FU injections to be given, or sutures to be lysed or removed. Also, if hypotony or a flat chamber occurs, it will not go undiagnosed for a prolonged period.

Complications of filtering surgery

Early and late complications of filtering surgery are listed in Table 8-1. Bleb-related complications may occur early (within 3 months of surgery) or late (after 3 months postoperatively). Early complications include wound leakage and hypotony, shallow or flat anterior chamber, and serous or hemorrhagic choroidal effusions. Late complications include bleb-related endophthalmitis, bleb leakage, ocular hypotony and associated maculopathy or choroidal hemorrhage, bleb failure, overhanging blebs, painful blebs, ptosis, and eyelid retraction. The filtering bleb can leak, produce dellen, or expand so as to interfere with eyelid function or extend onto the cornea and interfere with vision or cause irritation. Blebs may also encapsulate or fibrose, causing elevated IOP. Filtering blebs are dynamic; they evolve over time and must be monitored. All patients must be informed of the warning signs of endophthalmitis and instructed to seek ophthalmic care immediately should they develop a red eye or other signs of infection.

Late-onset bleb-related endophthalmitis is a potentially devastating complication of filtering surgery. The incidence of postoperative endophthalmitis associated with glaucoma surgery with or without antifibrosis drugs has been reported to range from 1.3% per patient-year for superior blebs to 7.8% per patient-year for inferior blebs. Risk factors for bleb-related endophthalmitis include blepharitis or conjunctivitis, ocular trauma, nasolacrimal duct obstruction, contact lens use, chronic bleb leak, male sex, and young age. Trabeculectomy performed at the inferior limbus is associated with an unacceptably high risk of bleb-related endophthalmitis. Use of adjunctive antifibrosis drugs such as 5-FU or MMC has been associated with increased risk of bleb-related endophthalmitis, perhaps because these blebs are often thin-walled and avascular. Patients may present with blebitis or with blebitis and endophthalmitis (Fig 8-12).

Hypotony after filtering surgery is usually due to overfiltration through the scleral flap. Aqueous leakage from a filtering bleb may occur as an early or late complication of surgery. Early-onset bleb leaks are usually related to ineffective wound closure or a

Table 8-1 Complications of Filtering Surgery

Early Complications	Late Complications
Infection	Leakage or failure of the filtering bleb
Hypotony	Cataract
Shallow or flat anterior chamber	Blebitis
Aqueous misdirection	Endophthalmitis/bleb infection
Hyphema	Symptomatic bleb (dysesthetic bleb)
Formation or acceleration of cataract	Bleb migration
Transient IOP elevation	Hypotony
Cystoid macular edema	Ptosis
Hypotony maculopathy	Eyelid retraction
Choroidal effusion	
Suprachoroidal hemorrhage	
Persistent uveitis	
Dellen formation	
Loss of vision	

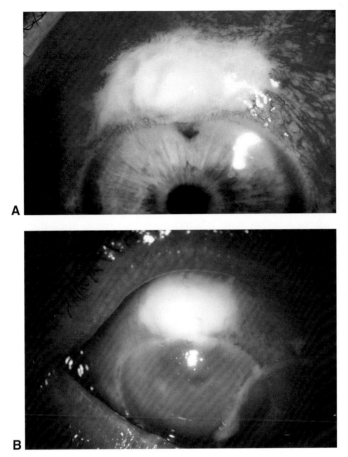

Figure 8-12 Bleb-related infection. Patients may present with blebitis, which is characterized by mucopurulent infiltrate within the bleb, localized conjunctival hyperemia, and minimal intraocular inflammation **(A)**. Bleb-related endophthalmitis **(B)** is characterized by diffuse bulbar conjunctival hyperemia, purulent material within the bleb, and anterior chamber cellular reaction, and sometimes by hypopyon formation and marked vitritis. *(Part A courtesy of Richard K. Parrish; part B courtesy of Keith Barton. Part B is reproduced with permission of Moorfields Eye Hospital.)*

conjunctival buttonhole. Late-onset leaks occur more frequently after full-thickness procedures such as posterior lip sclerectomy or after use of antifibrosis drugs. Untreated bleb leaks may lead to vision-threatening complications, including shallowing of the anterior chamber, PAS formation, cataract, corneal decompensation, choroidal effusion, suprachoroidal hemorrhage, endophthalmitis, and hypotony maculopathy. Clinical manifestations of hypotony maculopathy include decreased vision, hypotony, optic nerve and retinal edema, and radial folds of the macula.

Choroidal effusions may be treated medically with cycloplegics, with the injection of a viscoelastic substance into the anterior chamber, or by choroidal drainage. Suprachoroidal fluid is drained through 1 or more posterior full-thickness sclerotomies overlying the area of effusion, as the anterior chamber is deepened through a paracentesis. Numerous techniques have been described for managing bleb leaks, including the use of an oversize contact lens, aqueous suppressants, suture, tissue glue, autologous blood injection, and oral antibiotics from the tetracycline family. Excision of the bleb, in combination with a conjunctival graft or conjunctival advancement with or without a scleral graft, is also possible. The surgeon may also advance a conjunctival flap over the existing bleb.

The bleb may fail following filtering surgery. In eyes with failing blebs, reduced bleb height, increased bleb-wall thickness, vascularization of the bleb, loss of conjunctival microcysts, and increased IOP may be seen. Risk factors for bleb failure include anterior segment neovascularization, black race, aphakia, prior failed filtering procedures, uveitis, prior cataract surgery, and young age. Initial management of failing blebs often includes digital massage. In eyes that do not respond to this initial therapy, transconjunctival needle revision may restore aqueous flow.

The use of contact lenses with a filtering bleb presents special problems. Contact lenses may be difficult to fit in the presence of a filtering bleb, or the lens may ride against the bleb, causing discomfort and increasing the risk of infection. Several options can be considered for the patient who has myopia, needs a trabeculectomy, and prefers not to or cannot wear spectacles. Refractive surgery options include photorefractive keratectomy (PRK), laser in situ keratomileusis (LASIK), or intracorneal ring segments prior to trabeculectomy. Clear lens extraction (either before, after, or combined with trabeculectomy) is controversial. In some circumstances, hard or soft contact lens use under close supervision may be considered after trabeculectomy. Contact lens use is more often feasible in patients after implantation of a glaucoma drainage device than after trabeculectomy. When an initial filtering procedure is not adequate to control the glaucoma and resumption of medical therapy is not successful, revision of original surgery, a second filtering surgery at a new site, glaucoma drainage device implantation, or possibly cyclodestructive procedures may be indicated.

Au L, Wechsler D, Spencer F, Fenerty C. Outcome of bleb revision using scleral patch graft and conjunctival advancement. *J Glaucoma*. 2009;18(4):331–335.

Budenz DL, Hoffman K, Zacchei A. Glaucoma filtering bleb dysesthesia. *Am J Ophthalmol*. 2001;131(5):626–630.

Camras CB. Diagnosis and management of complications of glaucoma filtering surgery. *Focal Points: Clinical Modules for Ophthalmologists*. San Francisco: American Academy of Ophthalmology; 1994, module 3.

DeBry PW, Perkins TW, Heatley G, Kaufman P, Brumback LC. Incidence of late-onset bleb-related complications following trabeculectomy with mitomycin. *Arch Ophthalmol*. 2002;120(3):297–300.

Greenfield DS. Dysfunctional glaucoma filtration blebs. *Focal Points: Clinical Modules for Ophthalmologists*. San Francisco: American Academy of Ophthalmology; 2002, module 4.

Greenfield DS, Suñer IJ, Miller MP, Kangas TA, Palmberg PF, Flynn HW Jr. Endophthalmitis after filtering surgery with mitomycin. *Arch Ophthalmol*. 1996;114(8):943–949.

Haynes WL, Alward WL. Control of intraocular pressure after trabeculectomy. *Surv Ophthalmol*. 1999;43(4):345–355.

Tannenbaum DP, Hoffman D, Greaney MJ, Caprioli J. Outcomes of bleb excision and conjunctival advancement for leaking or hypotonous eyes after glaucoma filtering surgery. *Br J Ophthalmol*. 2004;88(1):99–103.

Combined Cataract and Filtering Surgery

Both cataract and glaucoma are conditions that show increasing prevalence with aging. It is not surprising that many patients with glaucoma eventually develop cataracts either naturally or as a result of the effects of glaucoma therapy. It should also be noted that cataract surgery alone may lower IOP in eyes with open angles and may lower it even more in eyes with phacomorphic narrow angles.

Indications

Cataract surgery may be combined with trabeculectomy in the following situations:

- cataract requiring extraction in a glaucoma patient who has advanced cupping and visual field loss
- cataract requiring extraction in a glaucoma patient who requires medications to control IOP but who tolerates medical therapy poorly or has inadequately controlled IOP
- cataract requiring extraction in a glaucoma patient who requires multiple medications to control IOP

The success of IOP control in combined surgery is reduced compared to that in trabeculectomy alone. Thus, in uncontrolled glaucoma, combined surgery is usually performed only in specific circumstances, such as primary angle-closure glaucoma uncontrolled with medications or after laser iridotomy when cataract surgery alone is unlikely to provide successful IOP control. Many surgeons perform trabeculectomy with cataract surgery when the IOP is stable but the patient is using 2 to 3 IOP-lowering medications. The goal in these cases is to avoid perioperative problems with elevated IOP and to achieve a long-term reduction in the number of medications required. However, many surgeons would perform cataract surgery alone in a patient who has controlled IOP using 1 medication, with mild to moderate cupping and little visual field loss.

Relative contraindications

Combined cataract and filtering surgery should be avoided in the following situations, in which glaucoma surgery alone is preferred:

- glaucoma that requires a very low target IOP
- advanced glaucoma with uncontrolled IOP and immediate need for successful reduction of IOP

Considerations

A combined procedure may prevent a postoperative rise in IOP. Combined procedures are generally less effective than filtering procedures alone in controlling IOP over time, although combined procedures that use small-incision phacoemulsification techniques with an antifibrotic agent appear to have better success rates than trabeculectomy combined with extracapsular cataract surgery. For patients in whom glaucoma is the greatest immediate threat to vision, filtering surgery alone is usually performed first.

Several clinical challenges are common in patients with coexisting cataract and glaucoma. Medical therapy for glaucoma may create chronic miosis, and the surgeon must deal with a small pupil. In patients with exfoliation syndrome, zonular support of the lens is often fragile, and vitreous loss is therefore more common in such complicated eyes. As with all surgery, the risks, benefits, and alternatives should be discussed with the patient.

Technique

Long-term control of IOP is better with combined glaucoma and cataract operations than with cataract surgery alone, and several surgical approaches to coexisting cataract and glaucoma are currently used. Although little evidence exists to compare the long-term outcomes of patients treated with these different approaches, it is reasonable for the surgeon to use the cataract procedure that he or she performs best, because the primary indication for surgery is the presence of cataract.

Trabeculectomy may be combined with phacoemulsification, which is performed through the superior trabeculectomy incision or through a temporal clear corneal incision. Also, cataract extraction may be combined with implantation of a glaucoma drainage device. In addition, there are several procedures that combine cataract surgery with surgery on the Schlemm canal, as for example, canaloplasty (see the section Nonpenetrating Glaucoma Surgery) and trabectome. In trabectome, electroablation of the trabecular meshwork is performed through a temporal corneal incision, a technique similar to that used in goniotomy, to lower IOP in OAG.

For the patient whose IOP is controlled medically, clear corneal cataract surgery alone may be the appropriate choice. As no violation of conjunctiva or sclera occurs with this procedure, there is little reason to perform an incidental trabeculectomy. Rather, standard trabeculectomy can be performed when dictated by independent indications.

Balyeat HD. Cataract surgery in the glaucoma patient. Part 1: A cataract surgeon's perspective. *Focal Points: Clinical Modules for Ophthalmologists*. San Francisco: American Academy of Ophthalmology; 1998, module 3.

Friedman DS, Jampel HD, Lubomski LH, et al. Surgical strategies for coexisting glaucoma and cataract: an evidence-based update. *Ophthalmology*. 2002;109(10):1902–1913.

Jampel HD, Friedman DS, Lubomski LH, et al. Effect of technique on intraocular pressure after combined cataract and glaucoma surgery: an evidence-based review. *Ophthalmology*. 2002;109(10):2215–2224.

Jin GJ, Crandall AS, Jones JJ. Phacotrabeculectomy: assessment of outcomes and surgical improvements. *J Cataract Refract Surg*. 2007;33(7):1201–1208.

Skuta GL. Cataract surgery in the glaucoma patient. Part 2: A glaucoma surgeon's perspective. *Focal Points: Clinical Modules for Ophthalmologists*. San Francisco: American Academy of Ophthalmology; 1998, module 4.

Weinreb RN, Mills RP, eds. *Glaucoma Surgery: Principles and Techniques*. 2nd ed. Ophthalmology Monograph 4. San Francisco: American Academy of Ophthalmology; 1998:65–85.

Surgery for Angle-Closure Glaucoma

The first clinical decision to be made following diagnosis of angle-closure glaucoma (ACG) is whether angle closure is due to pupillary block or another mechanism. The treatment of angle closure due to pupillary block, whether primary or secondary, is a laser iridotomy or an incisional iridectomy. These procedures provide an alternate route for aqueous trapped in the posterior chamber to enter the anterior chamber, which then allows the iris to recede from its occlusion of the trabecular meshwork (Fig 8-13). Laser surgery has become the preferred method in almost all cases. Both the argon laser and the Nd:YAG laser are effective, but the Nd:YAG laser has become the more popular instrument to use. Cataract extraction is also effective as therapy for angle closure secondary to pupillary block. Following the successful resolution of pupillary block, IOP may return to normal or may remain elevated. At this point, the indications for surgery become similar to those for POAG, except for possible surgical goniosynechialysis. When cataract surgery will result in aphakia or anterior chamber intraocular lens placement, a surgical iridectomy should be performed at the time of the cataract surgery.

For eyes with secondary angle closure not caused by pupillary block, the ophthalmologist should attempt to identify and treat underlying conditions before surgery. For example, an eye with rubeosis iridis from diabetic retinopathy should be treated with panretinal photocoagulation and consideration should be given to intravitreal injection of an antivascular endothelial growth factor (anti-VEGF) agent prior to glaucoma surgery. In early cases, the IOP elevation may be reversible. Even in the presence of complete synechial angle closure from rubeosis, neovascularization may regress following panretinal photocoagulation, allowing subsequent successful filtering surgery and reducing the risk of hyphema.

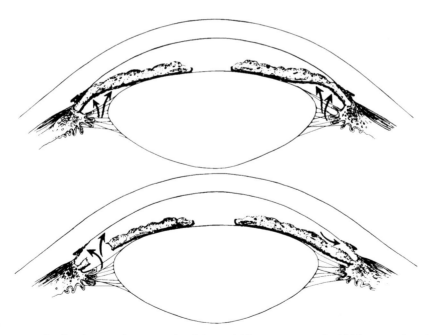

Figure 8-13 Angle-closure glaucoma *(top)*. Laser iridotomy or surgical iridectomy breaks the pupillary block and results in opening of the entire peripheral angle *(bottom)* if no permanent peripheral anterior synechiae are present. *(Reproduced and modified with permission from Kolker AE, Hetherington J, eds. Becker-Shaffer's Diagnosis and Therapy of the Glaucomas. 5th ed. St Louis: Mosby; 1983.)*

Laser Iridotomy

Indications

The indication for iridotomy is the presence of pupillary block. However, it is sometimes necessary to perform iridotomy for diagnostic as well as therapeutic purposes. For example, the diagnosis of plateau iris can be confirmed only when a patent iridotomy fails to change the peripheral iris configuration and relieve angle closure. Laser iridotomy is also indicated to prevent pupillary block in an eye considered to be at risk of this condition, based on gonioscopic findings or an angle-closure attack in the fellow eye.

Contraindications

An eye with active rubeosis iridis may bleed following laser iridotomy. The risk of bleeding is also increased in a patient taking systemic anticoagulants, including aspirin. The argon laser may be more appropriate than the Nd:YAG, should laser iridotomy be performed in such an individual.

Preoperative considerations

In the setting of acute angle closure, it is often difficult to perform laser iridotomy because of the cloudy cornea, shallow chamber, and engorged iris. The clinician should attempt to break the attack medically and then proceed to surgery. Corneal edema may be improved prior to laser iridotomy by pretreatment with topical glycerin. It is easiest to penetrate the iris in a crypt. The surgeon should take care to keep the iridotomy in the peripheral iris and covered by eyelid, if possible, or at the 3- or 9-o'clock position, to avoid monocular diplopia. Pretreatment with pilocarpine may be helpful by stretching and thinning the iris. Pretreatment with apraclonidine or brimonidine can help blunt IOP spikes.

Technique

The argon laser may be used for performing iridotomy in most eyes, but very dark and very light irides present technical difficulties. With a condensing contact lens, the typical initial laser settings are 0.1 second of duration, 50-μm spot size, and 800–1000 mW of power. There are a number of variations in technique, and iris color dictates which technique is chosen. Complications include localized lens opacity, acute rise in IOP (which may damage the optic nerve), transient or persistent iritis, early closure of the iridotomy, posterior synechiae, and corneal and retinal burns.

Iridotomy performed with the Q-switched Nd:YAG laser is preferred for most eyes. A patent iridotomy created with the Q-switched Nd:YAG laser generally requires fewer pulses and less energy than one created with an argon laser. Also, the effectiveness of the Q-switched Nd:YAG laser is not affected by iris color, and the iridotomy created by this laser does not close as often over the long term as one created by argon laser. With a condensing contact lens, the typical initial setting for the Q-switched Nd:YAG laser is 2–8 mJ. Potential complications include disruption of the anterior lens capsule or corneal endothelium, bleeding (usually transient), postoperative IOP spike, inflammation, and delayed closure of the iridotomy. To prevent damage to the lens, the surgeon must use caution with the Q-switched Nd:YAG laser when further enlarging the opening once patency has been established. The site of the iridotomy should be as peripheral as possible, at the point where the distance between the iris and lens is greatest.

Postoperative care

Bleeding may occur from the iridotomy site, particularly with use of the Nd:YAG laser. Often, compression of the eye with the laser lens will tamponade the vessel, thereby slowing bleeding until coagulation can occur. In rare cases when this does not work, it may be helpful to use the argon laser to coagulate the vessel. Postoperative spikes in IOP may occur, as with LTP, and they are treated as described in the section on LTP. Inflammation is treated as necessary with topical corticosteroids.

Murphy PH, Trope GE. Monocular blurring: a complication of YAG laser iridotomy. *Ophthalmology.* 1991;98(10):1539–1542.

Ritch R, Shields MB, Krupin T, eds. *The Glaucomas.* 2nd ed. St Louis: Mosby; 1996.

Shields MB. *Textbook of Glaucoma.* 4th ed. Philadelphia: Williams & Wilkins; 2000.

Spaeth GL, Idowu O, Seligsohn A, et al. The effects of iridotomy size and position on symptoms following laser peripheral iridotomy. *J Glaucoma.* 2005;14(5):364–367.

Laser Gonioplasty, or Peripheral Iridoplasty

Indications

Gonioplasty, or iridoplasty, is a technique to deepen the angle. It is primarily used in angle-closure glaucoma resulting from plateau iris. Stromal burns are created with the argon laser in the peripheral iris to cause contraction and flattening.

Contraindications

The contraindications are the same as those for laser iridotomy.

Preoperative considerations

An angle that is closed from plateau iris will not open with creation of a laser iridotomy, because the underlying mechanism is not pupillary block. Anterior segment ultrasonography may be helpful in making this diagnosis.

Technique

Typical laser settings for the argon green laser are 0.1–0.5 second duration, 200- to 500-μm spot size, and 200–500 mW of power. Laser gonioplasty can be used to open the angle temporarily, in anticipation of a more definitive laser or incisional iridectomy, or in other types of angle closure, such as plateau iris syndrome and nanophthalmos.

Ritch R, Tham CC, Lam DS. Argon laser peripheral iridoplasty (ALPI): an update. *Surv Ophthalmol.* 2007;52(3):279–288.

Postoperative considerations

Elevated IOP may occur in the postoperative period and should be monitored, as is done after other laser procedures. Anisocoria and iris pigment changes may also be noted. The clinician should mention this possibility to the patient during the preoperative consent process.

Incisional Surgery for Angle Closure

Peripheral iridectomy

Surgical iridectomy may be required if a patent iridotomy cannot be achieved with a laser. Such situations include a cloudy cornea, a shallow or flat anterior chamber, and insufficient patient cooperation.

Cataract extraction

When pupillary block is associated with a visually significant cataract, lens extraction might be considered as a primary procedure. However, laser iridotomy may stop acute pupillary block, so that cataract surgery may be performed more safely at a later time. Cataract extraction combined with goniosynechialysis may be effective in patients with chronic angle-closure glaucoma following acute primary angle-closure glaucoma and in patients with primary angle closure unresponsive to laser iridotomy.

> Harasymowycz PJ, Papamatheakis DG, Ahmed I, et al. Phacoemulsification and gonio-synechialysis in the management of unresponsive primary angle closure. *J Glaucoma.* 2005;14(3):186–189.

Chamber deepening and goniosynechialysis

When PAS develop in cases of angle closure, iridotomy alone may not lower the IOP adequately. Chamber deepening through a paracentesis may break PAS of relatively recent onset. A viscoelastic agent and/or an iris or cyclodialysis spatula may be useful, in a procedure known as *goniosynechialysis,* to break synechiae.

> Campbell DG, Vela A. Modern goniosynechialysis for the treatment of synechial angle-closure glaucoma. *Ophthalmology.* 1984;91(9):1052–1060.
>
> Shingleton BJ, Chang MA, Bellows AR, Thomas JV. Surgical goniosynechialysis for angle-closure glaucoma. *Ophthalmology.* 1990;97(5):551–556.

Other Procedures to Lower IOP

Incisional and nonincisional procedures to control IOP include glaucoma drainage device implantation, ciliary body ablation, and cyclodialysis, as well as viscocanalostomy, canaloplasty, and other nonpenetrating procedures.

Glaucoma Drainage Device Implantation

Many different types of devices have been developed that aid angle filtration by shunting aqueous to a site away from the limbus, such as the equatorial subconjunctival space. Glaucoma drainage device implantation generally involves placing a tube in the anterior chamber, in the ciliary sulcus, or through the pars plana into the vitreous cavity. This tube is usually connected to an extraocular plate, which is attached to the sclera in the equatorial region of the globe, between the extraocular muscles; some devices employ 2 plates. Aqueous flows out through the tube and into the subconjunctival space in the region of the extraocular plate.

Glaucoma drainage devices can be broadly categorized as nonvalved devices, which have no flow restrictor, or valved devices, which have a flow restrictor (Table 8-2). The most popular nonvalved devices are the Molteno (Molteno Ophthalmic Ltd, Dunedin, New Zealand) and Baerveldt (Abbott Medical Optics, Santa Ana, CA) designs. The most widely used valved device is the Ahmed (New World Medical, Inc, Rancho Cucamonga, CA). A recently published study comparing the Ahmed glaucoma valve (AGV) and the Baerveldt glaucoma implant (BGI) found that the average IOP after 1 year was slightly higher in patients who received the AGV; however, there were fewer early postoperative complications associated with use of the AGV than with the BGI. The size of the drainage device plate varies and can influence IOP control and complications postoperatively.

The anterior chamber tube shunt to an encircling band (ACTSEB), described by Schocket, is another type of glaucoma drainage device. ACTSEB uses an encircling element intended for scleral buckling, and tubing, which is attached to the encircling band. A variation on ACTSEB can be used in eyes with a previously placed scleral buckle: angiocatheter tubing is passed into the anterior chamber via a needle track near the limbus and then threaded into the capsule surrounding a previously placed scleral buckle.

Budenz DL, Barton K, Feuer WJ, et al. Treatment outcomes in the Ahmed Baerveldt Comparison Study after 1 year of follow-up. *Ophthalmology.* 2011;118(3):443–452. Epub 2010 Oct 8.

Weinreb RN, Mills RP, eds. *Glaucoma Surgery: Principles and Techniques.* 2nd ed. Ophthalmology Monograph 4. San Francisco: American Academy of Ophthalmology; 1998:65–85.

Indications

The devices mentioned and similar types of implants have generally been reserved for difficult glaucoma cases in which conventional filtering surgery has failed or is likely to fail. However, glaucoma drainage device implantation may be used as a primary filtration procedure. The 3-year follow-up results of the Tube Versus Trabeculectomy study showed that tube-shunt (glaucoma drainage device) surgery had a higher success rate compared to trabeculectomy with MMC. Both procedures were associated with a similar reduction

Table 8-2 Glaucoma Drainage Devices

	Molteno			Baerveldt		Ahmed		Eagle Vision
	Single Plate	Double Plate	M3	Single Plate		Single Plate	Double Plate	Single Plate
Surface area, mm²	133	265	175 230	250	350	184	364	365
Height profile, mm	1.65	1.65	1.50	0.84	0.84	1.90	1.90	1.75
Plate material	Polypropylene			Silicone		Polypropylene or silicone		Silicone
Flow restrictor	No	No	Ridge	No		Yes		No
Pediatric surface area, mm²	55			No		96		No

in IOP and use of supplemental medications. A glaucoma drainage device should be considered in the following clinical settings:

- *Failed trabeculectomy with antifibrotics:* It may be appropriate to perform a second trabeculectomy in some clinical situations. However, when the factors that precipitated the initial failure cannot be modified, or when it is not technically possible to repeat the trabeculectomy, implantation of a glaucoma drainage device may be the procedure of choice.
- *Active uveitis:* Although few randomized, prospective studies have been performed comparing trabeculectomy with antifibrotics to glaucoma drainage devices in the setting of active uveitis, the success rate of trabeculectomy is disappointingly low in most cases of active inflammation. In certain types of uveitis, for example, young patients with juvenile idiopathic arthritis, the success rate of trabeculectomy is low and glaucoma drainage device implantation is often the primary surgical treatment.
- *Neovascular glaucoma:* Eyes with neovascular glaucoma (NVG) are at high risk of trabeculectomy failure. In one prospective study, the 5-year success rate of trabeculectomy with 5-FU in NVG was 28%. When possible, panretinal photocoagulation is performed prior to glaucoma surgery in cases of NVG. When the IOP level is such that urgent surgery is required, or when the NVG does not respond to panretinal photocoagulation, a glaucoma drainage device is indicated. The management of NVG is likely to change with the use of anti–vascular endothelial growth factor agents. These medications may decrease the risk of perioperative intraocular bleeding.
- *Inadequate conjunctiva:* In patients who have undergone severe trauma or previous surgery involving conjunctiva (eg, retinal detachment surgery), trabeculectomy success may be reduced because these patients may have excessive conjunctival scarring. A glaucoma drainage device can be implanted, even in the presence of a scleral buckle. When a complete vitrectomy has been performed, the tube can be placed through the pars plana.
- *Aphakia:* The success rate of conventional filtering surgery in aphakic eyes is low, even when MMC is used. Many surgeons use glaucoma drainage device implantation as a primary procedure in uncontrolled aphakic glaucoma.
- *Contact lens use:* The need for contact lens use for vision rehabilitation is an important consideration. The use of a soft contact lens over a trabeculectomy bleb is a risk factor for bleb trauma and subsequent infection. The use of a soft contact lens following glaucoma drainage device implantation is not without risk, however, as the conjunctiva overlying the tube is more prone to erosion with contact lens use.

Contraindications

Glaucoma drainage device implantation may have a complicated postoperative course. Borderline corneal endothelial function is a relative contraindication for anterior chamber placement of a tube.

Preoperative considerations

The preoperative evaluation for glaucoma drainage device implantation is similar to that for trabeculectomy. During the ophthalmic examination, the clinician should note the findings of the motility examination, the status of the conjunctiva, the health of the sclera at the anticipated sites for the tube and external plate, the location of PAS near possible tube insertion sites, and the location of vitreous in the eye. The clinician should also note a previously placed scleral buckle.

Techniques

Although glaucoma drainage devices differ in design, the basic techniques for implantation are similar. The superotemporal quadrant is preferred over the superonasal quadrant, because surgical access is more easily achieved in the former. Valved devices must be primed before implantation. The extraocular plate is sutured between the vertical and horizontal rectus muscles, posterior to the muscle insertions. The tube portion of the device is then routed in 1 of 3 ways: anteriorly to enter the chamber angle; into the ciliary sulcus in a pseudophakic eye; or through the pars plana for posterior implantation in eyes that have had a complete vitrectomy. Typically, the tube is covered with tissue such as sclera, pericardium, or cornea to help prevent erosion through the conjunctiva. Dura should be avoided because of the potential risk of prion transmission.

For the nonvalved devices, there are a number of techniques to restrict flow in the early postoperative period, such as stenting the tube lumen or ligating the tube with a suture. Restricting flow is not necessary with devices that contain a flow restrictor, although hypotony and a flat chamber can still sometimes occur with them. Administering antifibrotic agents in doses similar to those used in trabeculectomy does not appear to improve the success of glaucoma drainage device surgery. For devices with 2 plates, the second plate and its interconnecting tube may be placed either over or under the superior rectus muscle; the distal plate is attached to the sclera in a manner similar to that in which the proximal plate is attached.

A confounding cause of hypotony can be leakage of aqueous around the tube at its entry site. In general, tubes should be introduced into the anterior chamber via a needle incision that is no larger than the diameter of the tube (23 gauge for most tubes). When the patient's eye has thin sclera or when the tube is introduced under a partial-thickness scleral flap, a tighter entry site (eg, 25 gauge) may be required.

Postoperative management

The IOP in the early postoperative period can be variable. With nonvalved devices in which the tube has been occluded, early IOP spikes are best managed medically. After sufficient time has passed for a capsule to form around the extraocular plate, the occluding suture is released for the nonvalved devices. As with trabeculectomy, topical corticosteroids, topical antibiotics, and cycloplegic agents are used. IOP elevation occurs around 2–8 weeks postoperatively, which probably represents encapsulation of the extraocular reservoir. Aqueous suppression can control the IOP, and this elevation usually improves or resolves spontaneously within 1–6 months.

Complications

Success rates have been encouraging, but the implant procedures share many of the complications associated with conventional filtering surgery. In addition, unique problems related to the tubes and plates arise. Early overfiltration in an eye with tube placement in the anterior chamber results in a flat chamber and tube–cornea touch. Tube–cornea touch can compromise the cornea; and even when no touch occurs, an area of corneal decompensation can appear near the tube. Eyes must be monitored for late complications such as tube erosion or plate migration. Ocular motility disturbances may also occur. Tube obstruction, plate migration, or tube erosion may require surgical revision. Table 8-3 lists

Table 8-3 Glaucoma Drainage Device Surgery Complications and Prevention/Management Options

Complication	Prevention/Management
Tube–cornea touch	Avoid by making the anterior chamber insertion parallel with the iris plane and using a tube occlusion technique to avoid a flat chamber. Pars plana and ciliary sulcus insertion avoid this complication.
Flat chamber and hypotony	Flat chamber and hypotony caused by overfiltration are best avoided by the use of a valved device, an occlusion technique, or viscoelastic agents. Aqueous leakage around the tube at the anterior chamber entry site is another important cause of hypotony. Avoid by ensuring that the entry site is watertight around the tube. A flat chamber with tube–cornea touch and serous choroidal detachment should be managed by early re-formation of the anterior chamber and correction of the overdrainage. To correct overdrainage, use tube occlusion techniques or correct entry site problems by repositioning the tube if necessary. Viscoelastic can help maintain the chamber. A flat chamber resulting from a complication such as suprachoroidal hemorrhage must be managed based on the clinical setting.
Tube occlusion	Avoid by beveling the tube away from uveal tissue (iris) or vitreous. A generous vitrectomy should be performed if needed. Although it is possible to use Nd:YAG laser to clear an occlusion, surgical intervention is often required.
Plate migration	Avoid by securing plate tightly to sclera with nonabsorbable sutures. If the plate migrates, the intraocular tube may become longer or retract. Plate migration toward the limbus requires repositioning of the plate in the equatorial subconjunctival space. Plate migration away from the limbus is rarely significant enough to warrant repositioning but may require a tube-extender if the tube retracts from the anterior chamber.
Valve malfunction	Test valves for patency before insertion of the tube. Several techniques have been described to unclog a valve.
Tube or plate exposure or erosion	Repair tube or plate exposure by removing any protruding sutures that have precipitated the erosion, securing tube tightly to sclera, covering tube with reinforcing material (eg, sclera, cornea, or pericardium), and mobilizing conjunctiva. Donor sclera must be adequately covered with conjunctiva, or further erosion may occur. If adequate conjunctiva is not available, conjunctival autograft or amniotic membrane may be used. Exposure increases the risk of endophthalmitis. In some settings, the tube should be removed if adequate coverage cannot be achieved.

several common complications of glaucoma drainage devices, along with methods for avoiding their development or managing them.

Gedde SJ, Herndon LW, Brandt JD, Budenz DL, Feuer WJ, Schiffman JC. Surgical complications in the Tube Versus Trabeculectomy Study during the first year of follow-up. *Am J Ophthalmol.* 2007;143(1):23–31.

Gedde SJ, Schiffman JC, Feuer WJ, et al. Three-year follow-up of the Tube Versus Trabeculectomy Study. *Am J Ophthalmol.* 2009;148(5):670–684.

Gedde SJ, Schiffman JC, Feuer WJ, Herndon LW, Brandt JD, Budenz DL. Treatment outcomes in the Tube Versus Trabeculectomy Study after one year of follow-up. *Am J Ophthalmol.* 2007;143(1):9–22.

Sidoti PA, Heuer DK. Aqueous shunting procedures. *Focal Points: Clinical Modules for Ophthalmologists.* San Francisco: American Academy of Ophthalmology; 2002, module 3.

Wilson MR, Mendis U, Paliwal A, Haynatzka V. Long-term follow-up of primary glaucoma surgery with Ahmed glaucoma valve implant versus trabeculectomy. *Am J Ophthalmol.* 2003;136(3):464–470.

Ciliary Body Ablation Procedures

Several surgical procedures reduce aqueous secretion by destroying a portion of the ciliary body. The secretory activity of ciliary body epithelium can be inhibited by treatment with cyclocryotherapy and thermal lasers such as continuous-wave Nd:YAG, argon, and diode (Fig 8-14).

Indications

Ciliary ablation is indicated to lower IOP in eyes that have poor visual potential or that are poor candidates for incisional surgery. Incisional surgery in blind eyes should be avoided,

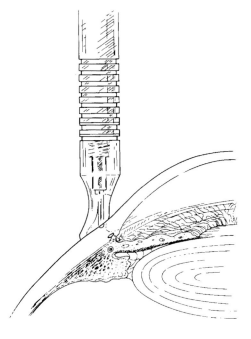

Figure 8-14 Cyclophotocoagulation. The diode laser handpiece attachment from one manufacturer is shown. After the edge of the probe is aligned with the limbus, approximately 17–19 applications are placed 270° around the limbus, with a power of 1.5–2 W and a duration of approximately 2 seconds. *(Reproduced with permission from Weinreb RN, Mills RP, eds.* Glaucoma Surgery: Principles and Techniques. *2nd ed. Ophthalmology Monograph 4. San Francisco: American Academy of Ophthalmology; 1998:165.)*

if possible, because of the small risk of sympathetic ophthalmia. Diode laser cyclophoto-coagulation (CPC) is often the treatment of choice for lowering the IOP in painful blind eyes or in eyes unlikely to respond to other modes of therapy. Interventions such as retro-bulbar alcohol injection, retrobulbar chlorpromazine injection, or enucleation are rarely performed now because of improved CPC techniques.

Contraindications

External ciliary ablation is relatively contraindicated in eyes with good vision because of the risk of loss of visual acuity from macular edema.

Preoperative evaluation

The preoperative evaluation for ciliary body ablation procedures is the same as that for incisional glaucoma surgery.

Methods and considerations

Cyclocryotherapy and Nd:YAG laser CPC are rarely performed now, as they have largely been replaced by transscleral diode laser CPC and endoscopic diode laser CPC, which is better tolerated, causing less pain and inflammation. Also, even though there is a degree of unpredictability with diode laser CPC, this method is considerably more predictable than its predecessors in its effect.

An *endoscopic laser delivery system* can be used with cataract surgery and in pediatric, pseudophakic, or aphakic eyes. In a small percentage of patients, it is possible to use a procedure in which the argon laser beam is focused through a goniolens and aimed at the ciliary processes.

Postoperative management

Pain following external CPC or cyclocryotherapy may be substantial, and patients may need to be provided with adequate analgesics, including narcotics, during the immediate postoperative period.

Complications

Each of these procedures may result in prolonged hypotony, pain, inflammation, cystoid macular edema, hemorrhage, and even phthisis bulbi. Sympathetic ophthalmia is a rare but serious complication.

Pastor SA, Singh K, Lee DA, et al. Cyclophotocoagulation: a report by the American Academy of Ophthalmology. *Ophthalmology.* 2001;108(11):2130–2138.

Nonpenetrating Glaucoma Surgery

Although the most widely accepted IOP-lowering incisional surgeries involve creating a direct communication between the anterior chamber and the subconjunctival space, non-penetrating surgery has also been proposed. Nonpenetrating glaucoma procedures were initially described in the early 1970s. The goal was to achieve IOP lowering while avoiding some of the complications of standard trabeculectomy.

Recently, interest in nonpenetrating surgery has been revived. Several variations in-clude a deep sclerectomy, which involves dissection and excision of a second, deep scleral flap down to a tissue plane just above the ciliary body and unroofing of the Schlemm canal. These nonpenetrating procedures include deep sclerectomy with or without a collagen implant, viscocanalostomy, and canaloplasty. In both viscocanalostomy and canaloplasty, the deep sclerectomy is augmented with injection of viscoelastic into the Schlemm canal. In viscocanalostomy, a cannula is used to inject viscoelastic into a limited section of the Schlemm canal. In canaloplasty, a flexible illuminated catheter is utilized to inject viscoelastic into the full 360° of the canal and to pass a suture through it; the suture is then tied, leaving the canal stretched. In deep sclerectomy, canaloplasty, and viscocanalostomy, the surgeon creates a superficial scleral flap and then removes deeper sclera and peripheral cornea underneath, leaving only a thin layer of sclera and Descemet membrane. This allows aqueous to percolate through the Descemet membrane into a scleral lake formed by the removal of the deep scleral flap.

Currently, there are limited long-term data from prospective, randomized trials comparing these new procedures with trabeculectomy. In theory, nonpenetrating surgery should avoid some of the complications associated with penetrating filtering surgery. However, the procedures are technically challenging, and most results suggest that the IOP reduction achieved with nonpenetrating procedures is less than that achieved with trabeculectomy. Proponents of nonpenetrating procedures argue that with fewer potential complications, surgery may be considered earlier in the disease process, and that the target IOP may therefore not need to be as low.

Chai C, Loon SC. Meta-analysis of viscocanalostomy versus trabeculectomy in uncontrolled glaucoma. *J Glaucoma.* 2010;19(8):519–527.

Cillino S, Di Pace F, Casuccio A, et al. Deep sclerectomy versus punch trabeculectomy with or without phacoemulsification: a randomized clinical trial. *J Glaucoma.* 2004;13(6):500–506.

Gilmour DF, Manners TD, Devonport H, Varga Z, Solebo AL, Miles J. Viscocanalostomy versus trabeculectomy for primary open angle glaucoma: 4-year prospective randomized clinical trial. *Eye.* 2009;23(9):1802–1807.

Lewis RA, Von Wolff K, Tetz M, et al. Canaloplasty: circumferential viscodilation and tensioning of Schlemm canal using a flexible microcatheter for the treatment of open-angle glaucoma in adults: 2-year interim clinical study results. *J Cataract Refract Surg.* 2009;35(5):814–824.

Netland PA; Ophthalmic Technology Assessment Committee, Glaucoma Panel, American Academy of Ophthalmology. Nonpenetrating glaucoma surgery. *Ophthalmology.* 2001;108(2):416–421.

Sarodia U, Shaarawy T, Barton K. Nonpenetrating glaucoma surgery: a critical evaluation. *Curr Opin Ophthalmol.* 2007;18(2):152–158.

Special Considerations in the Surgical Management of Elderly Patients

When deciding whether to proceed with surgery in an elderly patient, the surgeon must take into account a number of issues specific to this population. The first issue is determining the appropriateness of surgery. The surgeon must consider the severity of the disease and the risk of functional vision loss in relation to the patient's life expectancy. Also, the surgeon must assess the patient's ability to comply with medical therapy. A patient who is poorly compliant (due to memory loss, poor vision, tremor, or arthritis) preoperatively stands a high risk of being noncompliant in the postoperative phase and may well jeopardize the outcome as a result. In addition, the surgeon must consider whether the presence of a major systemic disease would affect the patient's ability to physically withstand the stress of surgery.

Once the decision has been made to proceed with surgery, the surgeon should determine which procedure is most likely to be successful and result in the fewest complications. The surgeon should consider the patient's ability to return to the clinic or office for multiple follow-up visits. If a patient is not mobile or has no easy transportation options, a glaucoma drainage device or nonpenetrating procedure may be a reasonable choice, as these procedures tend to require fewer postoperative visits than does trabeculectomy. Further, a limbus-based conjunctival flap is less likely to leak than a fornix-based flap and might be considered for patients with transportation issues. The use of anticoagulants and antiplatelet medications should also be considered, as the risk of serious complications from intraocular hemorrhage is increased with their use. Finally, the surgeon must consider compromised healing in elderly persons and be circumspect about the use of antifibrotics in this group of patients, whose tissues tend to be thinner and more fragile than those of a younger patient and whose diets may be more limited.

Basic Texts

Glaucoma

Allingham RR, Damji KF, Freedman S, Maroi SE, Rhee DJ. *Shields' Textbook of Glaucoma*. 6th ed. Philadelphia: Lippincott Williams & Wilkins; 2010.

Anderson DR, Patella VM. *Automated Static Perimetry*. 2nd ed. St Louis: Mosby; 1998.

Drance SM, Anderson DR, eds. *Automatic Perimetry in Glaucoma: A Practical Guide*. Orlando, FL: Grune & Stratton; 1985.

Epstein DL, Allingham RR, Schuman JS, eds. *Chandler and Grant's Glaucoma*. 4th ed. Baltimore: Lippincott Williams & Wilkins; 1997.

Harrington DO, Drake MV. *The Visual Fields: Text and Atlas of Clinical Perimetry*. 6th ed. St Louis: Mosby; 1990.

Levin LA, Nilsson SFE, Ver Hoeve J, Wu SM, Kaufman PL, Alm A. *Adler's Physiology of the Eye: Clinical Application*. 11th ed. Elsevier/Saunders; 2011.

Minckler DS, Van Buskirk EM, eds. *Color Atlas of Ophthalmic Surgery: Glaucoma*. Philadelphia: Lippincott Williams & Wilkins; 1992.

Ritch R, Shields MB, Krupin T, eds. *The Glaucomas*. 2nd ed. St Louis: Mosby; 1996.

Stamper RL, Lieberman MF, Drake MV, eds. *Becker-Shaffer's Diagnosis and Therapy of the Glaucomas*. 8th ed. St Louis: Mosby; 2009.

Tasman W, Jaeger EA, eds. *Duane's Ophthalmology on DVD-ROM*. Philadelphia: Lippincott Williams & Wilkins; 2012.

Thomas JV, Belcher CD III, Simmons RJ, eds. *Glaucoma Surgery*. St Louis: Mosby; 1992.

Zimmerman TJ, Kooner KS, Fechtner RD, Sharir M. *Textbook of Ocular Pharmacology*. 3rd ed. Philadelphia: Lippincott Williams & Wilkins; 1997.

Related Academy Materials

Focal Points: Clinical Modules for Ophthalmologists

Print modules are available through an annual subscription or limited back-year set. On-line modules are available through an annual subscription or for individual purchase. For a complete list of back issues, visit www.aao.org/focalpointsarchive.

Campagna JA. Traumatic hyphema: current strategies (Module 10, 2007).
Colwell JA. Intensive therapies in managing diabetes mellitus (Module 1, 2009).
Freedman SF, Yanovitch TL. Pediatric glaucoma (Module 3, 2012).
Giaconi JA, Coleman AL. Evidence-based medicine in glaucoma: clinical trials update (Module 3, 2008).
Heier JS, Shah SP. Pseudophakic CME (Module 6, 2012).
Mayer HR, Tsai JC. Management of neovascular glaucoma (Module 11, 2011).
Reynolds AC, Skuta GL. Current trends and challenges in glaucoma care (Module 6, 2008).
Sheth BP. Drugs and pregnancy (Module 7, 2007).
Smith MF. Laser treatment of glaucoma (Module 3, 2011).
Stiles MC. Update on glaucoma surgery (Module 3, 2012).
Tsai JC, Tello C, Ritch R. Angle-closure glaucoma update (Module 6, 2009).

Print Publications

Dunn JP, Langer PD, eds. *Basic Techniques of Ophthalmic Surgery* (2009).
Oetting TA, ed. *Basic Principles of Ophthalmic Surgery.* 2nd ed. (2011).
Rockwood EJ, ed. *ProVision: Preferred Responses in Ophthalmology. Series 4.* Self-Assessment Program. 2-vol set (2007).
Wilson FM II, Blomquist PH, eds. *Practical Ophthalmology: A Manual for Beginning Residents.* 6th ed. (2009).

Academy Maintenance of Certification (MOC)

MOC Exam Review Course (2011); www.aao.org/moc

Ophthalmic Technology Assessments

Ophthalmic Technology Assessments are available at www.aao.org/ota and are published in the Academy's journal, *Ophthalmology*.

Ophthalmic Technology Assessment Committee, Glaucoma Panel. *Aqueous Shunts in Glaucoma* (2008).
Ophthalmic Technology Assessment Committee, Glaucoma Panel. *Assessment of Visual Function in Glaucoma* (2011).

Ophthalmic Technology Assessment Committee, Glaucoma Panel. *Corneal Thickness Measurement in the Management of Primary Open-Angle Glaucoma* (2007).

Ophthalmic Technology Assessment Committee, Glaucoma Panel. *Cyclophotocoagulation* (2001; reviewed for currency 2009).

Ophthalmic Technology Assessment Committee, Glaucoma Panel. *Laser Peripheral Iridotomy for Pupillary-Block Glaucoma* (1994; reviewed for currency 2009).

Ophthalmic Technology Assessment Committee, Glaucoma Panel. *Laser Trabeculoplasty for Open-Angle Glaucoma: A Report by the American Academy of Ophthalmology* (2011).

Ophthalmic Technology Assessment Committee, Glaucoma Panel. *Nonpenetrating Glaucoma Surgery* (2001; reviewed for currency 2006).

Ophthalmic Technology Assessment Committee, Glaucoma Panel. *Novel Glaucoma Procedures* (2011).

Ophthalmic Technology Assessment Committee, Glaucoma Panel. *Optic Nerve Head and Retinal Nerve Fiber Layer Analysis* (2007).

Preferred Practice Patterns

Preferred Practice Patterns are available at www.aao.org/ppp.

Preferred Practice Patterns Committee, Glaucoma Panel. *Primary Angle Closure* (2010).

Preferred Practice Patterns Committee, Glaucoma Panel. *Primary Open-Angle Glaucoma* (2010).

Preferred Practice Patterns Committee, Glaucoma Panel. *Primary Open-Angle Glaucoma Suspect* (2010).

DVDs

Shields MB, Fine LC, Salim S, eds. *Glaucoma Filtering Surgery and Drainage Devices* (2010).

Online Materials

Focal Points Modules; www.aao.org/focalpointsarchive
ONE Network, Academy Grand Rounds, Retina; www.aao.org/cases
ONE Network, Online Courses, Retina; www.aao.org/courses
Ophthalmic Technology Assessments; www.aao.org/ota
Practicing Ophthalmologists Learning System (2011); www.aao.org/learningsystem
Preferred Practice Patterns; www.aao.org/ppp
Rockwood EJ, ed. *ProVision: Preferred Responses in Ophthalmology. Series 4.* Self-Assessment Program. 2-vol set (2007); www.aao.org/provision

---

To order any of these materials, please order online at www.aao.org/store, or call the Academy's Customer Service toll-free number, 866-561-8558, in the U.S. If outside the U.S., call 415-561-8540 between 8:00 AM and 5:00 PM PST.

Requesting Continuing Medical Education Credit

The American Academy of Ophthalmology is accredited by the Accreditation Council for Continuing Medical Education to provide continuing medical education for physicians.

The American Academy of Ophthalmology designates this enduring material for a maximum of 10 *AMA PRA Category 1 Credits™*. Physicians should claim only the credit commensurate with the extent of their participation in the activity.

The American Medical Association requires that all learners participating in activities involving enduring materials complete a formal assessment before claiming continuing medical education (CME) credit. To assess your achievement in this activity and ensure that a specified level of knowledge has been reached, a posttest for this Section of the Basic and Clinical Science Course is provided. A minimum score of 80% must be obtained to pass the test and claim CME credit.

To take the posttest and request CME credit online:

1. Go to www.aao.org/cme and log in.
2. Click on "Review or claim CME online" and then "Report AAO credits."
3. Select the appropriate Academy activity. You will be directed to the posttest.
4. Once you have passed the test with a score of 80% or higher, you will be directed to your transcript. *If you are not an Academy member, you will be able to print out a certificate of participation once you have passed the test.*

To take the posttest and request CME credit using a paper form:

1. Complete the CME Posttest Request Form on page 219 and return it to the address provided. *Please note that there is a $20.00 processing fee for all paper requests.* The posttest will be mailed to you.
2. Return the completed test as directed. Once you have passed the test with a score of 80% or higher, your transcript will be updated automatically. To receive verification of your CME credits, be sure to check the appropriate box on the posttest.

   Please note that test results will not be provided. If you do not achieve a minimum score of 80%, another test will be sent to you automatically, at no charge. If you do not reach the specified level of knowledge (80%) on your second attempt, you will need to pay an additional processing fee to receive the third test.

Note: Submission of the CME Posttest Request Form does not represent claiming CME credit.

• **Credit must be claimed by June 1, 2015** •

For assistance, contact the Academy's Customer Service department at 866-561-8558 (US only) or 415-561-8540 between 8:00 AM and 5:00 PM (PST), Monday through Friday, or send an e-mail to customer_service@aao.org.

CME Posttest Request Form
Basic and Clinical Science Course, 2012–2013
Section 10

Please note that requesting CME credit with this form will incur a fee of $20.00. (Prepayment required.)

☐ Yes, please send me the posttest for BCSC Section 10. I choose not to report my CME credit online for free. I have enclosed a payment of **$20.00** for processing.

Academy Member ID Number (if known): _____

Name: _____
      First   Last

Address: _____

_____
    City   State/Province   ZIP/Postal Code   Country

Phone Number: _____ Fax Number: _____

E-mail Address: _____

Method of Payment: ☐ Check   ☐ Credit Card   Make checks payable to AAO.

Credit Card Type: ☐ Visa   ☐ MasterCard   ☐ American Express   ☐ Discover

Card Number: _____ Expiration Date: _____

Credit must be claimed by June 1, 2015. Please note that submission of this form does not represent claiming CME credits.

Test results will not be sent. If a participant does not achieve an 80% pass rate, one new posttest will be sent at no charge. Additional processing fees are incurred thereafter.

Please mail completed form to:
American Academy of Ophthalmology, CME Posttest
Dept. 34051
PO Box 39000
San Francisco, CA 94139

Please allow 3 weeks for delivery of the posttest.

Academy use only:

PN: _____ MC: _____

Study Questions

Please note that these questions are *not* part of your CME reporting process. They are provided here for self-assessment and identification of personal professional practice gaps. The required CME posttest is available online or by request (see "Requesting CME Credit"). Following the questions are a blank answer sheet and answers with discussions. Although a concerted effort has been made to avoid ambiguity and redundancy in these questions, the authors recognize that differences of opinion may occur regarding the "best" answer. The discussions are provided to demonstrate the rationale used to derive the answer. They may also be helpful in confirming that your approach to the problem was correct or, if necessary, in fixing the principle in your memory.

1. In which of the following conditions does increased episcleral venous pressure *not* play a role in elevated intraocular pressure (IOP)?
   a. superior vena cava syndrome
   b. pseudotumor of the orbit
   c. thyroid eye disease
   d. primary open-angle glaucoma (POAG)

2. The highest prevalence of angle-closure glaucoma (ACG) is found in which of the following?
   a. individuals of Asian ancestry
   b. individuals of African ancestry
   c. individuals of European ancestry
   d. the Alaskan Inuit

3. Which of the following risk factors is probably the least significant for POAG?
   a. myopia
   b. race or ethnic origin
   c. family history
   d. level of IOP

4. All of the following statements regarding the Goldmann equation are true *except:*
   a. The facility of outflow is inversely related to the level of IOP.
   b. *F* denotes the rate of aqueous formation and is typically 2.0–2.5 microliters per minute.
   c. Episcleral venous pressure is normally 8–10 mm Hg and is directly related to IOP, especially in acute situations.
   d. *C* denotes the facility of outflow and is essentially the same as resistance to outflow through the trabecular meshwork.

5. Which of the following is an accurate statement about IOP?

    a. IOP is distributed normally when measured in large epidemiologic studies.

    b. IOP varies 2 to 6 mm Hg in individuals without glaucoma over the course of 24 hours.

    c. IOP is often transiently increased following alcohol consumption.

    d. IOP is linearly related to central corneal thickness.

6. The measurement of IOP

    a. can be obtained via applanation methods, which are based on the Imbert-Fick principle

    b. shows almost no variation throughout the day

    c. using applanation puts the patient at significant risk of permanent corneal damage

    d. is not affected by corneal edema, as long as the patient is lying down

7. Factors that may increase IOP include all of the following *except:*

    a. Valsalva maneuver

    b. aerobic exercise

    c. ketamine

    d. blepharospasm

8. During automated static perimetry, a patient responds when no stimulus is presented. What type of error is this?

    a. short-term fluctuation

    b. fixation loss

    c. false-negative error

    d. false-positive error

9. Which one of the following visual field testing strategies may allow an earlier detection of glaucoma compared with standard automated perimetry?

    a. suprathreshold testing

    b. optical coherence tomography (OCT)

    c. frequency-doubling technology (FDT)

    d. confocal scanning laser ophthalmoscopy (CSLO)

10. The optic nerve finding most suggestive of glaucoma is

    a. asymmetry of the cups

    b. progressive enlargement of the cup

    c. generalized pallor

    d. exposed lamina cribrosa

11. What is the mode of inheritance of Axenfeld-Rieger syndrome?

    a. X-linked

    b. sporadic

    c. autosomal recessive

    d. autosomal dominant

12. Which one of the following types of perimetry has been used to detect glaucomatous visual field loss earlier than conventional white-on-white perimetry?

    a. static suprathreshold testing

    b. tangent screen

    c. Goldmann perimetry

    d. short-wavelength automated perimetry (SWAP)

13. Which ocular condition is associated with an increased risk of complications with cataract surgery?

    a. exfoliation syndrome

    b. ocular hypertension

    c. pigment dispersion syndrome

    d. angle recession

14. Which multicenter randomized clinical trial evaluated the long-term effect of treating patients with newly diagnosed OAG with trabeculectomy versus medical therapy?

    a. Early Manifest Glaucoma Trial (EMGT)

    b. Collaborative Initial Glaucoma Treatment Study (CIGTS)

    c. European Glaucoma Prevention Study (EGPS)

    d. Ocular Hypertension Treatment Study (OHTS)

15. According to OHTS, which one of the following is associated with an increased risk of converting from ocular hypertension to POAG?

    a. a history of diabetes mellitus

    b. decreasing age

    c. smaller cup–disc ratio

    d. lower central corneal thickness

16. Which glaucoma is caused by the leakage of lens proteins through the capsule of a mature or hypermature cataract?

    a. phacomorphic glaucoma

    b. lens particle glaucoma

    c. ectopia lentis

    d. phacolytic glaucoma

17. Which is the correct order of normal angle structures viewed anteriorly to posteriorly during gonioscopy?

    a. cornea, nonpigmented trabecular meshwork, Schwalbe line, pigmented trabecular meshwork, scleral spur, cilary body band, iris root

    b. cornea, scleral spur, nonpigmented trabecular meshwork, pigmented trabecular mesh-work, Schwalbe line, ciliary body band, iris root

    c. cornea, Schwalbe line, pigmented trabecular meshwork, nonpigmented trabecular meshwork, scleral spur, ciliary body band, iris root

    d. cornea, Schwalbe line, nonpigmented trabecular meshwork, pigmented trabecular meshwork, scleral spur, ciliary body band, iris root

18. Which of the following is the best method to determine whether a patient is at risk of angle closure?

    a. gonioscopy

    b. darkroom prone-position test

    c. pharmacologic pupillary dilation

    d. darkroom test

19. In which of the following is peripheral iridotomy the treatment of choice?

    a. secondary angle closure following dense panretinal photocoagulation

    b. iridocorneal endothelial dystrophy

    c. phacoanaphylactic glaucoma

    d. phacomorphic glaucoma

20. In an eye with a narrow angle, which of the following most strongly argues in favor of performing a laser peripheral iridotomy?

    a. gonioscopic findings

    b. amount of glaucomatous optic nerve cupping

    c. amount of glaucomatous visual field loss

    d. IOP level

21. A 14-year-old boy with bilateral iris atrophy and corectopia is found to have elevated IOPs. His father has a similar condition. Which of the following is the most likely diagnosis?

    a. iridocorneal endothelial syndrome

    b. Lowe syndrome

    c. Axenfeld-Rieger syndrome

    d. Hallermann-Streiff syndrome

22. What anatomical modification is found in increased frequency in primary congenital glaucoma?

    a. increased axial length

    b. hyperopia

    c. hypoplastic optic nerve

    d. decreased corneal diameter

23. Which one of the following is the preferred initial surgical procedure for an infant with primary congenital (infantile) glaucoma and corneal clouding?

    a. goniotomy

    b. trabeculectomy

    c. cyclophotocoagulation

    d. trabeculotomy

24. Mutations in the *TIGR/myocilin* gene are associated with which of the following disorders?

    a. pigment dispersion syndrome

    b. exfoliation syndrome (or pseudoexfoliation)

    c. juvenile OAG (JOAG)

    d. nanophthalmos

25. Which of the following medications is contraindicated in the treatment of glaucoma in a toddler?

    a. dorzolamide

    b. brimonidine

    c. latanoprost

    d. timolol

26. Which class of glaucoma medications can induce uterine smooth muscle contraction and should therefore be avoided during pregnancy?

    a. β-blockers

    b. carbonic anhydrase inhibitors

    c. α-agonists

    d. prostaglandins

27. A 21-year-old woman with JOAG and 7 diopters of myopia complains of severe blurring of vision after using 1 drop of pilocarpine. What is the most likely cause of her symptom?

    a. increased hyperopia

    b. retinal detachment

    c. increased myopia

    d. a small pupil

28. Which of the following categories of primary ACG occurs without pupillary block?

    a. acute ACG

    b. intermittent ACG

    c. plateau iris syndrome

    d. subacute ACG

29. A 52-year-old woman with ocular hypertension is started on a monocular trial with a glaucoma medication. Which glaucoma medication is most likely to produce a decrease in IOP in the contralateral (untreated) eye?

    a. brimonidine

    b. timolol

    c. dorzolamide

    d. latanoprost

30. Which one of the following patients with a preoperative IOP of 50 mm Hg would be at greatest risk for developing a suprachoroidal hemorrhage following a trabeculectomy?

    a. a phakic patient with a postoperative IOP of 18 mm Hg

    b. an aphakic patient with a postoperative IOP of 5 mm Hg

    c. a phakic patient with a postoperative IOP of 5 mm Hg

    d. an aphakic patient with a postoperative IOP of 18 mm Hg

31. Which of the following glaucomas might not resolve after cataract extraction?

    a. primary ACG

    b. phacolytic glaucoma

    c. an eye with angle recession and phacodonesis after blunt trauma

    d. microspherophakia with glaucoma

32. The use of adjunctive antifibrotic agents is more commonly associated with which complication that can occur years after a trabeculectomy?

    a. encapsulated bleb

    b. aqueous misdirection

    c. bleb infection

    d. cystoid macular edema

Answer Sheet for Section 10
Study Questions

Question	Answer	Question	Answer
1	a b c d	17	a b c d
2	a b c d	18	a b c d
3	a b c d	19	a b c d
4	a b c d	20	a b c d
5	a b c d	21	a b c d
6	a b c d	22	a b c d
7	a b c d	23	a b c d
8	a b c d	24	a b c d
9	a b c d	25	a b c d
10	a b c d	26	a b c d
11	a b c d	27	a b c d
12	a b c d	28	a b c d
13	a b c d	29	a b c d
14	a b c d	30	a b c d
15	a b c d	31	a b c d
16	a b c d	32	a b c d

Answers

1. **d.** The primary mechanism of outflow resistance in primary open-angle glaucoma (POAG) is thought to be within the inner wall of the Schlemm canal, although some alterations in the uveoscleral pathway may also exist. In the other conditions, there is an increase in the venous pressure in the orbit, which is transmitted to the episcleral veins.

2. **d.** Available data show that, among white populations in the United States and Europe, the prevalence of primary angle-closure glaucoma (PACG) is approximately 0.1%; the prevalence of PACG among the Inuit population of the Arctic regions is 20 to 40 times higher. For most Asian population groups, the prevalence of PACG is between that for whites and that for the Inuit. Groups of African ancestry have a higher prevalence of OAG.

3. **a.** Although glaucoma is not equated with elevated intraocular pressure (IOP), elevated IOP is probably the most important risk factor for vision loss. Family history and racial or ethnic background are also highly important risk factors. Black Americans have a greater prevalence of OAG at all ages. There is mounting evidence for the genetic basis of many of the glaucomas. Other factors, such as myopia and diabetes mellitus, are probably less important risk factors for POAG.

4. **d.** The facility of outflow is the inverse of the resistance to outflow.

5. **b.** In individuals without glaucoma, IOP varies 2–6 mm Hg over a 24-hour period. IOP has a non-Gaussian distribution with a positive skew (tail to the right), and it is normally decreased after alcohol consumption, not increased. Although there is a direct correlation between corneal thickness and measured IOP, it is not linear.

6. **a.** Applanation tonometry is based on the Imbert-Fick principle and, performed correctly, is a very low-risk procedure. The other choices are incorrect because IOP varies 2 to 6 mm Hg throughout the day, and corneal edema can significantly alter the measurement of IOP no matter the patient's position.

7. **b.** Aerobic exercise has been shown to decrease IOP.

8. **d.** Automated static perimetry determines the threshold sensitivities at multiple points in the visual field. When a patient responds at a time when no test stimulus is presented, a false-positive error is recorded. When a patient fails to respond to a stimulus presented in a location where a dimmer stimulus was previously seen, a false-negative response is recorded. Short-term fluctuation is a measure of normal physiologic variation and intratest reliability. It is measured when the visual field analyzer double-determines 10 preselected points during the course of the test session. Fixation losses are identified when the patient fails to look at the central fixation light during testing.

9. **c.** Frequency-doubling technology (FDT) perimetry presents a low spatial frequency grating during visual field testing that preferentially activates the M cells. Whether it is because of isolation of specific cell populations that are susceptible to early damage in glaucoma or because of the reduced redundancy allowing earlier detection of defects, FDT perimetry may allow earlier detection of glaucoma than does standard automated (white-on-white) perimetry. Suprathreshold testing presents a stimulus at an intensity expected to be brighter than the patient's threshold and is designed for screening purposes to detect moderate to severe visual field defects. Optical coherence tomography (OCT) and confocal scanning laser ophthalmoscopy (CSLO) are newer techniques that can provide quantitative measurement of the optic nerve head and retinal nerve fiber layer, which

may aid clinicians in making an earlier diagnosis of glaucoma. OCT and CSLO are not visual field testing strategies.

10. **b.** Progressive enlargement of the cup is the optic nerve finding most suggestive of glaucoma. Although asymmetry of the cups can be a sign of early glaucoma, it can be seen in individuals without glaucoma as well and is often due to differences in the size of the neural canal. Generalized pallor is more commonly a sign of nonglaucomatous optic nerve injury. Exposed lamina cribrosa can be seen in glaucoma, but it is also present in individuals with physiologic cupping.

11. **d.**

12. **d.** In short-wavelength automated perimetry (SWAP), a blue stimulus is projected onto a yellow background designed to preferentially activate the koniocellular ganglion cell population and measure the sensitivity of short-wavelength mechanisms throughout the visual field. SWAP provides a more sensitive method than does white-on-white perimetry for detecting early visual dysfunction in glaucoma.

13. **a.** Patients with exfoliation syndrome (also termed *pseudoexfoliation syndrome*) are at increased risk of lens subluxation and vitreous loss during cataract surgery because of the reduced integrity of the lens zonular fibers. Patients with exfoliation syndrome should be carefully examined preoperatively for signs of phacodonesis. Segmental and complete tension rings are helpful intraoperative tools for stabilizing the lens capsule. In addition, these patients have a higher incidence of IOP spikes postoperatively and are more vulnerable to corneal edema and decompensation.

14. **b.** The Collaborative Initial Glaucoma Treatment Study (CIGTS) enrolled patients with newly diagnosed OAG and randomized them to initial trabeculectomy or treatment with glaucoma medications. After 5 years of follow-up, the rates of visual field progression were similar in the medical treatment group (10.7%) and surgical treatment group (13.5%). The Early Manifest Glaucoma Trial assessed the efficacy of glaucoma medical and laser therapy in patients with newly diagnosed glaucoma. The Ocular Hypertension Treatment Study (OHTS) and the European Glaucoma Prevention Study evaluated the efficacy of topical ocular hypotensive medications in delaying or preventing the onset of POAG in patients with ocular hypertension.

15. **d.** OHTS is a multicenter randomized clinical trial designed to evaluate the safety and efficacy of topical ocular hypotensive medications in preventing or delaying the development of POAG in subjects with ocular hypertension. This study identified baseline demographic and clinical features that predicted which participants were more likely to progress to POAG. Enrolled patients were randomized to observation or treatment with topical glaucoma medications to lower IOP by 20% and maintain an IOP of 24 mm Hg or lower. After 5 years of follow-up, 4.4% of treated patients developed glaucoma, compared with 9.5% in the untreated observation group. Higher IOP, lower central corneal thickness, larger cup–disc ratio, older age, and higher pattern standard deviation on visual field testing were identified as significant risk factors for the development of POAG in patients with ocular hypertension. In OHTS, diabetes mellitus was found to be associated with a lower risk of conversion to glaucoma.

16. **d.** In a mature or hypermature lens, soluble lens protein molecules are released through microscopic openings in the lens capsule into the anterior chamber. Secondary OAG may develop as lens proteins, phagocytizing macrophages, and other inflammatory debris obstruct the trabecular meshwork. Although medications should be used to treat the IOP

elevation, definitive therapy requires cataract extraction. In phacomorphic glaucoma, a large, intumescent lens induces ACG. Lens particle glaucoma occurs when lens cortex particles obstruct the trabecular meshwork following disruption of the lens capsule with cataract extraction or ocular trauma. Ectopia lentis refers to displacement of the lens from its normal anatomical position.

17. **d.** Knowledge of normal angle structures is essential for a proper understanding of gonioscopy. Expert opinion varies as to the best landmark to use for properly orienting the clinician to the angle structures, but most prefer to first identify either the scleral spur or the Schwalbe line. The Schwalbe line is best identified by observing the corneal light wedge reflection (the *parallelopiped,* or *corneal light wedge, technique*), which marks the junction of the corneal endothelium and the anterior border of the trabecular endothelium. For more information on and a video of normal angle structures, go to gonioscopy.org, a website dedicated to teaching gonioscopy through videography, and select "The Normal Angle."

18. **a.** Most clinicians find gonioscopy to be the best method for identifying angles that are potentially at risk for angle closure. Results of provocative testing may supplement gonioscopic findings, but gonioscopy is considered the gold standard by most experts.

19. **d.** Laser iridotomy is useful for treating angle closure when there is an element of pupillary block (eg, in phacomorphic glaucoma). Iridotomy is of no benefit when angle closure is caused by other mechanisms and may exacerbate the condition if outflow is further diminished by the inflammation inherent in the procedure.

20. **a.** In chronic ACG with relative pupillary block, gonioscopic findings are the key to diagnosis and management. IOP may be normal or elevated. In an eye with a narrow angle, the presence of elevated pressure alone is not an indication for laser iridotomy. In this case, coexisting OAG may be causing the IOP elevation, not the narrow angle. The extent of visual field loss or optic nerve damage does not indicate whether an iridotomy is needed. Patients with appositional angle closure or areas of peripheral anterior synechiae with relative pupillary block have a high risk of developing chronic angle closure and should have a laser iridotomy.

21. **c.** Axenfeld-Rieger syndrome is a group of bilateral congenital anomalies involving anterior segment structures of neural crest origin. Approximately 50% of cases are associated with glaucoma. Although this syndrome was initially separated into Axenfeld anomaly (posterior embryotoxon with multiple iris processes), Rieger anomaly (Axenfeld anomaly plus iris hypoplasia and corectopia), and Rieger syndrome (Rieger anomaly plus developmental defects of the teeth or facial bones, redundant periumbilical skin, pituitary abnormalities, or hypospadias), these disorders are now considered to be variations of the same clinical entity and are combined under the name *Axenfeld-Rieger syndrome.* In iridocorneal endothelial (ICE) syndrome, iris atrophy and corectopia may be present, but this condition is unilateral and not inherited. Lowe syndrome and Hallermann-Streiff syndrome are systemic congenital disorders that are commonly associated with glaucoma; however, iris atrophy and corectopia are not features of these syndromes.

22. **a.** Primary congenital glaucoma is caused by abnormal development of the anterior chamber angle. It is a rare disease, occurring in 1 in 10,000 births, but it accounts for approximately 50%–70% of congenital glaucoma cases. During the first 3 years of life, the collagen fibers of the eye are more elastic than they are later in life. As a result, elevated IOP causes the cornea to stretch, which leads to increased corneal diameter and enlargement of the

globe (buphthalmos). Optic nerve cupping and pallor are generally seen, but optic disc hypoplasia is not a characteristic feature of congenital glaucoma. An increase in axial length usually induces myopia, not hyperopia.

23. **d.** Primary congenital glaucoma is generally managed surgically, and goniotomy and trabeculotomy *ab externo* are the procedures of choice. Either is appropriate if the cornea is clear; a trabeculotomy should be performed if the cornea is cloudy. A goniotomy involves incising the anterior aspect of the trabecular meshwork via an *ab interno* approach under gonioscopic guidance. A clear cornea is required for adequate visualization of the anterior chamber angle during goniotomy. In a trabeculotomy, a trabeculotome or prolene suture is inserted into the Schlemm canal from an external incision and passed into the anterior chamber. Trabeculotomy is a type of angle surgery that can be performed with or without a clear cornea. Trabeculectomy and cyclodestruction are usually used in the management of primary congenital glaucoma when angle surgery has failed.

24. **c.** The first OAG gene identified was *GLC1A,* which was initially mapped in a large juvenile glaucoma family and has been localized to chromosome 1. Mutations in this gene produce the protein myocilin, which was also found to be upregulated in trabecular meshwork cells following dexamethasone exposure. For this reason, the gene was functionally termed *trabecular meshwork inducible glucocorticoid response (TIGR).* Mutations in the *TIGR/myocilin* gene have been reported in 3% of individuals with adult-onset POAG.

25. **b.** Brimonidine has been shown to cause systemic hypotension and apnea in children younger than 2 years.

26. **d.** Prostaglandins contract uterine smooth muscle and are used therapeutically to induce labor. They should therefore be avoided in the treatment of glaucoma during pregnancy, if possible.

27. **c.** Young, highly myopic patients may have substantially increased myopia with miotic therapy. This occurs because of a miotic-induced increased convexity of the lens and forward movement of the lens. Retinal detachment can occur after miotic therapy, but it would not be the most likely cause of severe visual blurring in this case. All patients with a normal iris develop a small pupil on miotic therapy. This can cause nyctalopia and is more troublesome in older patients with a cataract or other media opacity.

28. **c.** Elevation of IOP occurs with plateau iris syndrome without pupillary block and may occur despite a patent iridotomy.

29. **b.** The contralateral effect of topical timolol, and of topical β-blockers in general, is clinically significant and has been reported in a number of clinical trials, including OHTS (Piltz J, Gross R, Shin DH, et al. Contralateral effect of topical beta-adrenergic antagonists in initial one-eyed trials in the Ocular Hypertension Treatment Study. *Am J Ophthalmol.* 2000;130(4):441–453).

30. **b.** Suprachoroidal hemorrhage can be one of the most devastating complications of trabeculectomy. Bleeding originates from the short or long posterior ciliary arteries as they enter the suprachoroidal space from the intrascleral canal. Delayed suprachoroidal hemorrhage is usually preceded by hypotony and the development of serous ciliochoroidal effusions, which stretch and rupture one of the vessels where the vessel bridges the suprachoroidal space. Conditions that are associated with an increased risk of suprachoroidal hemorrhage include high myopia, aphakia or pseudophakia, hypotony, prior vitrectomy, advanced age, hypertension, anticoagulant therapy, and history of suprachoroidal hemor-

rhage in the fellow eye. The Fluorouracil Filtering Surgery Study found that the risk of suprachoroidal hemorrhage was strongly associated with the level of preoperative IOP and the magnitude of IOP reduction. Reducing the IOP as much as possible before filtering surgery and decreasing the magnitude of the immediate IOP reduction through the use of releasable sutures or laser suture lysis can help reduce the risk of this complication.

31. **c.** Cataract extraction would not be expected to improve pressure control in an eye with blunt trauma and direct trabecular damage. Angle recession may be present and would be evidence of trabecular damage. Phacodonesis is evidence of zonular disruption. In this patient, the lens is not contributing to the IOP elevation. In chronic PACG, relative pupillary block is induced by the tension of the iris sphincter muscle against the lens, which is positioned slightly anteriorly, in an eye with a relatively short axial length. Cataract surgery may improve glaucoma control or may completely eliminate glaucoma in these eyes. In phacolytic glaucoma, proteinaceous lens material that is released through microscopic openings in the lens capsule and engulfed by macrophages clogs the trabecular meshwork and causes secondary elevation of IOP. Cataract surgery may cure this form of glaucoma. In microspherophakia, the abnormal, spherical shape of the lens induces pupillary block, which a laser peripheral iridotomy or lens removal would be expected to relieve.

32. **c.** The incidence of encapsulated filtering blebs after guarded filtering surgical procedures without adjunctive antifibrotics is 8% to 28%. When a trabeculectomy with mitomycin C is performed, the incidence of encapsulation decreases to 2.5%. Aqueous misdirection can occur following guarded filtering surgery, with an incidence of 2% to 4%. However, aqueous misdirection tends to occur soon after the surgery and in patients with a history of chronic ACG, hyperopia, or nanophthalmia or after laser suture lysis or cessation of cycloplegic therapy. Cystoid macular edema may occur after trabeculectomy, but its incidence does not appear to be increased with the use of antifibrotic agents. The reported incidence of bleb-related infections is 5.7% per year, and this percentage increases significantly with the use of adjunctive antifibrotic therapy.

Index

(*f* = figure; *t* = table)